Merry Christmas

PACKING IN THE MOUNTAINS

(*By Charles Nahl, in A. Delano's "Old Block's Sketch Book"*)

FORTY-NINERS

The Chronicle of the California Trail

Fully Illustrated

BOSTON
LITTLE, BROWN, AND COMPANY
1931

With Unbounded Affection
I Dedicate this Book

" If it be romance, if it be contrast, if it be heroism that we require, what was Troy town to this ? "

— ROBERT LOUIS STEVENSON in *Across the Plains*

PREFACE

maps, the California Trail came to life.

These maps, showing accurately all the vagaries and intricacies of the old pathway, at once lent a new meaning to the diaries and journals of travelers over them. One saw, as moderns could never otherwise have seen, what made these trails veritable "roads of iron"; a thousand references in diaries hitherto meaningless or vague became understandable.

To prepare this chronicle of the California gold rush the California Trail was divided into eight sections, represented by the eight maps here reproduced on a scale of thirty miles to an inch. Then every available diary or journal was read for the light it might shed on pioneer experience in the region covered by Section I. In turn that process was repeated eight times. The result was a story of actual experience covering 2200 miles of plain, desert, butte, mountain, river, and ravine. In addition to consulting this source material the writer has traveled most of the trail himself, mile by mile, several times.

Thus a diary of a party of Forty-Niners came into existence. Every material fact in it is from some record left by an Argonaut of the gold-rush days, 1848–1853. Every illustration (with a single exception) is also contemporaneous — whether it be one of the priceless drawings made at the time by a gold-seeker, or one of the innumerable cartoons of the day made to picture the ignorance, foibles, and crazy whims of the multitude that, ignorant of the West, flung itself so hysterically out on those Western trails. The byplay which introduces some of our cartoons will be recognized for what it is — a vehicle for their introduction with less formality than might otherwise be secured. The songs sung along the way (here collected for the first time), being contemporaneous documents, reveal likewise the raw incident and local color of the trail in the wilderness or the Main Streets of Bogus Thunder, Ground-Hog Glory, or Hell's Delight.

Nothing, therefore, is modern in this book except the arrangement. When readers might have doubted the authenticity of an eccentric incident, the writer has inserted a footnote naming the author of old, and more specific details may be found in the Bibliography. It might be added that the writer has, now and then, made inferences which seemed reasonable in the premises; if it is known that chokecherries were picked in Ash Hollow, it is supposable that some made a chokecherry pie; again, if it is known that San Franciscans were sending their washing across the Pacific to China in 1849, it is supposable that the information had reached some emigrants on the way thither. Again, it is taken for granted that the experiences of hunters and pioneers who preceded the Forty-Niners had, by 1849, become traditions of the country and the trail. Numerous overland journals show an acquaintance with the writings of Townsend, Frémont, Burnet, Sage, Hastings, Coyner, and many other noted travelers. When the members of our 1849 expedition mention the real names of the persons they met, it is to be understood that the latter were actual emigrants of 1849.

Despite references in ribald song and ballad, and despite the accepted belief that emigrants "generally" were hostile to the Mormon sect, the reader will find practically every diary reference in our text to be distinctly favorable to the character and disposition of the Mormons. Actual references

detrimental to that sect in diaries of Forty-Niners (so far as
the writer knows) are almost negligible.   Rumors and hints
exist in plenty; specific allegations of wrongdoing, so far as
diaries are concerned, are next to unknown.

To Mr. and Mrs. Philip B. Stewart, founders of the Stewart
Commission, and Mr. Charles B. Voorhis, associated with
them, the author is indebted for the opportunity of making

THE INN, CLAREMONT, CALIFORNIA
April 20, 1931

CONTENTS

PART II

FROM THE CONTINENTAL DIVIDE TO CALIFORNIA

ILLUSTRATIONS

SECTION I
THE GOLDEN ARMY TAKES THE CALIFORNIA TRAIL

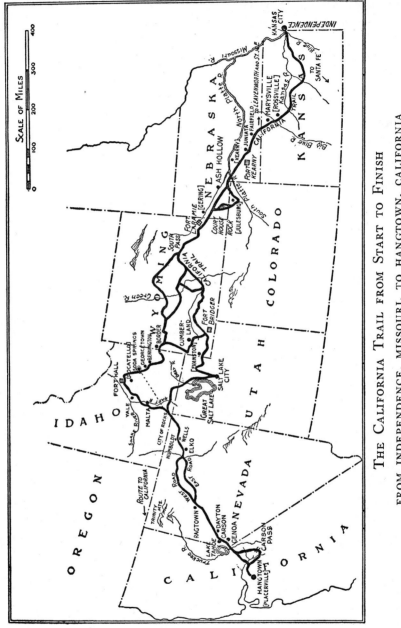

The California Trail from Start to Finish

from Independence, Missouri, to Hangtown, California

SECTION I

DEAR DAD:

Millions of stars are looking down on these rolling plains of Western Missouri where the many tracks of the California Trail curve out from this town of Independence across "the Line" into the Indian Territory beyond [over the present site of Kansas City, Missouri]. On every side, as far as you can see to-night, earthly "stars" — the camp-fires of all this multitude of eager, restless Forty-Niners — twinkle on the ground, being fed by members of the most excited army that was ever assembled in the New World, every one impatient for mud to dry and spring grass to grow so that these shaggy regiments can get on their way.

Had I fifty hands I could not jot down a tenth part of what I hear, or sketch a fraction of the memorable things I see which deserve attention. Never did Life and Death hustle each other on a narrower pathway. Look at one proof of this: a hundred feet from me, to the right, under a canvas thrown across a broken wagon wheel a man from Pennsylvania is dying of cholera; nothing anyone can do will help him. A hundred feet in the opposite direction a dynamic derelict whom we 've

[1] The reader is asked to remember throughout this diary that persons bearing nicknames are characters taken from contemporary cartoons. All real names belong to real emigrants.

nicknamed "Old Pickpan"[1] because his total baggage consists of a pickaxe and dish pan is celebrating to-morrow's departure for the land of gold by one last determined assault on Demon Rum, and nothing anyone can do will help him, either. Just now, between his cups and hiccoughs, he is — I had almost said "singing" — emitting the newly arrived ballad from London entitled "Oh, the Good Time Is Come at Last." Holding in each hand (as he fondly supposes) a nugget of gold, he chants amid antics: —

PICKPAN

"The Miser looks with wistful eye,
    The Spendthrift hails with glee, Sir,
This Golden Scheme now set afloat
    By many a Company, Sir.
In breathless haste they all set off,
    And like the Gilpin chase, Sir,
See Nations for the Ingots rare,
    To California race, Sir."

Across this vast, rolling bivouac ground you see the "Nations" celebrating, like Pickpan, or lying in windrows under blankets in every posture of repose; or you hear the wail of fiddles, the strumming of banjos, or the snap of cards laid down vindictively on improvised, lantern-lighted "tables." Our unquenchable songster continues his lyrical prophecy of finding gold in a land which would flow with something better, to his way of thinking, than milk and honey: —

"Instead of drinking pump water
    Or even half-and-half, Sir,
We all will live like jolly souls,
    And Port and Sherry quaff, Sir.

[1] "Pickpan" hails from the pages of an illustrated poem, *The Miner's Progress, or, Scenes in the Life of a California Miner* (Anonymous), published in Sacramento.

In 'spirits' we will keep ourselves, —
    The Mettle's coming in, Sir.
And not a man will now be found
    Who 'll say he wants for 'tin,' Sir."

In the light of a dying fire to the left we see a sturdy family at their even-prayer, with a fine old patriarch face uplifted to the starlight, describing an equal faith in future happiness, but

uttermost parts of the sea;
Even there shall thy hand lead me,
And thy right hand shall hold me. . . .
Yea, the darkness hideth not from thee;
But the night shineth as the day:
The darkness and the light are both alike to thee."

In a strange way the two voices — like those of different "Nations" — blend in the evening breeze, expressive of different, but unconquerable, philosophies: —

(From the right)

"Oh, the Good time has come at last,
    We need no more complain, Sir.
The rich can live in luxury
    And the poor can do the same, Sir.
For the Good time has come at last,
    And as we all are told, Sir,
We shall be rich at once now,
    With California Gold, Sir."

(From the left)

". . . Thou hast possessed my reins. . . .
When I awake, I am still with thee."

No earlier Cause ever called together in the New World such a strange medley of men, so curious a mass as this Golden Army. There they lie amid their fading fires of prairie grass, of tepee poles, of cottonwood stumps, of chokecherry wood, of sagebrush, of greasewood — rich men, poor men, beggar men, thieves; farmers, lawyers, doctors, merchants, preachers, workmen; Republicans, Whigs, Federalists, Abolitionists; Baptists, Methodists, Transcendentalists, Campbellites, Millerites, Presbyterians, Mormons; white men, black men, yellow men, Germans, Russians, Poles, Chileans, Swiss, Spaniards; sailors, steamboat men, lumbermen, gamblers; the lame, squint-eyed, pockmarked, one-armed; the bearded, the beardless, the mustachioed, side-whiskered, and goateed; singing, cursing, weeping, and laughing, in their sleep; squaws in royal blankets, prostitutes in silk, brave women in knickerbockers that reach to the shoe-tops, covered by knee-length skirts of similar material; the witty, nitwits, and witless; pet cats, kittens, canaries, dogs, coons; cherished accordions, melodeons, flutes, fiddles, banjos; fortune-tellers, phrenologists, mesmerists, harlots, card sharks, ventriloquists, and evangelists from almost every state, nation, county, duchy, bishopric, island, peninsula, bay, and isthmus in all the world — dreaming of gold where those California trails zigzag away over a hundred rough knolls [1] where the Kansas and Missouri rivers have quarreled for centuries for right of way.

To the left of our wagon train a tragedy of proportions is being enacted by candlelight in an open tent. An emigrant has been celebrating so seriously this epoch-making departure from civilization that he is now unable to take advantage of his last chance to write home because his hand has forgotten the gentle art of penmanship. He is sober enough to know he must write; his grief at thinking that it will be his last letter vies with his dismay at not being able to write it. The two procure him another drink which, automatically, forwards the matter, for nothing except dictation is now possible. But this proves slow work, because each draft either contains something objec-

[1] On the site of present-day Kansas City, Mo.

THE PUBLIC SQUARE, INDEPENDENCE, M———RTIES

(By Edmund Flagg, in George Willis Read———)

ours. One thing: he could not be kinder to me if he really was your brother, Dad, but I must say he circulates a *spirit*-ual cheer wherever he goes as no brother of yours could!

HE HESITATES TO TELL HIS WIFE

There in the moonlight stand fourteen very solid reasons why this Uncle Bob is going to California — that many substantial wagons, not counting Uncle's library-bedroom-on-wheels, which we call the "Ark," and the four-wheeled chuck wagon. The freighters are loaded with two thousand pounds of cargo, the profitable part being powder, shot, and percussion caps for the Californians — the powder being worth out there almost an ounce of gold ($18.00) per pound. There is Uncle's lure, combined with the adventure across a world none of us ever

"HURRA" '

saw and a grand voyage around the Horn for a homecoming.

A great many have joined the army of gold-seekers this year because of the reports of continued successes in the "Diggings" last autumn.

Foreigners have eagerly flocked across the seas, partly because of the hope to acquire wealth in the mines and partly because the recent unsettled conditions in Europe would have led to migration even if Mr. Marshall had

agents on the spot,   COMMODIOUS PALACES
have created a popu-
lar confidence in the reality of Marshall's discovery. Steamboat companies have flooded the landscape with alluring invitations to go to California in ease in their commodious floating palaces. No one cause explains it all — everything is calling to California!

Peering through my tent-flaps, I observe the commander-in-chief of our little company in this great army, Captain Meek, of the famous pioneer Meek family, and his two swarthy adjutant-generals, known familiarly as Wagonhound and Ox Bow, accompany Uncle Bob to his great Ark, and linger over a nightcap drawn from one of several casks of private stock which repose in the innermost recesses of that chariot.

There in the dark the last words are spoken, the last reckonings made, the last recountings summarized. "We" consist, as I said, of sixteen masterpieces of wagon building, including the Ark and a chuck wagon; four mules to a wagon and three to spare for each; one driver to a wagon; four muleteers-at-large; upward of thirty men and over a hundred animals. "Snug outfit," says Uncle, looking down our line of wagons, hopeful, sanguine. "We'd better be," said Meek, taking his nose out of his tin cup. "Right fit," said Uncle, a little later. "Can't be too fit," said Meek. I am reminded of the endless attention to detail of these last days on the part of this triumvirate of ours, Meek, Wagonhound, and Ox Bow, to make us approach Uncle Bob's dictum, "the best outfit on wheels."

THE NEWS REACHES
NEW YORK [1]

"No, we 're not so bad off," was Meek's comment in the end.

Those words meant a dozen things I knew and probably a hundred I did n't know. It meant that very few irritable, petulant men had been included among those hired to mulewhack us across the plains. It meant that the wagons were built of seasoned lumber. It meant that the tires were put on with a bolt in each felloe and a nut and screw on the bolt — so that when the spokes began to work in the hub they could be tightened by putting leather or something under the tire and drawing it up with the nut. It meant that hub and axles were large in proportion to the wheels, with at least three-inch arms. That the stakes were high so that, if lightened, the wagonbeds could be raised a foot or more from the bolsters when fording streams. That the beds themselves were caulked as tight as the best of boats. That the stakes holding the bed had iron braces forward and backward, to prevent their giving way on the steep pitches. That the half springs were strong and heavy, but not fastened to the bolster. That the forward wheels

---

[1] This and the accompanying street scene in front of the Herald Building are from a series of cartoons by "X. O. X.," entitled *A History of an Expedition to California,* published in New York in 1849.

were just about as high as the back wheels. That the bows of the wagon-top were fitted to staples on the main box. That a cord passing through rings on the outer covering of the wagon-tops and under the carriage knobs on the main box allowed the tops to be tightened at will, much as you would tighten the head of a drum. It meant that the mules' sweat collars were fas-

AND CREATES EXCITEMENT

tened to a Spanish tree and skirt only, with crupper, breast strap, and blankets to put under instead of a finished padded saddle. That for every man we carried a hundred twenty-five pounds of flour, fifty pounds of cured ham, fifty pounds of smoked side bacon; thirty pounds of sugar, six pounds of ground coffee, one pound of tea, a pound and a half of cream of tartar, two pounds of soda or good saleratus, three pounds of salt, a bushel of dried fruit, one sixth of a bushel of beans, twenty-five pounds of rice, sixteen and a half pounds of hard or "pilot" bread, and pepper, ginger, citric acid, and tartaric acid "to suit." [1]

[1] For pioneer outfitting details for plains travel see L. Sawyer, *Way Sketches*.

May Day, 1849. — The trouble in reading most such diaries of travel as this is that one gets a proper sense of location or position too late in the reading to make the latter properly intelligible. In the present case I am going to help you over-come that handicap by leaving a space before each section, or chapter, of this tale which Uncle Bob expects me to write; in that space I will, later on, give an outline log of the days of travel therein covered, with a map. Thus, when you read my story, you will be posted beforehand as to the main jumps we will make each day and can scan the line on a map before you traverse it — and not be "going it blind," as is so often the lot of diary-readers.

May 1. Cross Blue River [in eastern section of Kansas City, Mo.].

May 2. To Indian Creek [five miles northeast of Olathe, Kan.].

May 3. To Bull Creek [three miles southwest of Gardner, Kan., where the Santa Fé and California (Oregon) trails divide].

May 4. Across Wakarusa [four miles south of Lawrence, Kan.].

May 5. Spent in camp.

May 6. Twenty-two miles on prairie [four miles south of Tecumseh, Kan.].

May 7. Fourteen miles on prairie [southwest of Topeka, Kan.].

May 8. Crossed the Kaw [Kansas River near Rossville, Kan.].

May 9. Along the Kaw.

May 10. In camp.

May 11. Crossed first Vermillion [Red Vermillion].

May 12. Crossed second Vermillion [Black Vermillion, Bigelow, Kan.].

May 13. Crossed Big Blue [Schroyer, Kan., near Marysville].

You do not need artificial stimulants to feel a very genuine species of intoxication at pulling out from this great camp-ground near the Missouri River, crossing "the Line" into Indian Territory, and beginning the 2200-mile march. Uncle Bob insists that I describe what I see. Being an irresponsible, and the most perfect greenhorn in or out of the Know-Nothing Party, I accept the invitation of our guide, Captain Meek, to ride with him at the head of our train, which gives me a fine

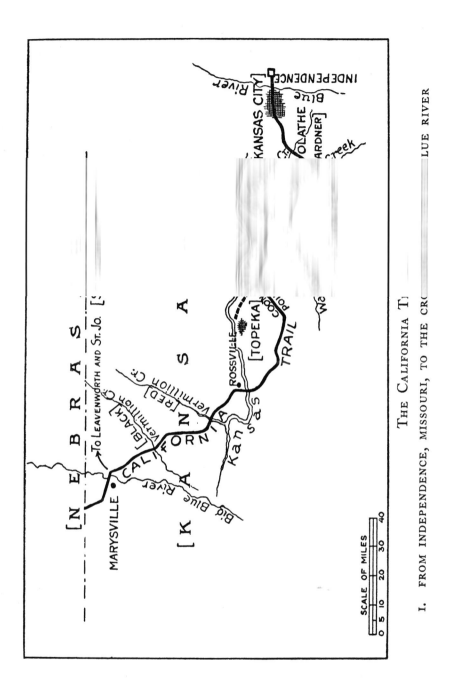

THE CALIFORNIA TRAIL

I. FROM INDEPENDENCE, MISSOURI, TO THE CROSSING OF THE BLUE RIVER

coign of vantage to "see"; but no candid ignoramus could journey three miles with this captain of ours, or his lieutenants Wagonhound and Ox Bow, without realizing the difference between looking and "seeing."

Amid the clouds of dust of other outfits also starting west this May morning, my "looking" seems to present to view a good many people coming back from California — on foot, on horseback, muleback, in hurrying wagons, carts, and even carriages. But when I am taught to "see" what is happening I realize that almost everyone starting out has forgotten something, and a hasty messenger is being sent back from the first tentative camp to secure it — more rope, another mule, horse, or ox, extra wagon-bows, horseshoe nails, cooking utensils, picket pins, and so on without end.

Our road, therefore, is as plain before us as a gangplank, and our need of Meek and Wagonhound as guides is, seemingly, slight; but for every other purpose imaginable they are godsends, even now at the start — and very much so just here, for they keep us from forgetting. I do not know just what it is that comes over their faces now and again, and which they seem to smother in their great beards; it is not quite a smile and it is anything but a laugh; but things that these untutored emigrants do, and some things that I say, seem to — well, how would you put it? — make their chins itch. They scratch them on their beards.

Like the rest, and even though excellently advised, we too make only a short day's journey to what you might call a "practice" camp on Blue River near by, not to be confused with the Big and the Little Blue, Meek tells me, beyond the Kaw or Kansas River. For pitching camp, and starting camp-routine, near the source of supply, gives you a chance to remember what you have forgotten while there is yet time to fetch and carry.

A Spaniard sits on a handsome mule, smoking a cigar; sharp conical hat with a red band; blue roundabout with little brass buttons. His duck pantaloons are open at the side as high as the knee, exhibiting his white cotton drawers between his knee and the top of his low half-boots.

In the rear come his Santa Fé wagons, like bruised and battered ships staggering into port, some driven by Spaniards, some by Americans resembling Indians, some by negroes, some by crosses of races both known and long forgotten. The dilapidated, bedraggled wagons and wagon-sheets and the terrible sores on the mules' backs speak to us ignorant ones of the grime and heat and — What do *we* know about it? Only what that

fire that was being fed by Indian boys; the shadows of the tatterdemalion group wavered like black ghosts on the sides of a hastily erected tepee, made of hides, ragged blankets, and odd pieces of clothing, from which came frantic words and noises. Partly because of the drugged condition of the group, and partly because of the exigency of the crisis, no barrier was raised to the approach of any of us passers-by.

Edging through a little knot of emigrants who were looking into the tepee (at a point where the impromptu coverings failed to overlap), I saw, helpless upon the floor, and near the point of death, a squaw of some eighteen years, who had swallowed nearly a pint of the pop-skull dispensed in the near-by grogshop under the name of whiskey.

Conspicuous among those about her was a large, obese, cross-eyed Indian, earnestly engaged in native performances for her recovery. A breechcloth was his sole garb. With eyes straining from their sockets and revolving in an unearthly manner, he stood first upon one foot and then upon the other, and then stamped the floor as if to crush it through. Grunting, screeching, bellowing, or beating his breast, and swelling meanwhile like a puffball, he bent over his patient and applied spittle to her mouth, throat, and breast. Taking an ample draught of water, he then bespattered her face and forehead with it. These extraordinary efforts seemed, however, to fail to produce their designed effect, and the poor girl grew weaker, her breathing fainter and more difficult.

It was plain that some powerful restorative had to be adopted or she would soon be beyond the reach of medicine. Standing for a minute or two in the attitude of reflection, an idea seemed to strike the "Doctor." Ah, he has it now! This cannot fail! Snatching a butcher knife and hastening with it to the fire, he heats the point to redness upon the coals. Balancing it between his teeth, at a toss he flings it vaulting above his head and backward upon the floor; recatching it, he then goes through the performance a second and third time. He now begins anew, with threefold energy, his grotesque and uncouth manœuvres. If he had stamped his feet before, he now stamps them with a determination hitherto unknown; if he had thumped his breast and beat the walls before, he now thumps and beats as if each blow were intended to prostrate the tent; if he had grunted, screeched, and bellowed before, he now grunts, screeches, bellows, and yells, till the very ground quakes with the reverberations of his demoniacal noise; if he had gagged, puffed, and swelled before, he now gags, puffs, and swells as if he would explode. Then, with an air of confidence, he rushes to his patient and commences a process of manipulation from her breast downwards, and reverse, and then repeats his previous operations with scrupulous exactness and unsparing effort, with every variation of minutiæ. But alas for the medicine man! The squaw dies then and there despite the omnipotence of his skill!

May 3. — Fifteen miles to Bull Creek. Looking across these great plains, I remember the inland lady who visited the Atlantic Coast and replied, when asked what she thought of the ocean, "It is n't as big as I expected." A bar of earth stretches from your feet to the horizon; it is n't very broad; while above you is the gigantic round kettle cover of blue. The plains seem small compared with the sky. And everybody seemed to think

A Wagon Train on the March

(*From Howe's "Historical Collections of the Great West"*)

they were level. "My stars," as Uncle Bob says, "there is nothing level about them except their looks!" Riding with Meek to-day down this Santa Fé-California trail,[1] the guide pointed out this continuous rise and fall of the track across what are rightly called the billows, or little ridges, of the prairie. "No, it's not high mountains ner great rivers ner hostile Injuns," says Meek, speaking in the vernacular of the plains,

— 123 days. How much a day, and every cussed day?"

I saw the point. Seventeen miles a day.

"Yaas," drawled the scout; "and every day, rain, hail, cholera, breakdowns, lame mules, sick cows, washouts, prairie fires, flooded coulees, lost horses, dust storms, alkali water. Seventeen miles every day — or you land in the snow and eat each other like Donner party done in '46."

Just before reaching our camping place on Bull Creek, we passed the point of separation[2] of the old Santa Fé Trail and the Oregon Trail — now known by the new name we are giving it, "The California Trail." Although used by wagons from 1822 onward, while the Oregon Trail did not see wagon-wheels in any number until 1841, there is not so much difference in the looks of the two great highways as they separate and wind off into the setting sun. As Meek pointed out to us, neither one can properly be called a trail, if by that you mean one track. Except at intervals (hundreds of miles apart), no one track can or does take care of the traffic. Usually the "trail" consists of three or four parallel roadways, or six or eight wheel-tracks, as the case may be. Our outfit proceeds now three columns abreast, five wagons in a column, with the chuck wagon bring-

[1] By present site of Olathe, Kan. [2] Near Gardner, Kan.

ing up the rear; and now in single file if the roadway makes
this necessary. At coulee or river crossings these tracks may
multiply into twenty — as new fording-places are opened when
the river banks at old crossing-places get "rotten." And on
many high plateaus there is not now, and never was, the sign
of a wagon-track at all; the wind covers every boot, horseshoe,
or wheel-track with sand an hour after it is made! The Santa
Fé Trail swerves southwest from near Bull Creek; the California Trail turns abruptly north from here to find a crossing
place over the Kansas River — the widest stream to be crossed
in the whole 2100 miles ahead of us.

May 4. — Our camp-fire last night felt good after a hammer-
and-tongs thunderstorm that struck us a mile or two from
camp. Dozens of outfits were scattered along the creek, and
we all pooled forces and made a fire worth remembering. Some
of Meek's old cronies were in other trains, and when you get
hardened liars like them loosened up by what Sir Robert has in
his noble Ark (into which he dived quick enough when the
squall struck), and purring around a spanking fire, you hear
stories with a real tang to them. If gold filled the waking
dreams of these wayfarers as did no other theme, the buffalo on
the plains came second as a chief topic of interest. Old Ox Bow
was on this theme of buffaloes as I came to the fire.

"Talk about sufferin'," said this tanned and grizzled speaker,
"I never seen nothin' to beat a buffalo what had been bitten
by a mad wolf. I 'll be as old as Independence Rock 'fore I
forgit the first one o' them we happened on. We met him
comin' down Squaw Creek to the Platte. He was runnin' in a
circle, almost at the height of his speed, and narrowin' it down
to nothin' at each gyration. Several of us rode out to him —
but he still continued a-frothin' at the mouth and protrudin'
his tongue, swollen to the full size of his jaws, eyeballs rollin'
like globes of clotted gore, and a-bellowin' with pain as regard-
less of us as of our granddaddies.

"Soon he commenced whirling round and round, with fal-
terin', half-stumblin' steps, and finally he keeled over before

us, in a last writhin' of mortal agony. In vain he struggled to rise, while his tongue bled from between his jaws, chafed raw in a crazy effort to close 'em, and his head, keeping time with the convulsive throes of his dyin' strength, tore up the prairie sod and lashed the ground in mad fury. Even us rough mountaineers was moved to pity and gladly ended his miseries with a friendly bullet that put a finish to his sufferin's and sent him

on the prairie ahead, but so fur off we was not able to determine what it was. As it come our way, by the aid of a glass we seen it was a band of wolves in full chase after a buffalo comin' directly toward us. As all was anxious to see the race, and maybe lay a bet or two on how it would end, the boys placed themselves in a position not to be noticed very handy by the wolves, and in a few minutes they had a fair view of the whole show. The buffalo was a well-grown young bull, in fine condition. There was about twelve wolves of the largest kind and they must have had a long and a tight race, as the hull party seemed much fagged. As they come on, the wolves closed around the buffalo, snappin' and snatchin' all the time; but they was observed not to seize and hold on like a dog. Their system of takin' the buffalo is to run 'em down; and when they git 'em out of breath, by constant worryin' and snatchin' (kept up by all hands), they drag it to the ground and then fill themselves with hot flesh even before he is dead. In this Popogie case they seemed to feed upon their buck as they run, for every thrust they made at him they took away a mouthful o' flesh, which they gulped as they run, and by the time they had brought him to the ground the flesh of his hind

[1] The Popo Agie flows into Wind River near Lander, Wyo.

quarters was cleaned off to the bone. So eager was them wolves for their meat, and so fierce was the contest, that they did not see us until we rode up within ten steps of 'em, and even then they did n't seem just scared to death, but scurried off a short distance and sat down and licked their jaws an' looked like they wanted to know which ones of us won the bettin'. The buffalo had suffered violence in every part. The tendons of his hind legs were clipped apart; the tuft of hair at the end of the tail was took away, with part of the tail; pieces of hide and flesh, as large as your hand, was jerked out of his sides in several places; his ears was about gone and he was minus one whole eye. Just before they succeeded in bringin' Mr. Bull to the ground one of the pack, a large, gray devil, was seen to spring upon his back, tear out a mouthful of his hump and then bound off. Goin' crazy may be hard dyin', but I 'll risk it for my part against bein' stripped alive."

A long silence ensued after this gruesome tale, while we listened to the crackling of the fire. At last Uncle Bob arose and, groaningly, stroked his stiffened legs. But he sent us all to bed in good humor when he stopped a moment where Meek was sitting and, putting his hand patronizingly on the latter's shoulder, said: "Good night, Big Chief; I hope you dream of nothing but gore."

The wear and tear of this covered-wagon life on the plains discourages many, although (who can doubt it?) we are journeying to a land unexcelled in all the world — even if there is n't a single nugget of gold within its boundary lines! This is illustrated by the yarn of a man who had lived in California, until he had reached the interesting age of 250 years. In most countries a man that old would be pretty feeble and decrepit, but not in California — Oh no! In fact such were the exhilarating, life-giving, and youth-preserving qualities of that climate that our hero at 250 was in the perfect enjoyment of his health and every faculty of mind and body. But he had become tired of life. The perpetual responsibility of managing a large fortune made him long for a new state of existence, unencumbered with this world's cares, passions, and strifes. Yet, notwithstanding his desire, — for which he daily and hourly prayed to his maker, — health and vigor typical of residents of California clung persistently to him. He could not shake them off. At times he contemplated suicide; but the holy padres (to whom he confessed his thoughts) admonished him that that was damnation; being a devout Christian, he would not disobey their injunction. A lay friend, however, no doubt the

and executor, upon pain of disinheritance, to transport his remains to his own beloved country and there entomb them. This requisition was faithfully complied with. His body was interred with much be-candled pomp and ceremony in his own California, and prayers were duly rehearsed in all the churches for the rest of his soul. He was happy, it was supposed, in Heaven, where, for a long series of years, he had prayed to be; and his heir was happy that he was there. But who can safely mock Providence? Being brought back and interred in Californian soil, with the health-breathing, youth-preserving, Californian zephyrs rustling over his grave, the energies of life were immediately restored to his inanimate corpse! Herculean strength was imparted to his frame and, bursting the prison-walls of death, he appeared before his chapfallen heir reinvested with all the vigor and beauty of early manhood! He submitted to his fate with Christian resignation and determined bravely to live his appointed time.[1]

Guided by Meek and Ox Bow, and sustained by Providence, we floundered across the Wakarusa by four o'clock in the afternoon. Between the yells of our fourteen wagon-drivers and

[1] This tale, although oft repeated by Forty-Niners, was originally published by E. Bryant in 1848. Is it not the first California "booster" story?

Uncle Bob's imprecations you ought to have heard us in Ohio.
So much ill-prophecy about this crossing had been circulated
during the day that Uncle Bob was fortifying himself for the
ordeal in his Ark up to, and including, the very event itself.
Fortunately none of his bones, kegs, or bottles were broken —
but oh, his groans!

May 5. — The storm of day before yesterday gave almost
every caravan a slowing up, if not a real setback. For some
crews it was a real calamity.

UNCLE BOB EQUIPPED

As a rule, we are all overloaded;
and no matter what condition
mules, horses, or oxen are in,
heavy wagons mired to the
hubs make a problem — for
their owners and for everybody
behind them. No one wants
to drive into wheel tracks a
foot and a half deep. So it's
try and get around, taking in
new ground and maybe bogging
down worse than your neighbor.
You see, now, why our "trail"
is rods wide; if it wasn't that
wide it might be that deep. We
roll on a mile or two and, finding a fair camp-ground, lay
by for a day's rest and drying
out.

How many are there of us? Everybody asks that question,
but any answer is a guess. Steamboatmen bringing folks to
the "jumping off places" like Independence, Westport, St.
Jo, and Council Bluffs, make probably the best guesses. The
word goes around that there are some 50,000 of us going overland this season, counting men, women, and children, the ratio
being sixteen men to one woman and three women to every
child. As to four-footed emigrants, they say that there are

36,000 oxen on the trails, and half that many horses; about 7000 mules and cows and 2000 sheep. The wagons are supposed, by rumor, to number 10,000. If I am any judge, unless they are all as strong as Uncle Bob's palatial chariot, two thirds of them will never see California. And by the noises that come from Uncle Bob, as he swings down, "come-hell-and-high-water," into some of these creek beds and barrancos. it is not

NOTIS

No vehacle drawn by moar than one animile is aloud to cros this Bridg in opposite direxions at the sam Time

Many outfits, which are water-logged, so to speak, by the rain, have taken advantage of high spots along our route to stop, dry out, collect lost cattle, and mend breakdowns. We who move along, therefore, get a view of this Grand Parade of Forty-Niners as through a kaleidoscope; probably many despondent overlanders are cheered (?) at the sight of others more forlornly circumstanced than themselves. I have no hope in the world of your getting a true idea of it all from what I write. Even I do not fathom it; so many things happen (or must be analyzed) at once, and everything is so hurly-burly — how can you see it as I do? Perhaps by mixing ideas, men, cattle, wagons, and mind in rapid-fire order, as follows, just as they appear to me : —

A frantic horse, galled by an overturned wagon, kicked a cow and broke her leg. The owners have killed the cow and are having a barbecue out on the clean, wet grass at the right of the trail. Everybody is invited to take a snack as they pass.

An ex-dragoon, judging from portions of his stolen raiment, stands happily off to one side with big pieces of roast beef in each hand and compliments his host to the tune of "Caroline of Edinburgh" with this snatch of a song: —

> "If you are going across the Plains,
>   With snotty mules or steers,
> Remember beans before you start
>   Likewise dried beef and ham;
> Beware of venison, cuss the stuff,
>   Too often it 's a ram."

Some religious brotherhood or other, traveling in company, have sought relief from the discomforts of the late storm, and the trials of this earthly pilgrimage in general, in a wayside prayer-meeting near us.

"O God, we know you 're on these here plains," rings out the voice of the good brother who has the floor, "but they ain't no church bells but only prairy dogs as large again as a fox squirl and make a noise somethin' like a squirl.

"Praise be to God our cows are both givin' milk. Be a comforter to my dear Elizabeth at home and make 'er take care of herself and the dear children and know that the Lord rules its harder on her than me she has been sorely afflicted with that misery in her poor sweet head an' has bad dreams but put no confidence in dreams, honey. I have had dreams. O God, my mind when I 'm asleep is like an uncaged bird and is ungovernable as the wild roe on these plains. I can see Sally Ketchem a-waitin' on her grandmother, O God, with her mild countenance. I can see little China a-wirin' over the floor. I can hear the prattlin' of dear little Nank. I can see that sweet smile o' Elizabeth's which without all this world's vain store would be no more to me than the chaff before the mighty storm. O God, tell Sister Nerve that we have her Edward a-cookin' and it would make her laff to see him puttin' in bread with his tongue between his teeth."

All camps look the same on a day like this — dunnage spread out in the sun, equipment being overhauled, clothes being mended, washing hung out to dry, sore backs or legs or hoofs of horses, mules, cows, or oxen being treated with the simple but effective trail remedies. Ours is a fair sample, and across the piles of household débris drifts the ribald song of one of Uncle's teamsters, glad of a day's rest from "gee-hawing": —

> "I never changed my fancy shirt,

with it the vicious compliments of a messmate over by the chuck wagon who is helping cook get supper. Having missed his aim, the exasperated critic resorts to word of mouth: —

"How come that Mr. Jenny Lind could n't have been drowned in the Wakarusie?"

The singer croons away with withering indifference: —

> "No matter whether rich or poor,
>   I 'm happy as a clam;
> I wish my friends could look
>   And see me as I am.
> With woolen shirt and rubber boots
>   In sand up to my knees;
> And lice as big as Chili beans
>   A-fightin' with the fleas."

Do you not agree with me? Who could describe it all? And would believe it, if one succeeded?

May 6–7. — Getting a good start, we forge straight north toward the Kaw and then turn abruptly to the southwest at some rough knolls [1] and make a wide swing into the plains away from the river — two days' march for a total of thirty-six miles. Most outfits are keeping intact until the Kaw is crossed.

[1] On the outskirts of Lawrence, Kan.

That seems to be the present goal, and if reorganizations are desired they will be effected there. But demoralization is evident already in several companies we have passed. One was violently disrupted yesterday for a reason which appeared unreasonable to most of us. The wife of one partner presented him with a son and heir; a file of ten wagons, whose owners were impatient at the delay, pulled out, leaving the rest to come alone or join another party. "They go not how, but headway is the word," [1] muttered old Ox Bow in the jargon of the plains. Already the trail is well-lined with graves, although the very vanguard of this great crusade could not have passed this way before April 1. Cholera has taken its full quota. Deaths occur every day, for almost every cause. A man was drowned in the Wakarusa as we crossed. He rode into the river with his feet in the stirrups. His horse reared and then fell into deep water; the rider lost his balance and was dragged in the water the while the horse floundered a long zigzag course downstream. A boy was killed this morning while trying to pull a gun out of a wagon muzzle foremost. We are nooning just beyond two graves which we passed half a mile back — a memento of frontier justice. A board carried the striking epitaph that the party under it was murdered. Below were also scratched these words: "The murderer lies in the next grave."

As we went into camp to-night just below a glorious sunset a brilliant scene rivaling old Sol's incomparable departure attracted the attention of all. It was a party of Kiowa Indians, divided into numerous bands, setting off (it was alleged) to war. Each troop was led by a beautiful young female gorgeously decorated, mounted upon a prancing fat Indian pony and bearing in her hand a delicate staff or pole about ten feet in length, at the point of which was suspended a gilt ball or a variety of large brass trinkets together with bright feathers and flowers of various hues. Chiefs dressed in befitting regalia followed immediately in the rear of the feminine ensign-bearers, their bows and arrows in hand. Then came the women and

[1] V. K. Pringle, *Diary*.

children and the pack animals belonging to the party and, last of all, the warriors. It is pageants like this (says Meek), with every thread of finery that can be wrought, bought, or pilfered thrown to the breeze, that impress onlookers and creep into song and story and give the red man his place in popular imagination despite the indescribable squalor, filth, vermin, and disease that are so common a spectacle in every Indian

impressionable Uncle Bob incongruously hailed each division of the parade with an uplifted kerchief; but neither these demonstrations, nor his deep salutes, caused the flicker of one eyelash to soften the stolidity of that stern deportment.

"The path of glory leads but to the grave," he exclaimed oratorically, as he turned toward our fire.

"Grave nothin'," said a voice near by. The speaker was a grizzled old longshoresman of the Pickpan ilk who, with a lone companion, a faded old mare, and a rickety express wagon, was headed Californiawards. "You'll prob'ly find the hull caboodle o' them Kiowas down the road five mile, a-fortune-tellin'; they get up these here goin'-to-war pee-rades fur show — it's good business."

While speaking, the quaint old stager kept a furtive eye on his comrade, who was making a theoretical failure of disengaging his feet from a blanket but a very practical success at telling that piece of bedding what he thought of it.

"My buddy wanted an eye-opener this mornin'," he said, apologetically, gazing back over his shoulder, "an' now he wants a' appetizer; it 'ud be all right if the traders sold real whiskey, but this here red alkali — it makes your stomach all goose-flesh. For all o' their a-dilutin' the stuff, mebbe half an' half, with water, only reg'lar Gila Monsters like us kin

get any comfort out'n it. I gin Bill his eye-opener in this,"
and he held up a gill tin cup, "but I kep' three fingers in it so 's
to be easy on him. Howsomever he seen through the trick
an' now is fussin' fer a cup brimmin' full. An' he 'll get it,
too," grinned the old wagoner with a tricky look of pride, as
he exposed the inside of the cup to Uncle Bob's view. It
was half full of hard tallow. "Ye learn them crookednesses
from the traders; their systems ain't no straighter'n their
whiskey."

Among the topics in everyone's mouth in these camps none
is more often discussed than the Mormons. I have tried to
jot down some points on this subject which I will string together
right here. Among us "Gentiles" the prejudice against this
sect is unbelievably strong, especially among Missouri and
Illinois people. You can't get back of that, either to explain,
deny, or excuse it. Brigham Young took out his first overland
party to Great Salt Lake two years ago. Scores of hundreds
have followed him to the Promised Land by every one of these
main trails, especially the Mormon Trail from Council Bluffs
(following north shore of the Platte River) to Fort Laramie,
where that trail joins the Old Oregon Trail, now our California
Trail. A typical anti-Mormon fire-eater was talking to-night
here in our camp on this prairie.[1] According to him, at least
five thousand Mormons were crossing, had crossed, or were
about to cross the Kansas River just ahead of us, every man-
jack of them armed with a rifle, a bowie knife, and a brace of
large, revolving pistols, not to mention ten brass field-pieces
which were being carried as an additional protection; these
"ghouls in human guise" were declared to be bitterly hostile
to American emigration toward the Saints' new El Dorado,
Salt Lake City, and they are prepared to mow down all who
venture in that direction. Moreover, if any would-be California gold-seeker escaped their rifles, bowie knives, pistols, or
brass cannon, other impassable foes lurked on the plains!
The Kansas Indians were marshaled at one point on the trail
to cut down all adventuresome gold-seekers; if these failed,

[1] South of Topeka, Kan.

five Englishmen, emissaries of the British Government, had just gone forward on the California Trail with many wagon loads of Indian goods for the purpose of inciting other hostile tribes to rob, pillage, murder, and worse! Only one fortunate chance of life and happiness remained to all who were afflicted with the gold mania, according to this speaker, and that was to purchase a lot in the new town of ——— located three miles

who, after learning the ins-and-outs of overland travel, are taking full advantage of the situation to make money from the American migration. This they do in some cases honestly and in some cases by typical "Yankee" cunning and trickery. From Meek, Ox Bow, and Wagonhound I learn that the following are the chief ways by which the migration is being "cheated," "robbed," and "plundered" by the Saints: —

1. They have found the main crossing-places of streams, where at all times ferryboats are useful and where, in case of high water, they are absolutely necessary — as the crossings of the Kaw, the South Platte, the North Platte, and of Green River. They have monopolized these crossings by building ferryboats; and they charge what seems to the emigrants high prices for ferriage.

2. Knowing the California Trail well, they know about where the horses, mules, and oxen belonging to the migration will become most footworn and "played out." From their own stocks of recruited animals, and from the Taos–Santa Fé country to the south, they have gathered large herds of fresh animals, which they swap at such points with emigrants at the rate of three for one, or better, if they can. These worn-out animals are put right out to graze and recruit themselves without cost

in a couple or three weeks — to be exchanged again at a like profit.

To the unprejudiced person these projects seem to be a simple use of good judgment and business ability; but to all others they seem a "wicked," "vile," and "heathenish" extortion in every case.   Take your choice.

Two other instances are cited of Mormon profiteering from the migration which depend for success upon the gullibility of emigrants.   One is the writing and selling at the "jumping off" places (like Independence and Council Bluffs) of "guide books," — a half-dozen sheets of paper sewed together, — which purport to give all the trail information that the emigrants need, distances of proposed day's marches, location of wood and water and forage grounds.   These "guides" are said to be about as good as most, which is practically nothing; for every stream and camping-place is altered by every outfit that stops at it, and each week that goes by (supposing nine hundred people pass a given site each day during May, June, and July) sees a complete change in the face of the country. The Mormon guide-makers are not to blame for this — but, oh! to hear the cursing that arises from a company which expected on a given night to reach "good spring; wood to be had to the left; good grass across the creek" when they find the spring sucked dry, the wood supply used up, and the whole camp-site a forbidding mass of wheel-tracks covered with débris!   Least defensible of all is the selling of Mormon sun-glasses in those eastern outfitting points for one dollar at the ominous threat of blindness that will ensue to all from constant exposure to the prairie sun!   Those shoddy spectacles — made of plain glass set in a perforated leather strap which you bind about your head — cost the makers not over five cents and are as useless of productive good as any wooden nutmeg made in Connecticut or flannel sausage concocted in Vermont.

Made twenty-two miles to-day.

May 8. — On the trail at "crack o' dawn" to-day to get to the Kaw ferry ahead of the bulk of to-day's emigration.   Ignorant as they make 'em, I asked Wagonhound if the crossing involved much danger and was surprised to hear that the bigger the river the smaller the trouble and danger, at least in fair weather. The Kaw is the biggest stream we cross on the road to California. Unless you caulk your wagon-beds and row yourself across, it is just a question of waiting your turn at the ferry. The difficulty at such a river is the conges-

story there in the heat and dust of a bright man who combined a knowledge of geography and "horse sense" and became wealthy. Knowing that all animals turn back down the trail for home if they get free, and knowing that none of these would swim the Kaw River, he built a fence across the neck of land at the point of the Kaw and Missouri with a gate in it that was shut at night. There he sat on his pants and got rich. Hardly a day, it is said, but some horse, cow, or ox did not turn up and turn in. This story was then denied up and down the line. Ox Bow contributed one just as hard to swallow. It was that an emigrant party left a sick ox, with food, to die, and went on. Days later it came lowing and running into camp. Instead of turning around or dying, it had come ahead fifty miles.

Ox Bow says that we'll be surprised how many chances emigrants will have on the road to swap tired animals for fresh ones, and when all hope of this seems gone the Indians will have "Rocky Mountain horses" to trade way out on the Bear River.[1] They are California ponies that have been taken to Oregon, where they have gained two hundred pounds in weight in a moist country. They are called Cayuse ponies.

[1] O. Cross, *Report*.

It took us near three hours to cross; current moderate; two hundred fifty yards wide. We climb up and move out along the Kaw to camp.

May 9. — One of those curiosities of plains travel happened along the Kaw to-day right out of the blue, which made merriment for dozens of us and, incidentally, introduced us to an Iowa outfit with three jolly girls in it — and you've got to go through what we are experiencing in order to realize what a boon it is to meet some nice girls. Everybody on the trail is so busy, or so afraid of the roughs and toughs, that you might travel across the continent and never have a decent girl speak to you. This Iowa family is the Johnson outfit, horses and mules, sound and strong and going through good. There's the old folks, a brother, two husky boys, and three sisters. What happened was this. Three girls are walking on in advance of their company and pass another wagon. Two of them get into conversation with someone in that train. The third strides on ahead and secretes herself behind some jutting rocks. A tall man in a long bedraggled rain coat hurries onward, carrying a sleeping baby to its mother in a wagon ahead. Thinking that it is her companions coming up, the hidden girl jumps out from her hiding place with an echoing "*Boo.*" The baby wakes up with a wail, the man trudges on cursing, and the girl, covered with blushes, goes back to fall in the arms of her friends, who are nearly expiring with laughter.

As chance would have it, we nooned by that same outfit and I met "Boo" Johnson, as she will forever be remembered by us. She and her sisters are fine girls. "Boo," too, is keeping a diary. We have agreed when opportunity occurs to compare notes.

It is interesting to see how appealing and how popular are the songs which echo the desire to return to, or be taken back to, home — with these thousands who are going so far in the other direction! Of such songs Christie's "Carry Me Back to Old Virginny" ranks high in favor. Perhaps the very contrast of grinding away through these walls of alkali dust and raking oyster-beds, of itself alone, would make this song a favorite even if it did not echo the "carry me back" ache for "home and mother":—

> On the floating scow of old Virginny,
>   I work'd in from day to day,
> A-rakin' amongst de oyster beds,
>   To me it was but play ;

> ⸻, ⸻ ⸻ ⸻ ⸻ ⸻ ⸻ ⸻,
>   To old Virginny's shore.

> If I was only young again,
>   I 'd lead a diff'rent life ;
> I 'd save my money, and buy a farm,
>   And take Dinah for my wife ;
> But now old age, he holds me tight,
>   My limbs are growing sore ;
> So take me back to old Virginny,
>   To old Virginny's shore.

Made twenty-two miles to-day.

May 10. — As planned, we rested to-day for what Meek calls a "tough pull" up-country across the Vermillions to the Big Blue. Many outfits have a physical overhauling and reorganization on crossing the Kansas. We need none, having unconsciously drifted into a well-working crew under Meek, Ox Bow, and Wagonhound as administrative officers. One glance at a caravan like ours would convince anyone that it was being well conducted — wagons and gear in good order and animals in sufficient quantity to give rest to all when rest is needed. You see the difference when direct comparison is permitted by the close location of camps. Several unpleasant difficulties and altercations have occurred to-day in near-by camps from the perverse obstinacy of some of the men, who refuse obedience to the orders of their Captain. A committee, appointed to adjust such matters in one camp, has been in session the whole of this evening, but we have not heard the result of their investigations. A troublesome dispute between two emigrants in the outfit has been brewing for several days; one of the partners owned the wagon and the other the oxen. The owner of the oxen insists upon his right to break the partnership at any time and to take his animals from the wagon. The proprietor of the latter denies this right. Things came to a crisis on the road to-day and, in a personal encounter, the ox-owner attempted to take the animals from the wagon and leave that vehicle to move along by the best mode its owner could invent. We await with interest the decision of these Solomons. You can well see that if a man is predisposed to be quarrelsome, obstinate, or selfish, these traits are certain to be developed on a journey over the plains. The trip is a sort of magic, if not tragic, mirror, exposing every man's qualities of heart connected with it.

UNCLE BOB HEARS
A NEW SONG

May 11–12. — We were awakened early by our caroling teamster chanting the chorus of one of the three most popular songs of this migration : —

"Oh dearest Mae, you 're lubly as the day;
    Your eyes are bright,
    Dey shines at night
When de moon am gone away."

You can always tell when we 've had a day of recuperation by the spirit of the men — yes, and of the animals, too — the morning after. Uncle Bob's convivial soul is piqued by these migration-songs and he is making a collection of them; when

May 13. — Off for the Big Blue,[1] which, they say, you can cross easily by harnessing the mosquitoes to your teams; they fly above the water and haul you over — take Wagonhound's word for it.

Long pull. Here we begin to meet people who are turning back, discouraged. They had seen enough of "the Elephant." No one seems able to explain that expression — which is the commonest heard along the California Trail. "I sup-

pendence as: "They 've seen too much of the Elephant," or "The Elephant's tracks got too close." In rare instances the continent is referred to as "the Elephant," and the continental divide ahead of us (South Pass) as the top of the Elephant's back.[2]

Graves are more frequent these last days. Some are curiously ornamented. Over the head of one was placed an inverted pair of huge elk antlers. They were full four feet high and formed an arch over the head of the grave. A board bearing the name, age, and date of the death of the person who slept beneath was fastened across the horns. Another grave was indicated by an elk's horn with the inscription carved on the horns. Another, that of a Dr. Bryan, had a block of stone placed at the head of the grave. This must have been brought several miles, as there was no appearance of stone near the spot. We saw, whitening on the plains, bones of animals which had died on the way. These bones very often bear some inscription written by those who have gone ahead, to friends in the rear, giving them various kinds of information; thus the bones of those animals which at least tried to carry

[1] Present site of Marysville, Kan. [2] E. P. Hatheway, Ms. *Letters.*

emigrants to California are now usefully employed as messengers of thought.

Uncle Bob bought a horse from one emigrant who turned back after having traveled seven hundred miles; he said he had "seen the Elephant and eaten its ears." This man had his mother-in-law along, a somewhat opinionated old lady who said we had all better turn back, for if grass began to give out, what would become of us if we went on until our teams were not able to turn back; she said she was "going back, for she had made a living before she had ever heard of California and the rest might go on and starve their teams to death if they like." As we got near the Big Blue, we met two wagons returning to the Missouri. These people were already discouraged, and thought it more advisable to return than to attempt a journey of two thousand miles and run the risk of never reaching their place of destination. Many had started very unprepared, while others were entirely unacquainted with a prairie life and were not built to accomplish a journey fraught with many obstacles. Later we met two men who were returning to their homes in Tennessee, having heard of the death of some relatives, which required them to go back. This gave us opportunity to send letters back to our friends, who, hearing of the existence of the cholera along our route, would doubtless feel anxious and be relieved on hearing of our safety thus far. The men were loaded with letters from the emigration. Near the Big Blue we found a large spring of water called Alcove Spring,[1] as cold and pure as if it had just been melted from ice. It gushed from a ledge of rocks which formed the bank of the stream and, falling some ten feet, its waters were received by a basin fifteen feet in length, ten in breadth, and three or four in depth. A shelving rock projected over this basin, from which fell a beautiful cascade of water ten or twelve feet high.

Meek warned the party against drinking as cold water as this spring afforded in any quantity when overheated on the plains ahead of them.

[1] Near Schroyer, Kan.

"I'll never forget," he said, "a fellow over at Thousand Springs one summer.   He had said if he ever got to cold water again he was going to drink enough to last a camel the rest of the way to Oregon.   He kept his word at those Springs and we buried him there the same day."

Reached the Big Blue late, but got across.   The mosquitoes here have been lied about.   None are as large as turkeys; the biggest one I saw was no bigger than a crow.   All night trains

they have met a real test of hard pulling, strain on animals, tackle, and gear; those that are ill-equipped, and those which are overloaded, have learned their lessons, and those to whom homesickness proves a veritable disease have been warned thus early to turn back.

The sight of a number of broken-down outfits here led some in our company to speak in a self-satisfied way about our being well prepared for the hard grind ahead of us.   Quick as a flash Meek answered the speaker: —

"Yes, and some of us better be.   Some must be strong enough to make their way steadily and meet the responsibilities of the road with an easy conscience.   For we will overtake hundreds, if not thousands, that are a-foot and hungry, animals and cattle dead, wagons bogged and broken down.   Some of us must be strong enough (for our own safety) to help a goodly fraction of these.   Write this down in your hat in big letters. If those kind of people get too tired and too hungry and too great in number, something breaks that don't belong to harness or wagons, — breaks inside-like, — and our lives, let alone our property, won't be worth a pinch of alkali.   We must help our full share of all such.   Otherwise we'll have

the gruesome feeling of going forward — if they let us go —
over the dead bodies of fellow men. This California Trail
is a lot like the Trail of Life. So many are poor; so many are
ignorant; so many are foolish. Those who are well fixed can't
hardly feel comfortable in mind if they never 'lend a hand,'
supposing the mob lets 'em keep their hands and heads."

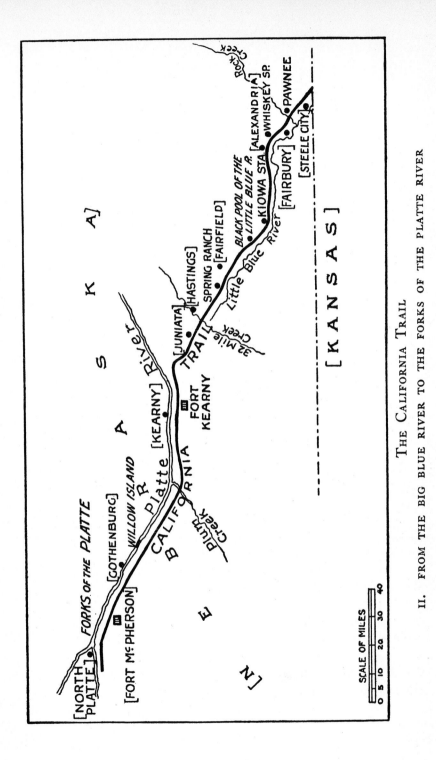

THE CALIFORNIA TRAIL

II. FROM THE BIG BLUE RIVER TO THE FORKS OF THE PLATTE RIVER

SECTION II

OFF FOR THE "COAST OF NEBRASKA" AND BUFFALO LAND

— thus glimpsing our route as you read from foresight rather than "hindsight" : —

May 14. Crossing high divide to the Little Blue River.
May 15. Same.
May 16. Reach Little Blue [Fairbury, Neb.].
May 17, 18, 19. Up Valley of Little Blue [near Hastings, Neb.].
May 20. Across divide [Juniata, Neb.] to Platte River.
May 21. Up the Platte [opposite Kearny, Neb.].
May 22. Up the Platte.
May 23. Up the Platte, crossing Plum Creek.
May 24, 25, 29. Up the Platte [passing future site of Fort McPherson to near North Platte, Neb.].

May 14. — It was upgrade with a vengeance to-day — to get out of the Big Blue valley and across into that of the Little Blue. This climb, and the rough character of the country, made the lightest wagon seem a heavy one to horses, mules, or oxen. A more sincere effort to lighten loads by discarding useless baggage was evident from the plunder along the road. But some thrifty Scots, Hebrews, and Yankees — which ? — could not reconcile themselves to this "waste." We were treated to one spectacle that would have been devastatingly funny had not the toil endured neutralized the humor. It was that of an agile old miser to whom everything that could be found, no matter how heavy, and particularly any old iron, was great gain. With a courage worthy of good cause, he retrieved everything that he could lift and tossed or heaved it into the wagon. And with equal regularity his companions threw each object out on one side while the old man was in search of more on the other.

No normal imagination can fancy the utterly strange things that happen to outfits on a voyage like this. We met a man to-day whose two horses were drawing a crazy, cart-like vehicle which, on inspection, proved to be the front wheels of a wagon with half a wagon-bed balanced on the axle. He and his partner had camped on these hills the night before. "The moon was shining," he said, "but there were clouds occasionally passing, so that at times it was quite dark. We had been picketing our four horses and came to the wagon, which was facing the animals down on the slope. Bud was armed with a 'Colt's Army,' while I had a double-barreled shotgun loaded with buckshot. I was sitting on the doubletree on the right side of the wagon-tongue, which was propped up with the neck-yoke. Bud sat on the tongue about an arm's length ahead of me. I was holding my gun between my knees with the butt on the ground. Bud was getting off one of his stories and had about reached the climax when I saw something running low to the ground toward the horses. Thinking it was an Indian on all fours trying to stampede the animals, I instantly leveled my gun, and, as I was following the shape to an opening, my gun came in contact with Bud's face at the moment of discharge. He fell backward, hanging to the wagon-tongue by his legs and feet. My first thought was that I had killed him. He recovered in a moment and began cursing and calling me vile names, accusing me of attempting to murder him. During these moments, in his frenzy, he was trying to get his revolver out from under him, swearing he would kill me. Taking in the situation, I dropped my gun, jumped over the wagon-tongue as he was getting to his feet, and engaged in a desperate fight for that revolver. We were sometimes struggling on the ground, then on our knees; he repeatedly struck me in the face and elsewhere, still accusing me of trying to murder him. As I had no chance to explain things, the struggle went on; finally I threw him and held him down until he was too much exhausted to continue the fight any longer, and, having wrested the revolver from him, I helped him to his feet. In trying to pacify him, I led him out to where the object ran

then flipped a copper cent to see which should have the front part of the wagon. After the partnership had been dissolved, each went to work, fixed up his part of the wagon as best he could, and drove on alone!

One of the funniest ruptures in friendship that we have heard of occurred on the pretty, but mosquito-ridden, Big Blue. Some of the boys belonging to one outfit sought temporary relief in the river while the mosquitoes hovered over them, whetting their daggers all the time. During the bath a most original wager was made betwixt two young fellows. One bet that he could remain exposed without his clothes longer than the other. It was agreed that both could smoke cigars. So, after each got a

UNCLE BOB STUDYING HIS POSSIBLE SUPPER

light, they sat down on the river bank, close to each other, wincing as stings were inflicted on a tender quarter, and smoking with a fiercer energy in proportion as the pain became more excessive. Both held out manfully for minutes, when one, in the very act of giving up the contest, accidentally touched the rear of his adversary with the end of his cigar, causing the latter to jump into the river in agony, swearing that "the great-grandfather of the whole flock had stabbed him." When a healthy blister developed where only a mere sting should have appeared, the murder was "out" and war to the death was declared.

The tragedies of the trail, occasioned by bad temper, impatience, and a disposition unfit for campfire companioning, are the main theme of the rigadoon "Crossing the Plains," one verse of which the roustabout soldier at that free-for-all barbecue was singing. The other verses, relating to the uncivil wars we hear of being fought in these camps, run : —

> "How do you like it overland?"
>   His mother she will say;
> "All right, excepting cooking,
>   Then the devil is to pay.
> For some won't cook and others can't,
>   And then it 's curse and damn,
> The coffeepot's begun to leak
>   And so 's the frying-pan.
>
> "It 's always jaw about the teams,
>   And how we ought to do;
> All hands get mad and each one says;
>   'I own as much as you.'
> One of them says, 'I 'll buy or sell,
>   I care not what may come;'
> Another says, 'Let 's buy him out,
>   The lousy son-of-a-gun.'
>
> "I 'd rather ride a raft at sea,
>   Wish I 'd gone around the Horn,
> Than try to cook with buffalo wood —
>   Take some that 's newly born.

> The desert 's nearly death on corns
> While walking in the sand,
> And drive a jackass by the tail —
> God damn this overland."

May 19. — If you will look at the map you will note one of the significant points to remember about this Little Blue River on which we have spent nearly a week so pleasantly that I ~~have simply fished and fished and~~ explored instead of writing in my

lines running east and west, and that they are conducted on north and south lines. The explanation of this is horses — the prime requisite and mainstay of Indian existence. All the Sioux lie above the Pawnee, and below you find the Osages, Kiowas, Comanches, Arapahoes, and Cheyennes; farther south are the tribes below the Arkansas and reaching on toward Texas and Mexico — the source of supply of horses. The lower tribes steal from the Mexicans and, in turn, each tribe to the north steals from its southern neighbor. This helps to explain why the Santa Fé Trail has seen more bloodshed in almost any week than the Oregon Trail ever saw in a year — it is on the line toward Mexico. As a pathway of war, these trails down this natural thoroughfare of the Little Blue have thus been worn deep for centuries.

Next to its strategic position is the fertility of the Little Blue. The soil is rich and all travelers comment on its verdure. But, by the same token, such a country offers heavy going in the spring — which is the season the emigrants pass here; few will ever forget the veritable gouges cut by wagons around such low spots as "the Black Pool of the Little Blue." We heard of it before we arrived and we 'll never hear the last of it, at this rate!

We have seen bold ravens, as they call crows out here, but we never saw one pay for the penalty of voracity with his life until yesterday. Three of these birds, in a flock of twenty or more, were so insatiable in their hunger for camp refuse that they approached with great effrontery. One of the three in his rapaciousness exceeded all bounds and was callous even to chastisements inflicted upon him by his bold comrades. Eventually, however, they gave up hope of keeping the disgraceful gormandizer within limits and promptly turned executioners and killed him on the spot.

While quietly wending our way along the Blue a day or two ago, I saw for the first time an antelope and was somewhat disappointed in its appearance. There was not that beauty in its form that I expected to find from the descriptions so often given "of the swift-footed antelope." In comparison with the deer I consider it by no means as handsome nor as delicately proportioned. At a distance, however, it seems much the same. The head is much like that of a sheep; the body appears shorter than the deer, with hair much coarser and longer. It stands very erect and leaps with much quickness, gathering its feet apparently at the same time immediately under it. Its curiosity exceeds that of any animal, Meek affirms, except the mountain goat. When this one first saw me it approached almost within gunshot, when, stopping for a few minutes, it ran off for a short distance and turned again, apparently to satisfy its curiosity. It then ran parallel to the road, getting sometimes ahead and then returning; if I stopped suddenly, or there was anything seen to attract its attention still more, it would run directly towards me until its curiosity was fully satisfied, and then it would bound off with great rapidity over the prairie until out of sight. It is much lighter in color than the deer, particularly on its sides, breast, and hind-quarters; this, with a black stripe which it has about the eyes, gives it a striking appearance, though not adding much to its beauty.

Uncle Bob has become impressed with the fact that our road, which is never exactly straight for fifty feet at a stretch, makes almost a straight line when you survey it for twenty-five miles of its length.[1] Commenting on this, Guide Meek gave us a lesson in Western geography that will make our journey more interesting. He said that the reason why the Oregon and California trails to the Pacific coast were so easily traveled was due to the fact that nowhere along the way do the highest mountains coincide with the Continental Divide. In other words, on that divide, streams originate and flow (either east or west) through those ranges which have the highest moun-

other part of the Union. Indeed, the road has already been graded by the hand of Nature. How long will our Government hesitate, and neglect to avail itself of such superlative advantages, in construction of a thoroughfare which will bring the mineral treasures of California to the doors of the Capitol, and roll the vast tides of Asiatic commerce through the centre of our states and territories? This subject ought to arouse our nation to immediate action, before the current of trade becomes permanently fixed in some other direction. The profits of a railway to the Pacific Coast would soon refund the money expended in its construction. Besides which, such a road would be a stupendous monument to the enterprise and greatness of our Republic — would be in keeping with the progressive spirit of the age, and would bind together the extremes of the Union with strong bands of iron. So get ready, Dad, to follow us across the plains by rail!

The reports from Oregon, first put in circulation by Dr. Marcus Whitman, of the profits to be had in sheep-raising across

[1] The California Trail left present-day Wyoming not over eight miles from a straight line from the point where that State was entered 450 miles away; crossing, meanwhile, the Rocky Mountains and the Continental Divide.

the Rockies have induced quite a number to drive flocks westward. We passed one numbering two hundred on Sandy Creek
to-day. The drivers have their troubles, but sheep do not seem
to sicken on the march as cattle often do. They get early
morning starts — as soon as daylight comes. Bad feed
affects them more quickly than it does cattle, but those which
suffer with sore feet improve more rapidly when rested than
cattle. The drovers find wolves their worst foes. One told
me that it is unbelievable how cleverly a wolf can take a sheep
out if one strays ahead of the flock unguarded. He will hide
behind a rock and all you see is a gray streak of lightning;
in the very air, while leaping across the road, so it seems, a
mouth reaches down for a sheep's throat, and beast and his
prey are a hundred yards away in the sagebrush! We think
of sheep as very timid, but these men say that in storms, or
any other cataclysms which produce stampedes (like mad
dogs running amuck), their sheep remain still and never
stampede.

A fine big dog which everyone admired passed us yesterday
going back down the trail, homeward. No amount of whis-
tling, calling, or cajoling in the least altered his fixed purpose
to regain the Missouri, or maybe the Connecticut, River, who
knows? He'd "seen enough of the Elephant," as many
remarked.

We have met several parties of Pawnee Indians along the
Little Blue, for the most part as stolid and indifferent as so
many bronze idols. We were delayed one afternoon by the
crippling of a luckless emigrant's wagon in a narrow pass ahead
of us; I loitered behind with Ox Bow, who remained with
some of our tools to help the comrade get on his wheels again,
and, happening to wander wide of the trail through a patch
of berry bushes, I accidentally witnessed a little scene that
came to few eyes — and one unforgettable, so far as I am
concerned.

Down the cross-trail to the ford came about a hundred
Pawnees, men and women, with a string of pack mules loaded
with corn. When they reached the ford, we had passed out of

sight, and, psychologically, the Indians were in a "state of
nature" and they acted the part.   All semblance of strain and
pose departed and a prettier little piece of forest comedy I
shall never behold.   The squaws, who, in our presence, are so
invariably dumb or sullen, abandoned the rôle as quickly as
though it were an uncomfortable garment, and plunged into
the water.   Some ran and splashed joyously; some swam;
some dived and popped out unexpectedly to bespatter a man

of it we gain by seeing them only, so to speak, on parade.   One
thing is sure: no maltreated, overlorded, and overworked
"drudges" could so suddenly and so spontaneously have
portrayed every sign of playful happiness.

I saw a horse to-day whose owner had trained it to point like
a "pointer" dog.   Let an Indian or a dog or wolf be smelled or
sighted, and out shot head and tail in almost a perfectly rigid
line!

We met some Mormons at the Black Pool of the Little Blue
on their way to Independence to get their families.   They were
bringing back with them Mrs. John Watts and baby of Des
Moines, Iowa, whose husband was taken from her by cholera
on the plains.   Their story illustrates the sacrifice and great-
heartedness possible among these thousands of travelers on the
gold road, albeit so many are callous and heedless of the sufferings of others.   With tears streaming down her face and her
baby in her arms, the widow had no concern for her terrible
loss nor fears of the long journey back to her distant relatives
which compared with her dread of burying her loved one on the
prairie without a coffin.   To her distraught mind, that seemed
desertion and desecration unthinkable.   Frantically she begged

the men in her company to secure wood for even the plainest of rough boxes, offering them one hundred dollars for something never to be had short of a miracle. If the world had been hers she would have given it for a wooden box in which to encase that loved partner taken from her as by a stroke of lightning.

No boards were procurable without destroying the bed of one of those "ships of the desert," an emigrants' wagon. But heroes were at hand — if only to satisfy the whim of a woman's broken heart. Joseph Reese and Benjamin Troutman, both of Des Moines, gave Mrs. Watts their wagon-bed. The gift was accepted with a gratitude no one present will ever forget; and the whole camp attended the funeral service of John Watts, at which John D. Chambers offered a prayer after a hymn had been sung. With an ingenuity worthy of so good a

UNCLE BOB READING THE "CALIFORNIA STAR"

cause, Reese and Troutman fashioned a frame made out of a network of willows and fitted it snugly on their running gear. The Mormons said that an old plainsman who witnessed the episode declared that Watts got a burial fit for a king and that in thirty years on the prairie he had never before seen a person buried in a coffin.

An emigrant had loaned Uncle Bob a copy of the *California Star* for April 1, 1848, and in it Sir Robert found a very solemn admonition to emigrants not to quarrel or take short cuts, but to stick to "The Old Road" — which was the title of the editorial.

Twice has he read this to the camp, at large, from the mouth of his tent, or marquee, as he calls it.

We cannot too strongly urge [ran the article] upon Emigrants the importance of keeping the well-defined "*old road*" to California. Their safety, and that of their property, depends upon this. Parties that have followed this road have reached the country without difficulty. Last season [1847] all succeeded in bringing their wagons in. The last companies arrived at the first settlements before the

season a new route across the country to the headwaters of the Sacramento. . . . Emigrating bodies should be especially guarded against the baneful effects of social discord. That unanimity of action is indispensable to their actual safety, let the fate of those who sank beneath the snows of Sierra Nevada attest. In reviewing the history of these unfortunate people, and tracing the disaster at once to a basis, it is shown that social harmony had long been extinct. It is enough that the physical fatigues are disposed of, without fresh harassing the mind with strifes, jarrings and disunion. To feverish irritability (produced by days and weeks of continued travel) the emigrant may be left entirely unprotected and alone. Misguided, and becoming belated on the road, he may encounter danger in its most appalling form — most earnestly are the emigration cautioned against the alarming consequences of social discord.

This topic — the story of the Donner party tragedy of 1846 — is in the mouth of every emigrant. Meek has promised to tell us "the facts of the case" sometime, but up to now he has not done so. All he has said, so far, is to offer this very unusual suggestion: "As to the news of the freezing to death of those in the Donner party, and the eating of human flesh by others in order to keep alive, it really amounts to this: those who died really gave their lives, unknowingly, as a sacrifice for many.

Perhaps hundreds of lives have been saved by that terrible
event, for nothing else could have so impressed these thousands
who are now going to California this year with the stern necessity of grinding on with regularity every single day so as not
to get caught in those Sierra Nevada snow-banks, which sometimes are thirty feet deep.   Had some not died because of
failure to push on, this warning would never have come in time
to be of use in this year of the great migration.   Many might
have been caught as a result.   Now everyone has been warned
and all know the great good sense in the advice given seven
years ago by Dr. Marcus Whitman: 'Nothing that holds you
back will do you any good.'   Least of all," added Meek,
"bickering and quarreling."

Our crew keeps a very even temper, but now and then Nature
takes her toll, and last night articles and tools of camp-life,
left loose on the ground or on temporary clotheslines, were
whisked away to adjoining counties, states, and nations —
requiring delay in to-day's departure.   Uncle Bob says little,
but Providence put it in his way to reprimand the camp for
carelessness — and a "jangling of tongues" due to carelessness
— in this indirect but unforgettable manner.

A morning scene on the Little Blue: fragrant groves of wild
plum trees, luxurious green grass, enormous wagon-wheel ruts
in the sward as though cannon balls had ricocheted along the
ground; a "misty, moisty morning" after a sockdolager (as the
Yankees say) of a pour-down as day dawned.   The teamsters
lie under their blankets, here and there, in every posture of
healthy repose, having merely pulled their heads in as the big
drops splashed on their faces.   The wet blankets smoke in the
sun like multicolored melon beds.   The echoing call of a ribald
sentry in a far-off camp: "Five o'clock and all is wet."

May 20. — "The last leaving of the Little Blue."   Surely
few who ever read these lines (unless they were of this army
of hurrying gold-seekers) can have any real understanding of
what they mean.

We left this morning all that the words "the East" signifies

— ascended our last five miles of the Little Blue and then climbed up through a sort of natural gap to the top of the divide and were, you might say, ushered instantly into the presence of the "Great West."   It was twenty-five miles to the Platte River.   The migration calls this curious new world we are entering the "Coast of Nebraska."   The signs of change were plain, even if the term "Coast" seemed very mystifying: dry air, sky that suggests infinity as does none other; hard,

from the sand, the

flying in the neighborhood of the river could hardly feel at home except on a "coast" — so we will let it go at that.

We strike the Platte near the "tail" of Grand Island, said to be the longest island in the world — measuring ninety miles from head to foot.   The river is wider than we expected, but very odd — shoaly and turbid, flowing rapidly over beds of quicksand, which, in the eddies, form into bars and conical-shaped tumuli, making the water an inch or two deep here and chin deep there.   Disputing ownership (for half a minute) with an enormous, handsomely striped garter snake, we go into camp; but not with the expectation that any entrenchments we can dig or battlements we can erect will in the least awe the brave reception army of mosquitoes which await us!

Platte River, and its tributary, the Sweetwater!   We shall follow them to the summit of the Rocky Mountains; our dreams (if we survive the "mosquito fleet") will be of buffalo, Chimney Rock, Fort Laramie, Red Buttes, Independence Rock, and the South Pass to California.   We are really in the Great West!

May 21. — It almost seemed as though our animals caught the fresh spirit of adventure which possessed us all upon reach-

ing the Platte; they were stirring early and we struck camp in
time to make fourteen miles to the new Fort Kearny (formerly
Fort Childs), in command of the famous Captain Bonneville,
before noon.   This post should be of some help to the migration, if the grogshops at the east and west entrances to the
reservation — Dogtown and Dobytown — do not neutralize
its effects for good!   Be that as it may, no one could be in
command here more likely, or more willing, to proffer wise
advice to emigrants than Bonneville.[1]   The renewed life of the
camp pleases everybody, whereupon Captain Meek urges that
what lies ahead up the Platte will draw heavily on our supply
of enthusiasm!   By the way, speaking of Dobytown, there is
a significant expression on the plains for the no-account loafers
who hang about the
camps and army posts.
They are called "doby-
men."   As though the
Lord might have run out
of clay when their time
came!

As for my enthusiasm,
it has been trebled many
times.   I have met a
trail-mate in a thousand.
"Boardy," as he will
stand in my Diary, hails
from Long Island and
belongs to the few chosen
who can tell you not only
what is happening but
why — and in language

MR. JEREMIAH SADDLEBAGS,

befitting any circum-
stance, incident, or exi-
gency.   In the regiments which he accompanied up the south
bank of the Platte River he, too, has found gay and glorious
specimens of excited humanity, but none to excel three whom

[1] O. Cross, *Report.*

he pointed out to me as "Brown," Jingo,"[1] and "Jeremiah Saddlebags."[2]   It is not for us, God wot, to go behind the facts in such cases; names change, you know, at the crossing-places of the Missouri River.   How or

might be that the undoubtedly gifted Saddlebags inveigled his comrades into the adventure, for many orators like him have harangued innumerable audiences in every part of the land to form, or join, gold associations and go to California in person or underwrite the expenses of agents who, by their discoveries, should make all the stockholders rich.

But, as there is no explaining names, so, also, there is no explaining reasons and motives which induced men to join this Golden Army — whether after much deliberation or, perhaps, hastily, owing to local revolutions as potent in the lives of individuals as European revolutions are in the lives of whole nations.

At any rate, as we swung down those last miles into this

---

[1] Our source of supply for the merry Brown-and-Jingo cartoons is the anonymous *The Adventures of the Firm of Brown and Jingo in California: Compiled entirely and with the strictest adherence to truth from Mr. Brown's own private Journal — without that gentleman's permission (and here Mr. Brown is recommended for the future NOT to leave his Journal in charge of the bar keeper wherever he goes).* (Published in San Francisco.)

[2] The heroic Saddlebags was the creation of J. A. and D. F. Read and plays the leading part in a series of cartoons entitled *A Journey to the Gold Digging Region.* (Published in Cincinnati.)

"Fort" the new additions to our moving panorama, adding fresh individuality with every new outfit or every curious

SADDLEBAGS HARANGUES HIS AUDIENCE

eccentric, created once more the "feel in the air" that a nation was moving westward.

ON HEARING THAT CRADLES WERE USED FOR WASHING GOLD, SADDLEBAGS BUYS ONE

"Fort" Kearny consists at present of a number of long, low buildings, constructed principally of adobe bricks, with nearly flat roofs; a large hospital tent; two or three workshops (of enormous help to those emigrants whose wagons have suffered severely) enclosed by canvas walls; storehouses similarly constructed; and several long adobe stables with roofs of brush. Its two companies of infantry, and one of dragoons, are housed, officers and men, in tents. Boardy, who has been on the ground several days, said he was holding converse here with a young dragoon dandy — all burnished up brightly and having as yet small acquaintance with his duties beyond dressing the part —

when a typical Nebraska "twister" came across the Platte
with a black cloud and struck Fort Kearny a glancing blow.

WHOSE DAUGHTER HE WAS ENGAGED TO MARRY, DEMANDS AN
EXPLANATION

The tent in which the two took refuge trembled spasmodically,
and then, ripping up all anchors, ballooned almost instantly into
the air.   The young jackanapes's spur caught in the canvas;
straight across the grounds, with head bouncing now and then
on the ground, went the would-be Brigadier-General and
brought up with a resounding crash against the adobe stables.

Made seventeen miles to-day all told; camped some three
miles beyond the Fort; even
Uncle Bob, not to mention our
new-found friends, found it
slow work to get by Dobytown
with its new supplies of merchandise.

May 22. — Now, if never before, we have plain proof that
a nation is moving westward.
Our tracks are almost countless
and trains in any number are

BROWN AND JINGO LOITERING
AT DOBYTOWN

behind, in front, and beside us; beyond this great sandy slough called the Platte a continuous line of covered wagons marks the "Mormon Trail." But the river gives some poor wood (driftwood) to burn — and water. Many are circling far to right and left to gather buffalo dung to burn for lack of wood. It serves well for cooking, but is useless in the case of many emigrants in need of a big fire in order to reset wobbly wagon-tires.

When nooning to-day we met a boy who was sent across the Platte by his father (an emigrant on the Mormon Trail) to find some alleged relatives who, it was rumored, had passed Fort Kearny on our route. He told a fair tale about an attempt of the Pawnees to work what is maliciously called a "Mormon trick" on emigrants at Shell Creek, northeast of the Fort.

"When our company came to this creek," the boy said, "we found a band of Indians squatting by an old bridgehead. The bridge had been swept away by a flood and they proposed to collect 'presents' from all who wanted to cross there.

"It seemed as though we 'd have to fork over, but old Dad was too much for them. Telling everyone to stand by and shut up, he went back to his buggy and fished out an old copy of Frémont's *Journal*. In a pocket in its cover was Frémont's map; with that, and a terribly sharp-pointed pencil, he formed a party of axemen and went straight into the Indian camp and told his men to go ahead and cut puncheons to replace the old stringers. The men had the sand to go to work with, Dad giving orders right and left. An old chief soon came up and poked Dad on the shoulder, but it took a lot of pokes to gain attention. Then a parley began, but not until Dad had given orders to the men not to stop work.

"Finally Dad asked in a low tone for the Great Big Chief. He came, surrounded by braves armed with tomahawks, swords, guns, and bows and arrows. Dad spread out the map. With every word he gave it a thump with that pencil.

"'You made a treaty with the Big White Chief in Washington,' he said. 'It gave our people the right to go to California, and I am leading these men there. It is our great White Father's pleasure that they should go. This is the way. There is your signature to the Treaty.' He pointed to the old signatures on the Frémont map, which some of the Indians recognized.

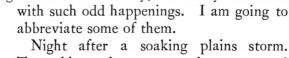

TRAVELING LIGHT

our way. We left a supply of tobacco with the Pawnees which Dad raised among the members of the train."

We keep forging ahead monotonously, but always are faced with such odd happenings. I am going to abbreviate some of them.

Night after a soaking plains storm. Tents blown down; ground too wet and soft to hold the tent-pins.

Wet puppy playing with a good boot that everybody is hunting for.

Sick man leering out of the rear of a wagon, looking calomel-y.

Man falls under a wagon's wheels; leg broken in two places. Dr. Gillespie sets it — for the long, discouraging trip home.

Fanciful cones and nebulæ of sand along the Platte River banks.

Man too much physicked has hiccoughs that the doctor cannot stop. Crowd stands around, suggesting.

UNCLE BOB FEEL-
ING NOT SO WELL

Man gets back to his train perfectly naked, holding a sage-brush skirt around his waist; was fishing; skulking Pawnees took his clothes, leaving — just him.

Cattle very thin — due to drinking muddy Platte water.

Storm drove cattle twenty miles off the road. Owners delayed a week hunting for those which Indians had not sequestered.

Cattle with leather "boots," made to protect the feet from mud and sand; you smear them with grease and tar to make them "waterproof."

One company lost seventy cattle out of a hundred; drifted with the storm.

Company waiting for return of man and boy — lost hunting cattle. Women in hysterics; absentees been gone three days.

Boys gathering driftwood from river banks, throwing it in a wagon which stops and waits whenever a likely pile is seen. It dries in the wind while traveling on.

Cattle "alkalied"; men forcing vinegar or bacon down their throats.

Little girl and mother playing in a wagon; wagon starts; girl goes down right between the wheels; little hands and feet come up, terribly lifelike, as the wheels pass over and crush her.

Man, not too strong after sickness, scared by a fake "Indian attack" of playful rowdies, hid under an overhanging bank. It fell in on him. If they "bring him to" he will be a wreck mentally if not physically.

Fort Kearny soldiers beseeching emigrants for whiskey when actually ill for want of plain flour and sugar.

Emigrants following frightened cattle at night by lightning across the plain.

Prairie dog broth extolled by many. At that rate rusty horseshoe soup will be a delicacy by this time next month.

Horses crazed for water rush uncontrolled into the Platte; some sink until nothing is out of water except what they wanted to put in — their noses; being hauled out with teams and ropes.

Piles of buffalo "chips" drying in the sun; as useless as wood is when wet.

Stockings being knit of buffalo hair (shed in May) gathered from the sagebrush; some wear two years.

"Shaved behind the skin" — said of the prairie when the grass is too short for grazing.

Traders, trappers, and actual Californians (going back East over our trail) bring with them the doggerel ballads which the

I soon fell in with a lot from Pike:
The next was 'Damn you, back, whoa, haw,'
A right smart chance from Arkansaw.

"On the Platte we could n't agree
    Because I had the mis-i-ree.
We there split up, I made a break
    With one old mule for Great Salt Lake.

"The Mormon girls were fat as hogs,
    The chief production cats and dogs;
Some had ten wifes, others none,
    Thirty-six had Brigham Young.

"The damned old fool, like all the rest,
    Supposed his thirty-six the best;
He soon found out his virgin dears
    Had all been Mormons thirteen years.

"On I traveled through the pines,
    At last I found the northern mines.
I stole a dog, got whipped like Hell,
    Then away I went to Marysville.

"Because I would not pay a bill,
        They kicked me out of Downieville;
    I stole a mule and lost the trail
        And fetched up in the Hangtown jail.

"Canvas roof and paper walls,
        Twenty horse thieves in the stalls;
    I did just like I done before —
        Coyoted out from 'neath the floor."

May 23–24. — Last night out of nowhere someone brought a few half-burned tepee poles that were dry enough to burn. A camp-fire was a luxury after the lack of one for some nights, owing to wet wood. In a moment's time ours was crowded, and Ox Bow, who rather likes to talk to a real audience, expanded awhile very interestingly on the never-ending debate of the relative merits of white man's and red man's instinct and cleverness. "The hoss ain't lived between whose ears I ever saw an Indian buck who could do anything but poison and steal better 'n a white man who had had a fair chanst to learn," he was saying, as I came up; "an' at that I 've saw thousands o' whites you did n't dare to sleep along side of with yer mouth open if you had a gold tooth.

"Now, fer instance, take them Shoshonys out on Bear River; we held a reglar circus day with 'em once back in '43, but 'longside mountain men they could n't come up to taw in any dee-partment.[1]

"Fer a start we put on a shootin' contest, with three posts a-stuck in the ground, about twenty-five yards apart, standin' six feet out of the ground and ten inches thick. The top o' each post was squared for a distance of about twelve inches. The arms used first was to be Colt's six-shooters, horses to be put at full speed and pass the posts not closer than ten feet, every man to fire two shots at each post. Some o' our boys sunk two bullets in each post and every man jack of 'em put in at least one. I tried it twice, but the best I could do was one bullet in each post. The Indians had several pistols equal to ours, but

[1] W. T. Hamilton, *My Sixty Years on the Plains.*

only three of them hit each post, putting one shot in each. Many Indians hit but one post out of six shots.

"Comin' to rifles, we licked 'em still worse, shootin' at all distances from twenty to three hundred yards. Our best rifles were the Hawkins, and they carried three hundred and fifty yards. Bets was always made and the Indians always wanted the last shot. Nine times out of ten we won; their alibi always was that their 'medicine was n't strong that day.'

scouts, who are nowadays never fooled by 'em.

"Indians are also smart in pointin' their arrows with flint, which they poison by dippin' the point in liver which has been daubed with rattlesnake poison. I have heard tell that they extract a poison from roots, but I never swallered that. Jack-rabbits and ground squirrels are their favorite grub and I 've noticed large numbers of them hung up in their villages. They hunt squirrels with blunt-pointed arrows. They are mighty cute at imitatin' the actions of wolves; puttin' a large wolf hide on their backs and crawlin' on their hands and knees, they imitate the wolf very closely. But mountain men are up to all such tricks and many an Indian has come to grief while trying the game on us.

"When it comes to fightin', Indians can't stand a white man's charge. They are yaller at close quarters — get bewildered-like. In a fight, the closer you are to an Indian the safer you are and the less danger of gettin' hurt; in a pinch he can't collect his thoughts. I have heard tell that Indians can hold their own in hand-to-hand conflicts; mebbe so, mebbe so; but old mountain men don't believe it. Fifty whites of experience can rout almost any number of 'em. But at poisonin' we had

to hand it to 'em, specially their arrows. We was always supplied with ammonia, which was good medicine for poison; we
used it by scrapin' the wound with the point of a knife and
dosin' on the ammonia, as well as freely breathin' its fumes."

A smouldering tepee stump now and then burst into a blaze,
lighting up the bearded faces of the men. Beyond, at a dis-
stance, horsemen were night-riding a mixed herd of oxen, mules,
and horses, some of which were being sold to emigrants every
hour or two.

"It ain't no wonder them red men out yonder on the plains is
such first-class hoss and cattle thieves," went on Ox Bow, after
a silence, "fur they go to school the hull year round to the
grandest perfessers o' deception and deceit that the Good Lord
ever give legs to run er stand on, and I mean prairie wolves."
The old man spat almost indignantly at the blaze. "There
ain't a man born east o' the Missouri would 'a' believed what I
seen with my own eyes while trappin' on the Bonte off Laramie
Peak two years ago come Christmas."

"Can I get a couple of travelin' mules?" interrupted an
emigrant of a drover on the edge of the fire. The latter nodded
and, mounting a pony, trotted away toward the night-riders.

"I was pestered with the idee," went on Ox Bow, "that the
camp ought to have a mountain sheep for a holiday dinner, but
after travelin' and climbin' miles it come over me that I did n't
like mutton nohow and I sat down on the point of a small hill.
By accident I was jest in time to see a show. First thing I
noticed was an onusual fussin' among some wolves on a near-by
rise o' ground where some fifty or a hundred o' those sneakin'
marauders seemed to 'a' met in a sort of convention. Off to one
side two V-shaped lines o' low hills led out from the river bottom into the prairie for five or six miles, makin' a widening
valley, at the fur end o' which a band of antelope were grazin'.
The chief topic o' the wolf convention seemed to have reference to these-here; for in a short time the rally broke up and
its members looped off to the two rows of hills shelterin' the
V-shaped valley I mentioned, and, settin' themselves down one
at a time upon both rows at reg'lar intervals, two ringleaders

went beyond them antelopes and commenced operations by driftin' down on them prey from the far side in such a way as to scare the whole band back along between the hills where the wolves was posted. This done, the chase begun in reglar' relay-fashion without no delay. As any antelope can outrun any wolf, each wolf in turn performed his level best by pursuin' them on up the valley until relieved by the wolf at the next station and he by the next one and so on, alternate, care being

with some good Christmas venison and a fresh gence o' wolves."

A shot rang out in the night air over where the cattle were, soon followed by the hoof-beats of two startled, rangy mules being led up toward our fire by the drover who went after them. He seemed all snarled up in ropes, holding two tethering ropes (with a mule at the end of each) in one hand and the end of a long taut lariat in the other.

"Hold them damn mules," he growled testily to the waiting emigrant on the outskirts of the ring. Relieved of the tethering ropes, he swung his fidgety pony right into the crowd and forced it the length of his lariat beyond the fire. The end of the lariat was tied around an Indian's moccasined foot; above the foot the fringed legging was in place, but the blanket had been dragged over the horse thief's head. In the firelight the blanket, with its big, telltale bloody spot in the centre, was jerked away by many hands.

The face of the dead thief was that of a white man.[1]

"Well, hello, little joker," said Ox Bow, brushing back the dead man's hair. "Fur God's sakes ain't the poor Injun got enough to answer fur without your makin' it wuss for him?"

[1] H. Allyn, *Diary*.

May 25. — Boardy and I have long talks, trying to analyze this thing right before our eyes — this migration — and make real sense out of what provides nonsense for the cartoonists and our own pencils and sketch pads. What are the real motives of these hurrying thousands, self-seeking or wealth for others? How many will reach their goal? Live to thank or regret the day? The way these various dispositions meet the unheard-of trials of the trail is a never-ending source of interest. Our talk this morning, at the head of the train with Meek, was prompted by overtaking picturesque old Pickpan and noting

his irresistible purpose to "make his way." He will arrive in the Land of Gold in a prosperous state! We found him to-day minus axe but lord of a tasty wagon and two tolerable mules. But was he driving it? Oh no! He had taken

PICKPAN'S TEAM AND PARTNER

in a partner to do that while he was hurrying ahead "in character," plying his trade of acquiring sympathy — and useful possessions.

You would not believe the arts and ruses adopted by some of our companion gold-seekers in order to make their way. One has a magic lantern containing the picture of "The Queen of all the Indians: The Most Beautiful Indian Maiden in the West." You wouldn't believe the number of lovelorn, lonesome men and boys in these camps who will hand over a coin to look in the little machine a minute by the watch! Boardy couldn't resist the temptation to see what the lantern contained — for professional purposes, of course. The lanternman will certainly arrive in California a prosperous individual!

I find in reading these pages over that I have really given you

no account of the many forms of amusement and relaxation
indulged in by us in camp.   Unless "drowned out," as we have
been twice lately, scarcely a camp-ground but what resounds
with the fiddle, flute, or accordion.   One is never out of the
sight of a card game.   Some companies while away many
hours in practising for and presenting skits, rowdy comedies,

THE MOST BEAUTIFUL INDIAN

and, sometimes, rather good plays.   Of course parts played by
"colored gem'men" are most popular, and the take-offs on our
life a-trail and in camp draw hilarious howls from the roistering
assemblages which gather as by magic whenever the strains of
"Oh! Susanna" or "Dearest Mae" drift from impromptu
"stages" across these camping-places.   Southern trains, and
those from sections like southern Illinois and Missouri into

which Southerners have migrated, are usually able to furnish good banjo-players and, not infrequently, slaves who are unable to keep from "Jim Crowing" even after a long day's dusty march — if a banjo strikes up at night! We often meet, pass, or are passed by, such trains as those of Captain English from Lexington, Missouri, or Mr. Hammer's from Bloomington, Illinois, or Colonel Kinkead's. Hammer should be called "Tinkler" because of his skill with the banjo; and you should see Colonel Kinkead's negroes "jump Jim Crow" or "Jim Crack Corn" when those strings begin to tinkle! [1] Others at home may be discussing squatter sovereignty, but the kind you hear in these camps is "Jim Crow" squatting or "Crack Corn" squatting — and it only makes for fun, not angry argument.

Yesterday a lay-over of a few hours was necessary because of a wrecked wagon ahead of us at a bad crossing; Meek and Ox Bow helped the emigrant in trouble to get out of the hole and also to repair the damage. It was a congested place on the trail, and who did we find camping near by but our long-lost religious brotherhood of those days back on the Blue!

From one of them we heard a "sermon," very unexpected as to both source and subject. It seems that some of the order had been taking this world too lightly — joining in these camp-fire sings and toying with "filthy" playing cards. One of the elders had acquired, goodness knows how, an extract from the Clayton diary of 1847 containing a part of a sermon preached by Brigham Young not fifty miles from where we were to his backsliding Mormon brethren just two years ago this month — when the famous original party of 147 were going overland to spy out the new Paradise for the Saints at present Salt Lake City.

In the first place I did n't know that the Mormon elders were ever guilty of such besotted crimes as dancing, card-playing, and giving minstrel shows; and, in the second place, we didn't know Brigham was such a ripping good Calvinist — if that is what you call folks who think that if anything is fun it is wrong.

"You are always saying the Mormons do this and don't do

[1] A. Delano, *Life on the Plains*, and L. Sawyer, *Way Sketches*.

that," this brotherhood elder began; "and you seem to believe, with many others, that what between polygamy and robbery they are the worst scoundrels unhung that ever came west. But I want you to know what kind of a leader they had when they crossed these plains two years ago and how he handed it

A REGIMENT OF BETTER HALVES ON THE MARCH TO
SALT LAKE CITY

(*From "A Journey to the Gold Digging Region" by J. Read*)

to them right over there across the Platte for engaging in devilment just as you have been doing.   This is what he said: —

"I remarked last Sunday that I had not felt much like preaching to the brethren on this mission.   This morning I feel like preaching a little, and shall take for my text, 'That as to pursuing our journey with this company with the spirit they possess, I am about to revolt against it.'   This is the text I feel like preaching on this morning, consequently I am in no hurry. . . .

"Nobody has told me what has been going on in the camp, but I have known it all the while.   I have been watching its movements, its influence, its effects, and I know the result if it is not put a stop to.   I want you to understand that inasmuch as we are beyond the power of the Gentiles where the devil has tabernacles in the priests and the people, we are beyond their reach, we are beyond their power, we are beyond their grasp, and what has the devil now to work upon?

Upon the spirits of men in this camp, and if you do not open your hearts so that the Spirit of God can enter your hearts and teach you the right way, I know that you are a ruined people and will be destroyed and that without remedy, and unless there is a change and a different course of conduct, a different spirit to what is now in this camp, I go no farther.   I am in no hurry. . . .

"But here are the Elders of Israel, men who have had years of experience, men who have had the priesthood for years, — and have they got faith enough to rise up and stop a mean, low, groveling, covetous, quarrelsome spirit?   No, they have not, nor would they try to stop it, unless I rise up in the power of God and put it down. I do not mean to bow down to the spirit that is in this camp and which is rankling in the bosoms of the brethren, and which will lead to knock downs and perhaps to the use of the knife to cut each other's throats if it is not put a stop to.   I do not mean to bow down to the spirit which causes the brethren to quarrel.   When I wake up in the morning the first thing I hear is some of the brethren jawing each other and quarreling because a horse has got loose in the night. I have let the brethren dance and fiddle and act the nigger night after night to see what they will do, and what extremes they would go to, if suffered to go as far as they would.   I do not love to see it. The brethren say they want a little exercise to pass away time in the evenings, but if you can't tire yourselves bad enough with a day's journey without dancing every night, carry your guns on your shoulders and walk, carry your wood to camp instead of lounging and lying asleep in your wagons, increasing the load until your teams are tired to death and ready to drop to the earth.   Help your teams over mud holes and bad places instead of lounging in your wagons and that will give you exercise enough without dancing.

"Well, they will play cards, they will play checkers, they will play dominoes, and if they had the privilege, and were where they could get whiskey, they would be drunk half their time, and in one week they would quarrel, get to high words and draw their knives to kill each other.   This is what such a course of things would lead to.   Don't you know it?   Yes.   Well, then, why don't you try to put it down?   I have played cards once in my life since I became a Mormon to see what kind of spirit would attend it, and I was so well satisfied, that I would rather see in your hands the dirtiest thing you could find on the earth than a pack of cards.   You never read of gambling, playing cards, checkers, dominoes, etc., in the scriptures, but you do read of men praising the Lord in the Dance, but who ever read of praising the Lord in a game at cards? If any man had sense enough to play a game at cards, or dance a little, without wanting to keep it up all the time, but exercise a little and then quit it and think no more of it, it would do well enough, but you want to keep it up till midnight and every night, and all the time. You don't know how to control your senses. Last winter when we had our seasons of recreation in the council house, I went forth in the dance frequently, but did my mind run on it? No! To be sure,

trifling, covetous, wicked spirit dwelling in our bosoms! It is vain; vain! Some of you are very fond of passing jokes, and will carry your jokes very far. But will you take a joke? If you do not want to take a joke, don't give a joke to your brethren. Joking, nonsense, profane language, trifling conversation and loud laughter do not belong to us. Suppose the angels were witnessing the hoe down the other evening and listening to the haw haws the other evening, would they not be ashamed of it? I am ashamed of it. I have not given a joke to any man on this journey nor felt like it; neither have I insulted any man's feelings but I have hollowed pretty loud and spoken sharply to the brethren when I have seen their awkwardness at coming to camp. . . .

"Now let every man repent of his weakness, of his follies, of his meanness, and every kind of wickedness, and stop your swearing and profane language, for it is in this camp and I know it, and have known it. I have said nothing about it, but I now tell you, if you don't stop it you shall be cursed by the Almighty and shall dwindle away and be damned. . . .

"Here are the Elders of Israel who have the priesthood, who have got to preach the Gospel, who have to gather the nations of the earth, who have to build up the kingdom so that the nations can come to it, they will stoop to dance as niggers. I don't mean this as debasing the negroes by any means; they will hoe down all, turn summersets, dance on their knees, and haw, haw, out loud; they will play cards, they will play checkers and dominoes, they will use profane language, they will swear! Suppose when you go to preach, the people should ask you what you did when you went on this mission to seek out a home for the whole Church, what was your course of conduct? Did you dance? Yes. Did you hoe down all? Yes. Did you play cards? Yes. Did you play checkers? Yes. Did you use profane language? Yes. Did you swear? Yes. Did you quarrel with each other and threaten each other? Why yes. How would you feel?"

There was some talk in camp to-night about the number of people who ridicule the whole California gold craze and think those of us who are starting overland are the biggest lunatics ashore, while those who are going around the Horn are the biggest ones afloat.

"Well," piped up a man from another outfit, "just before I left home my uncle, who loaned me some money for the trip, wrote me, saying: 'I think you are a fool for going, but you 've got as much right to make a fool of yourself as anybody. But don't say you were not warned. I enclose a clipping from the California *Star* printed in Sacramento, not fifty miles from where the supposed gold was found, and not three months after it was supposed to be found. I don't reckon reading it will make you stay at home and return me my money, but don't ever say you were not warned.'"

The man unfolded the clipping, which was cut from the *Star* of May 20, 1848 (one year old only last week), and read it out loud: —

"A fleet of launches left this place on Sunday and Monday last, bound 'up the Sacramento River' close stowed with human beings led by the love of 'filthy lucre' to the perrennial yielding Gold Mines of the North where any man can find upwards of two ounces a day, and two thousand men can find their hands full — of work! Was there ever anything so superlatively silly? Honestly . . . we are inclined to believe the reputed wealth of that section of country . . . all sham — as superb take in as was ever got up to 'guzzle the gullible.' "

There was something rather pitiful in the silence with which these words were received, by men and women wearing their hearts out to get to — a "sham!"

It was just like stern old Meek to turn the tables on this well-meaning pessimist — Meek, who never was afraid to look a thing in the face.

"How long did that newspaper live, neighbor," spoke up our noble Captain, "after it printed that story?"

SECTION III

ROLLING ON TO OLD FORT LARAMIE

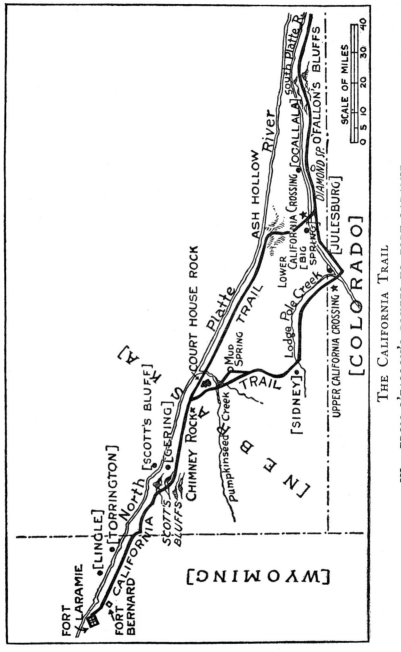

THE CALIFORNIA TRAIL

III. FROM O'FALLON'S BLUFFS TO FORT LARAMIE

SECTION III

therefore follow my gregarious family, especially if you consult the map. Meek tells me we will scarcely
have twelve more interesting days, at any stage of our 2000-
mile trip, than these twelve next ensuing.

May 27. 23 miles up the Platte [North Platte, Neb.].
May 28. 25 miles. Passed Forks of the Platte.
May 29. Cross South Platte at "Lower California Crossing"
　　　　[Brulé, Neb.].
May 30. To Ash Hollow — up North Platte [Lewellen, Neb.].
May 31. 22 miles up North Platte.
June 1. 22 miles to near Court House Rock.
June 2. In camp.
June 3. 22 miles to near Chimney Rock.
June 4. Up North Platte.
June 5. Marshall Pass [Gering, Neb.] and Scott's Bluffs [Scotts-
　　　　bluff, Neb.].
June 6. Up North Platte [Torrington, Wyo.].
June 7. 17 miles to Fort Laramie [Wyo.].

May 26. — We will pass the famous landmark the Forks of
the Platte to-day or to-morrow, according to Meek. The way
these old plainsmen can *see*, after all these years of looking into
the sun without the aid of "Mormon goggles," almost amounts

to clairvoyancy. I was out last night with Ox Bow on a mission of mercy, hunting lost cattle, several miles into the plain southward of the main track, for a sick emigrant. When we started back in the darkness for camp I wondered that the old hunter never seemed to give a thought to direction. When questioned he told me that if a dozen other circumstances would not take us home — like the "horse sense" of our animals or the inclination of the grass or the fact that most horse-tracks in the sand pointed toward the river or the topography of the region as fixed in the man's mind the while we were riding out — he would know it by the direction of the movements of the clouds, as the prevailing wind was always from the southwest. Eyes! And when I asked how he could tell our tracks from camp (made an hour before) from others, he made me get off and study the tracks we were following. Most of these were filled with sand. Then he pointed to one made by our horses' hoofs; the sand was *still sifting* into them!

For the past week the emigrants have been overhauling their guns. Buffalo land begins around these famous Forks of the Platte. Trains well-stocked like ours pay small attention to this — particularly if desirous of making good time. In these last years the great herds have been driven far south of the Platte; a real hunt — such as would interest Wagonhound or Ox Bow — would delay our outfit a week, and that Uncle Bob would not countenance.

But the sight of a drove north of the river this afternoon was too much for Boardy and me. Stripping off everything but our shirts and shoes, we gaily proceeded to walk across — the river being considerably over a mile and a half wide and very rapid. We got above our waists immediately near the shore, but, after wading fifteen or twenty yards, it began to shoal until we were not knee deep. The sand was very shifty, and the current rapid, making the footing insecure and toilsome. A few yards more brought us again into deep water, and thus it kept alternating from an ankle ripple to a chin-deep surge, the water being so muddy we could not forsee the difference of depth in any case.

We struggled on for half an hour without seeming to have made very much progress toward the opposite shore, and our boots and shoes were getting filled with sand and sharp gravel. This crippled us and caused such pain that we had to make an effort to get them off; but, as the shortest pause in the quicksand made us sink right down, it was a matter of extreme difficulty, especially with me, who happened to be the wearer of boots. I managed, however, to get one off after some stagger-

he had landed on to a shoal bar where he again got to his legs and was able to make a fresh start.   After an hour and twenty minutes of wading and floundering we at length reached terra firma, but so completely used up that we had to rest for a quarter of an hour before we were up to the mark for attack.   After freshly capping my rifle we proceeded to where we could again see the herd and were amazed to find that it had drifted so far that we could never hope to reach and pursue it and recross the Platte again before night fell; and no one wanted to try to ford that river after dark.   The return across that mile and a half of river, bog, morass, swamp, bayou, and lagoon exhausted our strength — but oh, the knowledge we had acquired! Take our word for it, if Old Platte has n't enough water on top to drown you he 'll drag you down to where it is if he can. There is more truth than fiction in the saying that it "flows bottom side up."

But in camp to-night, amid the chuckles indulged in by our old-timers at Boardy's description of our "Advance at Waterloo," as he called it, the talk naturally drifted around buffalo-hunting and the camp arts of the hunter.

The winter camp of a hunter is usually located in some spot

sheltered by hills or rocks, for the double purpose of securing the full warmth of the sun's rays and screening it from the notice of any strolling Indians that may happen in its vicinity. Within a convenient proximity to it stands some grove, from which an abundance of dry fuel is procurable when needed; and equally close the ripplings of a watercourse. The hunter's shanty faces a huge fire and is formed of skins carefully extended over an arched framework of slender poles, which are bent in the form of a semicircle and kept in place by inserting their extremities in the ground. Near this is his "graining block," planted on a slope, for greater ease in preparing his skins for the finishing process in the art of dressing; and not far removed is a stout frame, made of four pieces of timber so tied together as to leave a square of sufficient dimensions for the required purpose, in which a skin is usually stretched to its fullest extension, with the mountaineer busily engaged in rubbing it with a rough stone or "scraper," to fit it for the manufacture of clothing.

Facing his shanty, upon the opposite side of the fire, a pole is reared upon crotches five or six feet high, across which lie a choice selection of the dainties of his range — "side ribs," shoulders, heads, and "rump-cuts" of deer and sheep, or the "dépouille" and "fleeces" of buffalo. Over the camp-fire dainty bits of hissing roasts may hang, while the lord of the range sits upon the head of a mountain sheep whose huge horns furnish the legs and arms of his throne.

Carefully hung in their place are seen the hunter's riding and pack saddles, with his halters, "cavraces," "larrietts," "apishamores," and all the needful material for camp and traveling service; at no great distance away his animals are allowed to graze, or, if suitable nourishment of other kind be lacking, are fed from the inner bark of cottonwood trees leveled for that purpose.

The usual mode of dressing skins prevalent in this country among both Indians and whites is very simple in its details and is easily practised. It consists in removing all the fleshy particles from the pelt and divesting it of the thin, viscid substance upon the exterior known as the "grain"; then, after permitting it to dry, it is thoroughly soaked in a liquid decoction formed from the brains of the animal mixed with water; whereupon it is stoutly rubbed with the hands in order to open its pores and admit the mollient properties of the fluid.   The task in hand is completed by alternate rubbings and distensions until it is completely dry and soft.   In this manner a skin may be dressed in a very short time, and, on application of smoke,

lying promontory.   We continue to follow (as the map shows) the main trail on the south shore of the South Platte.   There are crossing-places along here to the promontory between, but the ground over there is likely to be soft and marshy, for it is a dozen miles before the land between the Forks rises to a great bare shoulder which widens as the two separate into individual drainage areas.

But if the main trail avoids treacherous ground by sticking to the south side of the South Platte, do not think it is easy traveling.   Here begin the weird sand formations which make strange pictures against the sky for a hundred miles.   The name here is O'Fallon's Bluffs — ridges of sand through which our route winds with wagons sinking axle deep in many places. Now we run behind them; now we swing north and pass between them and the river.   The result is just chaos; teams stuck, animals exhausted; families and outfits camping in the sand on every hand and in all conditions of despondency and despair.   By double-teaming we manage to forge on; our delays are due to hauling others out.

Explain the psychology of the thing as you will, misfortunes curiously work both ways; for things can get so badly off as to bring laughter to any lips — and save the day. I was reminded of this as we were nooning to-day after pulling an old Illinois boy out of a small sand crater. As we drew up he had asked for help in order to get out of our way.

"Is n't it a nicely graded road ahead?" queried Meek, playfully, of the distracted old man.

"Graded road!" he snorted, glowering at our guide. "My God, that road has n't been graded since the devil was a little baby."

But it took our warbling teamster, whose pet name appears to be Carlo, to illustrate cheerfulness in the midst of adversity as, sitting on a high mound, soaked with perspiration, the sand sifting unceasingly into both boots, he held aloft a piece of cheese and hardtack, or "Obsidian Cak[e," and chortled: —

A DESERT DREAM OF HOME AND
PANCAKES

"They 're all my fancy painted
        'em,
    They 're lovely, they 're
        divine !!
But they 're destined for
    another's mouth,
    They never can be mine.
I love them as man never
        loved,
    Yet I cannot touch or take;
Oh, my heart, my heart is
        breaking
    For the love of Buckwheat
        Cake."

"Did ye ever try ungent fur that, Carlo?" growled his buddy. "If it kills lice outside yer throat it might kill that what ails ye inside yer throat."

But there was no blighting that kingly spirit: —

"The dark brown cake is laid upon
  A plate of spotless white;
And the eye of him who tastes it,
  Now flashes with delight.
Oh, cake that 's buttered for me,
  Why can I not partake?
Oh, my heart, my heart is breaking
  For the love of Buckwheat Cake." [1]

of buffalo came sweeping up from the river, and Dolly [2]
joined a large number of men (some driving wagons in which
to bring back meat) who went in pursuit.

It was a magnificent sight to behold the solid-moving masses
of buffalo as they swept by herd after herd, over the broad
prairie. All of us were instantly in pursuit at the utmost speed
of our animals. Horses and riders appeared to partake equally
in the excitement. Rifles were heard cracking in all directions,
some men shooting from their horses and others leaping down
to shoot from the ground. The pursuit was continued for
several miles. The men who remained with the train had their
share of the sport too, for long after the horsemen were out of
sight herd after herd continued to come sweeping past the train,
breaking it up and running between the wagons. The drivers
had their hands full to manage their teams. They found it
necessary to turn their wagons crossways with the road, heading the teams in the direction the buffalo were running. In this
way they succeeded in controlling them, though the mules
danced and snorted furiously, becoming almost unmanageable.
The men on foot were surrounded on all sides by buffalo and
were well pleased if they could keep themselves from being

[1] Parody by Tom Bar.   [2] Near Brulé, Neb.

trampled. Some of them "bellowed" most lustily with a view to alarming the animals and turning them in another direction. Some played upon the buffalo with their pistols, though with little effect.

In the middle of that night a horde of the buffalo again crossed the Platte close to our camp, lowing and bellowing, making the ground tremble as if under the paroxysm of an earthquake, and causing all our animals, without a single exception, to stampede — Uncle Bob's prized bell-mare and all. Every man save six, who were indispensable for guarding the wagons, had to turn out in pursuit. Fortunately the night was clear, and, though we could not overtake them, we could see the course they took up a ravine leading to the other side of the bluffs. It was dawning day when we reached the top, and, though far out of sight, the fresh tracks and manure told Wagonhound the direction they went. From another range of hills we saw them about five miles off on the prairie. They did not attempt running further and we easily approached and secured the bell-mare, who had all her faithful mules around her. But nine of the horses were still wanting, so six of us mounted again, and after scouring the plains for two hours we found them all quietly grazing on a dip of land, where they waited unconcerned till we caught them.

We came to the Lower Crossing of the South Fork late in the day, where we found a number of wagons on both sides of the river. Some had crossed, others were then crossing, but with much trouble, for the rains had greatly swollen the river, thus increasing the risk of losing the wagons. If we had not realized it before, we now saw the reason for the careful caulking of our wagon-beds which Captain Meek had attended to in person. So many outfits were on this side waiting for a more favorable opportunity to get across that the banks seemed to be lined with trains; others could be seen across the river, and even on top of the divide which separates the two Forks. The sight made one wonder whether grazing could be found for such an immense number of cattle as must necessarily be thrown together when outfits are compelled to stop for water.

The South Platte here is 1090 yards wide, and we began to think at one time that the first wagons Meek sent across would not reach the opposite bank in safety. After this he had ten mules attached to each wagon; and as long as the leading wagon kept moving, the rest followed very well and got across much better than anyone supposed. The mules frequently got into the quicksand; but extra-duty men stationed ⸺ Meek in the river at the worst places were ready to give

than three feet deep, the ⸺

that deep was exceedingly deceptive. Meek said it was not uncommon to see teamsters down in the water at the same time with their mules and becoming so entangled with the harness that it appeared impossible to extricate them. It rained throughout the evening; but we were over in safety, much to the gratification of everyone — for most emigrants dread the crossing of this stream more than the balance of the journey.

Around our fire that night, by the "Lower California Crossing," was told one of the most pitiful stories of the plains. Here it is; and skip it! The speaker repeated it in the words of Edwin Bryant, who was the "Doc" of the incident.

"'Will ye come, Doc, will ye?' the man begged me. I could not refuse his request; for, although I insisted in the most serious possible way that I was not a physician, much less a surgeon, no answer can satisfy a terrified father, and by the use of simple remedies and applied common sense I had acquired during the journey a reputation for which I was not to be envied if any real crisis arose."

The speaker sat on the ground before the fire; his wind-beaten furrowed face bespoke the plainsman, but his language was not the frontiersman's brogue or jargon.

"The case to which I was thus hastily summoned against my will was an accident to a boy in an adjoining outfit encamped about a mile away. I supposed, of course, that it had just occurred. When I reached the tent of the unfortunate family to which the boy belonged, I found him stretched out upon a bench made of planks, ready for an operation which they expected I would perform. I soon learned, from the mother, that the accident which caused the fracture had occurred nine days previously, and that some person professing to be a 'doctor' had wrapped some linen loosely about the leg and made a sort of trough, or plank box, in which it had been confined. In this condition the child had remained, without any dressing of his wounded limb, until last night, when he called to his mother and told her that he could feel worms crawling in his leg! This, at first, she supposed to be absurd; but when the boy insisted, an examination of the wound for the first time was made, and it was discovered that gangrene had set in and the limb of the child was fairly swarming with maggots! They then immediately dispatched their messengers for me.

"I made an examination of the fractured limb and ascertained that what the mother had stated was correct. The limb had been badly fractured, and had never been bandaged; and from neglect gangrene had supervened; and the child's leg, from his foot to his knee, was in a state of putrefaction. He was so much enfeebled by his sufferings that death was stamped upon his countenance, and I was satisfied that he could not live twenty-four hours, much less survive an operation. I so informed the mother, stating to her that to amputate the limb would only hasten the end and add to the boy's pains while living. I declined, at the same time, peremptorily, all participation in a proceeding so useless and barbarous under the circumstances. The poor woman implored me, with tears and moans, not thus to give up her child without an effort. I told her again that all efforts to save him would be useless and would only add to the anguish which was now actually killing him.

"This could not satisfy a mother's affection. She could not thus unresistantly yield her offspring to a lonely grave in the wilderness. A Canadian Frenchman who belonged to the same emigrating party was present, and then stated that he had formerly been an assistant to a surgeon in some hospital and had seen many operations of this nature performed; he volunteered to amputate the child's limb if I declined doing it and the mother eagerly clutched at this straw of hope and frantically desired him to proceed. I could not repress an involuntary shudder when I heard of this proposition which won the con-

the operation should be performed above the knee. During these demonstrations the boy never uttered a groan or a complaint, but I saw from the change in his countenance that he was dying. The operator, without noticing this, proceeded to sever the leg above the knee. A cord was drawn round the limb, above the spot where it was intended to sever it, so tight that it cut into the flesh. The knife and saw were then applied and the limb amputated. A few drops of blood, only, oozed from the stump; the child was dead." [1]

The gruesomeness of the tale, the speaker went on to say, was alleviated by the fact that Mr. Bryant, the narrator, added that on that same night, and not a mile from the scene of that tragedy, he was called to another train to help bring a new California emigrant into the world. This being successfully accomplished, rustic merry-making on the part of the whole train followed — because its numbers had been happily increased. Later, in another neighboring train, the "doctor" had also attended a wedding ceremony, where, amid the gay festivities, he had looked across the plain and seen the lights of

[1] Edwin Bryant, *What I Saw in California*. Mr. Bryant later became the first Mayor of San Francisco.

the funeral procession which was taking the remains of the little boy to its last resting-place. All in one night, in adjacent trains: a death, a birth, a wedding!

As Wagonhound had left Uncle Bob's chariot to be brought over the Platte on the following day, Boardy and I went back to the ford in the morning to see him bring it across — confident that we should have an illustration of the thing we love most to see, expert plainsmanship in action.

First Wagonhound called for two of our men who should mark the exact point on our side where exit was to be made. When they took their stations, he put five span of picked mules to the Ark with a rider on the near leader and wheel mules, riding himself below the team to prevent them from swerving with the stream. In this order the outfit went in; but, notwithstanding digging away the south bank, the wagon made a drive that nearly drove the tongue mules under water; and if there had not been a good man in the saddle who upheld them with a powerful arm, the consequences might have been highly disastrous, as the chariot went broadside to the current. It occasionally swayed with portentous violence, almost floating when it got into deep water; and again, as it reached a shoal, the flood rushed through the spokes with a terrific noise. The mules in like manner were alternately swimming and walking, the length of the team, again, constituting its greatest safety; for when the wheel mules would be out of their depth, the lead and middle ones might not be over knee deep, and vice versa, so that there were always some on the strain to keep the vehicle in motion, otherwise it would have sunk in the quicksand and been lost. The danger against which it was impossible to take any precaution was that of overturning when the wheels on one side got on the steep slopes of the many ridges and bars of sand formed by the different eddies. Twice it was fairly poised, and I held my breath in fear, thinking an upset inevitable, which might have involved the loss of the wagon and mules — and possibly some of the riders, tangled in the harness as they necessarily would be. After fifty minutes' hard tugging the leaders reached land. While climbing the bank their sides

sobbed with distress; but the nature of the bottom forbade a
respite, and with Wagonhound dashing his riding horse past
them, and all of us joining in a teamster's chorus, they charged
the obstacle, and brought up their load over halfway when
overtasked nature, unable to sustain the impulse, let the
motion diminish until the wheels could be scarce seen to move.
An instant's pause, and back it must inevitably go.   At this
critical moment the lead mules just gained the level ground,

lightening of the ...g

brought from a fine spring on the south side of the river [2]
afforded a part of the conviviality.   The iron and sulphur in it
are found to be a curative for the commonest of our trail com-
plaints.

While our leaders carry out a semblance of a military guard,
its real purpose is to keep skulking Indian (and white?) thieves
from getting to our mules and horses.   It takes on, therefore,
more of the character of a civil than a military organization,
and when our men are congratulated in a tangible way, as
to-night, by Sir Robert, for meritorious conduct under water,
or above it, the character of our organization is not only civil
but polite.

Our chortling Carlo is on the firing line near Boardy and me
to-night, substituting for that (incapacitated) messmate of his
who so dreads to hear him sing.   Consequently we have
pointed caroling from the gloom beyond.   As, for instance: —

"I like a lazy partner,"

[1] Cf. W. Kelly, *An Excursion to California*.   The writer's description of this episode
is of moment to-day for the contrasts it presents to the numerous screen pictures of
such events purporting to be historical.
[2] On the later famous Beauvais Ranch.

— this being particularly addressed to a specific wagon with a prostrate form lying under it, —

> "So I can take my ease,
>   Lay down and talk of going home
>   As happy as you please.
>   Without a thing to eat or drink,
>   Away from care and grief,
>   I'm fat and sassy, ragged too,
>   And tough as Spanish beef."

The prostrate form, faintly animated by that "ruling passion strong in death," strives to reach a missile, but the effort ends only in a groan.

The tough beef-eater takes up the same refrain from another angle: —

> "You have to stand a watch at night,
>   To keep the Indians off;
> About sundown some heads will ache
>   And some begin to cough.
> To be deprived of health we know
>   Is always very hard;
> Though every night someone is sick,
>   To get rid of standing guard."

As things now began to fall about him, our serenader took heart, and ere we lapsed into unconsciousness we had several more samples of muleteer melodies, but none poorly chosen for the vindictive purpose intended, as witness this, sung to the air of "Boatman Dance": —

> "Being brave, I cut and carved,
>   On the desert nearly starved;
> My partner he laid down and died,
>   I had no blankets, so I took his hide."

There was originality, too, in the wording, as note: —

> "My partner fell in love with a Chilean girl,
>   Her eyes were gray, her hair did curl;
> But her nose turned up when she saw his chin,
>   Says, 'You're a dirty bullwhacker, you can't come in.'"

Then followed an endless ballad about the pride of Pike County, Missouri, "Sweet Betsey," known by the title, "Sweet Betsey from Pike," and sung to the air of "Villikins and His Dinah." We, of course, slept through most of it (as you will, Dad), but Uncle made me get a copy of it from Carlo for the official files : —

"Oh, don't you remember Sweet Betsey from Pike,

"Their wagon broke down with a terrible crash,
And out on the prairie rolled all kinds of trash;
A few baby clothes all done up with care —
'T was rather suspicious, though all on the *square*.

"The shanghai ran off, and their cattle all died;
That morning the last piece of bacon was fried;
Poor Ike was discouraged, and Betsey got mad,
The dog dropped his tail and looked wondrously sad.

"They stopped at Salt Lake to inquire the way,
When Brigham declared that sweet Betsey should stay;
But Betsey got frightened and ran like a deer,
While Brigham stood pawing the ground like a steer.

"They soon reached the desert, where Betsey gave out,
And down in the sand she lay rolling about;
While Ike, half-distracted, looked on with surprise,
Saying, 'Betsey, get up, you 'll get sand in your eyes.'

"Sweet Betsey got up in a great deal of pain,
Declared she 'd go back to Pike County again;
But Ike gave a sigh and they fondly embraced,
And they traveled along with his arm round her waist.

"They suddenly stopped on a very high hill,
    With wonder looked down upon old Placerville.
Ike sighed when he said, and he cast his eyes down:
    'Sweet Betsey, my darling, we 've got to Hangtown.'

"A miner said, 'Betsey, will you dance with me?'
    'I will that, old hoss, if you don't make too free;
But don't dance me hard; do you want to know why?
    Dog on you! I 'm chock full of strong alkali!'

"This Pike County couple got married, of course,
    And Ike became jealous — obtained a divource;
Sweet Betsey, well satisfied, said with a shout,
    'Good-bye, you big lummox, I 'm glad you 've backed out.' "

ASH HOLLOW, *May 30.* — It is very difficult indeed to make anyone who has not crossed the plains believe how depressing the continuous level floor becomes to all who have been accustomed to have their horizons bounded by something to see. It is a long pull for such folks from the Big Blue, let us say, to O'Fallon's Bluffs; and, despite the heartbreak caused by the sands in those Bluffs, the relief in contour of horizon which they gave to the eyes of many was helpful. Imagination is piqued by a definite boundary, a mental hazard, a topographical question-mark. When imagination lags, a dullness follows. Easterners have to grow into the way of thinking that could make Dr. Marcus Whitman of Oregon say, "All my plans require time and distance"; the nephew to whom he wrote those words never understood them.

If you will examine my map you will see that we are crossing a letter V, the point (lying to the east of us) being at the Forks of the Platte; the space between the two sides is a steadily increasing and high-uplifted triangle between the North Platte, to which we are journeying, and the South Platte, which we have just crossed.

This massive fifteen-mile-wide shoulder between the rivers is our first hint of the Rocky Mountains in the far distance; it is bare, wide, and just now beautifully painted with lupine.

Then suddenly the ground, so to speak, gives way from

beneath you! The gigantic plain breaks. A new world flashes into view — a lovely, wooded dell, dotted by shady cedar and ash trees beside the silvery North Platte. But all that is five hundred feet below you! And the accursedest set of roads

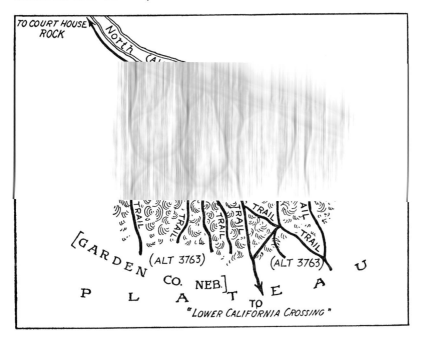

TRAILS LEADING TO ASH HOLLOW, NEBRASKA, DOWN TOIL-SOME DESCENT OF 463 FEET WHICH WAS AT ITS WORST AT WINDLASS HILL

lead to it through horrible, precipitous ravines of rock and sand hub deep!

Nothing more quickly than famous Ash Hollow [1] could have broken the monotony of level plains — or the legs of horses, mules, and oxen, let alone the arms, legs, and collar-bones of men. No camp on the California Trail, Meek tells us, will be more distinctly remembered by us than Ash Hollow.

Beautiful as is the lovely green prospect below on the river, it will not remain in memory one bit longer than that 450-foot

[1] Opposite Lewellen, Neb.

drop from the crest through those craggy, cedar-covered ravines filled with wagon wrecks! I rode ahead with Meek, who went onward to reconnoitre the condition of the many descending trails. Several teams had congregated along the summit, men and animals alike peering over, debating which route to take, or watching those who, having committed their all to Providence, had set sail down the slope amid shrieks, prayers, and curses! We watched one of these. Its leaders had debated the propriety of detaching the bodies of their wagons from the wheels and sliding them down; but, as the driver of the wagon in front volunteered a trial with rough double-locking and holding back with anchor ropes, the experiment went forward after taking out all but the wheel-span mules, which were left in merely to guide the ship. The result was successful until the bottom was reached. Then a frayed rope parted and the wagon slid, or, more properly speaking, fell on top of the mules, upsetting and killing the one on the off-side and breaking the collar-bone of the teamster, who was also otherwise badly bruised. The wagon-bows were all smashed and its contents went hopping down the steep. The wagon escaped any seriously disabling fracture, thus enabling the emigrants to reload it and proceed without much delay. Two more moderate descents brought one into a lovely wooded dell, so watered and sheltered that vegetation of every description thrived. Here, as if to compensate for the taxing experience of descent, were wild roses, chokecherries, gooseberries, currants, and shrubs forming the underwood of the majestic ash trees, which confer the name upon the Hollow.

Meek found a track which had not been used by more than one or two caravans since the last rain, and, when our outfit came up, sent men down ahead to smooth the roughest places. Cleverly making a windlass of a jacked-up wagon-wheel, Uncle Bob's house was let down and all our wagons came later with no other harm than that caused by a stampede near the bottom of a team belonging to one John Corum, the result of which was one mule's broken leg and a wagon-tongue broken off short.

Ash Hollow will also be remembered by most Forty-Niners for the congestion of teams and the log cabin or "Ash Grove Hotel," the walls of which had become a sort of general post-office. Numerous advertisements in manuscript were posted on its walls descriptive of lost cattle, horses, etc., etc.; and inside, in a recess, a large number of letters had been deposited, addressed to persons in almost every quarter of the globe, with requests that those who should pass would convey them to the

North Platte, save for divergences of from one to nine miles. The river channel, as we forge northward, becomes narrower, but the soil of its banks remains sandy and barren. The stream keeps, however, the general appearance of the lower Platte. I noticed in several places the clusters of small islands such as Boardy and I took refuge on during our "attack" on the buffalo. As we looked down from bluffs here and there, these presented a cultivated appearance; the green foliage of the willows, in contrast with the white sand, looked like serpentine walks of shrubbery in the distance, and the barren soil looked like cultivated ground — especially around a trading post called "Fort Bernard," a few miles from Fort Laramie.

By the way, Boardy's heroes, Brown and Jingo, whom we lost sight of soon after leaving the Dobytown saloons, have been heard from. Finding the footing heavier than expected, they and Jeremiah "bought in" partnership with a train overtaken on O'Fallon's Bluffs, and are coming along by the alternate road which ascends the South Platte to the "Upper California Crossing" [1] and meets our road near Chimney Rock. There are two routes on the map. Meek says there is little to

[1] At Julesburg, Colo.

choose between them when the river is not on a rampage. Our route has the Ash Hollow descent to make; the "Upper" route offers very heavy going in wet weather in the Pumpkin-seed Creek country south of Chimney Rock. For everyone going east on this California Trail the "Upper" road is, of course, much preferable; for no one wants to ascend Ash Hollow, although it can be done with wagons lightly loaded.

The steady grind forward for these two days from Ash Hollow, in sand so deep at times that twenty-two miles a day was swift traveling, proved monotonous enough. Boardy and I annexed ourselves to a band of buffalo-hunters on the second day — agreeing to meet the train again at Court House Rock, where a day's stop-over was planned to air out our provisions and trim the wagons. Riding south with them, we sighted buffalo east of Mud Spring [1] on the upper road, but we were not sufficiently expert at horsemanship to keep up at the head of the procession. Yet we got on the ground in time to see how buffaloes are cut up by these men who make a living by selling the meat to emigrants. It is nothing short of wanton butchery. Contrary to what I had heard was usual, the skinning process commences by making an incision along the top of the back-bone and separating the hide downward so as to get more quickly at what are considered the choice parts of the animal. First the "bass," a hump projecting from the back of the neck just before the shoulders, which is generally removed with the skin attached; it is about the size of a man's head, and, when boiled, resembles marrow, being exceedingly tender, rich, and nutritious. Next come the "hump" and the "hump ribs," projections of the vertebræ just behind the shoulders, some of which are a foot in length. These are generally broken off by a "mallet" made of the lower joint of one of the forelegs cut off for the purpose! After these come the "fleece," which is the portion of the flesh covering the ribs; the "depuis," a broad, fat part extending from the shoulders to the tail; the "belly fleece"; some of the ribs, called "side ribs," to distinguish them from the hump ribs; the thigh, or marrow-bones, and the

[1] At Simla, Neb.

tongue. Generally the animal is opened and the tenderloin
and tallow, only, secured. All the rest, including the hams
and shoulders, — indeed, by far the greater portion of the animal, — is left on the ground. When buffalo are plenty, the
hump, bass, and tongue — very frequently only the latter —
are taken, and occasionally a marrow-bone for a tidbit.

This is butchering, "mountain fashion," and a most barbarous fashion it is. The bulls are never killed for food except in

wants. Indeed, of the four killed, but three were butchered
(that is, the choice parts only taken away), and the men left
the ground to hurry back to the road, having two pack mules,
and all the riding horses, loaded down with meat, the fourth
buffalo being wholly untouched.

From near Mud Spring, in clear weather, one can very plainly
see to the northeast the outer rampart of the great castellated
area of the ancient plateau which the winds, storms, and frosts
of the ages have filed and sandpapered down until there is left,
among the better known, only such spectacular "ruins" as
Court House and Chimney Rocks and Scott's Bluffs. Among
the books carried by the emigration relating to the West (a
topic that should deserve a page or two sometime), one written
by R. B. Sage states that eight years ago trappers noticed
changes which a single storm had effected in the contour of
Court House Rock (or "McFarlan's Castle," as he terms it)
near Gonneville's Creek.[1] The present name of the Rock is
said to have been applied to the pile by St. Louis parties "from
a fancied resemblance to a well-known structure in their own
city." It rises in an abrupt, quadrangular form to a height

[1] The name of a trapper killed on the bank of present-day Pumpkinseed Creek.

of two hundred or more feet, occupying an area of two hundred yards in length by one hundred and fifty broad, and stands on a perfectly level site in the open prairie.

As we lay over in camp one day here (June 3), Boardy and I had a chance to examine this region with some care.   On the top of Court House Rock is an elevation which has the appearance of a flattened dome.   The formation is of soft sand and clay, intermixed with lime and easily cut with a knife.   Of more human interest to us than the Rock was a cliff, near the main trail, of the same formation, — full of water-worn fissures, — and over the top someone had carved the words "Post Office."   Some of the crevices had been made boxlike in shape with a knife, and here we found letters deposited for people coming along later in the migration!   One of these lay open, its covering having been lost.   It was written at Fort Laramie and was left here by some carrier who evidently was turning off the main track or was going buffalo-hunting or had decided to right-about again for California.   The salutation was torn, but the address was intact.   Before rewrapping it securely we read it, as others had: —

We have had a good trip so far we have had no bad luck whatever I have not had to wet my feet at any stream that we have crossed as to Indians I do not believe that we have been in the least danger as yet   we are now in the country of the Souix   they say that they are entirely friendly   we have seen four villiages of them some distance back   they were on the South side of the river   came in I suppose to trade with the emigrants. . . . Fort Laramie   we landed here day before yesterday Sabath about eleven o'clock found that we were greatly mistaken in what we had before understood when we crossed the Platt   down at Fort cearny [1] we understood that we was clear of the Platt but the farther we came up the more we became convinced that we was under a great mistake   it is said that a mountain goat can't go up this side of the river and consequently we had to cross at this point [Laramie] we could have crossed the same evening that we came up but put it off until Monday consequently Sunday knight a little after dark there was persons

---

[1] Fort Kearny.

crossing Horses. . . . they overloaded the boat and sunk it and broak the roap by which they was crossing [Ms. torn] and mules three of the men swam out the others went down with the boat about four miles and drifted on an island and they got them off the next morning so there was no life lost that time but you need not be alarmed if you hear of persons drowning for such carelessness and running of risks I have never seen it is now four o'clock and we are about to leave I will just say that we are all over safe I will wright at the next ferry[1] and I will try and give you more Satisfaction no Saint Jo road and I will give you now a little history of our travis thus far as near as I can recolect we left the bottom 5 miles above Saint Jo the 9th between 8 and 9 oclock we travled 15 miles over the crookedest Road that I have ever seen and campted on a litle creek called Musketoe and in one mile and a half from the Misouri River the grass so short that our catle gets none to do any good we started with a bout 12 bushels of corn to the team. Friday the 10th was on our jeorny at an early hour and after travling 6 miles came to wolf creek it is a small Stream 12 feet or 14 feet wide very deep and swift curent with a tall Bridge blonging to the Iowa indians who] charge 25 cts for a wagon and team we then travled 6 miles and came to the Iowa mishion or agency it is a beautifull place there is a large Farm in a high state of cultivation established by the georvnament for the purpose of learning the Red men of the west to cultivate the Soil there is al so a School or mishionary establishment for teaching the children of those wild Sons of Adam we travled the 11th 15 miles camped ¾ mile south of the road in a litle grove the grass still very scarce the Road to day has been more straight and the Prairie more levle and very Rich and the most beautiful country that I have ever seen traveled the 12th 12 miles and camped on a branch of the minewah a very beautiful litle stream — the weather still fare and cool travled the 13th 13 miles

[1] At the present site of Casper, Wyo.

camped in the open plains north of the road the weather warmer than usual travled the 14th 14 miles crossed the nimehaw a fine stream 20 feet wide running through as fine a country as I have everr seen and a considerable quantity of timber for this country the roads very good though a great deal of dust travled the 14th today 15 miles camped again in the open plains the 16th left camp at an early hour traveled 22 miles and camped on the east side of the big Blue it is a beautiful stream a bout 40 yards wide and near three feet deep the crossing at this time is good the water is clear with a bold curent.

Chimney Rock rivals its sister pinnacle to the east in height if not in breadth. It is a curious spire or chimney, which has been, undoubtedly, at one time a portion (probably a projecting shoulder) of the main chain of bluffs bounding the valley of the Platte and has been separated from it by the action of water. It consists of a conical elevation of about one hundred feet high, its sides forming an angle of about 45′ with the horizon. From the apex rises a nearly circular and perpendicular shaft of clay, now from thirty-five to forty feet in height. The cone has been formed by the disintegration of the softer portion of the bluff, arranging itself at its natural angle in a conical form while the remainder of the earth has been carried away by the floods and distributed over the plain, leaving the broad valley which is at present found between it and the main bluff. That the shaft has been very much higher than at present is evident from the corresponding formation of the bluff as well as from the testimony of all our *voyageurs*, with whom it was for years a landmark or beacon visible for upward of eighty miles on clear days.

An Englishman present on the spot vetoed the idea of a "chimney" in tones no one misunderstood and said that the Wellington Testimonial in the Phœnix Park, London, elevated on a Danish Fort, would give a much more correct idea of its configuration, though not of its proportions. The rock is said to have been reduced by sandstorms fifty feet in the last nine years. Boardy immediately remarked that he would sketch it as it was 500 years ago as soon as he found a drawing pad 277 feet long.

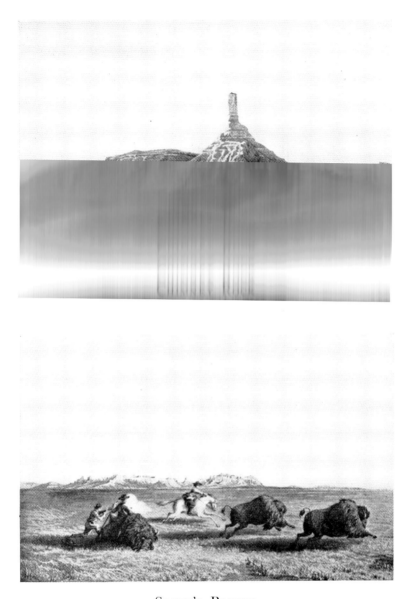

SCOTT'S BLUFFS

(Sketches by Frederick Piercy, in "Route from Liverpool to Great
Salt Valley")

To us the landscape hereabouts was more impressive than any outstanding pinnacle. To the right of this lonely tower, as you face the river from it, the wilderness is fascinating. There are four high elevations of architectural configuration, one of which would represent a distant view of the ruins of the Athenian Acropolis; another the crumbling remains of an Egyptian temple; a third, a Mexican pyramid; the fourth, the mausoleum of one of the Titans. In the background the bluffs

no effort of the imagination was required to suppose ourselves encamped in the vicinity of the ruins of some vast city inhabited by a race of giants, contemporaries of the Megatherium and the Ichthyosaurus. When "my" railroad shall pass this place the lovers of Nature's works will come here in crowds to feast their eyes on scenery worthy of a pencil of a Poussin or a Michael Angelo.[1]

Scott's Bluff, *June* 5–7. — Far beyond, toward Fort Laramie, a massive uplift, of which these sentinels at Pumpkin-seed Creek are the outposts, curls about at its extremity next to the South Platte like the end of a gigantic shepherd's crook. This fantastic freak of landscape gardening has received the name of Scott's Bluff, from a melancholy circumstance. A number of years since, a party belonging to the American Fur Company were descending the upper part of the river in canoes when their frail barks were overturned and all their powder spoiled. Their rifles being thus rendered useless, they were unable to procure food by hunting. After suffering extremely

---

[1] Present route of the Burlington Railroad (Alliance–Wendover Branch). For above classical allusions see such writers as E. Bryant and W. Kelly.

from hunger, they arrived at Laramie's Fork about sixty miles above the heights just mentioned. Here one of the party of the name of Scott, said by some to have been its commander, was taken ill. His comrades there discovered a fresh trail of white men who had evidently but recently preceded them. By a forced march they thought to overtake this party and thus be able to reach the settlements in safety. Scott, however, was incapable of moving. They determined, therefore, to abandon him to his fate and succeeded in overtaking the party of which they were in quest, but are said to have concealed their faithless desertion of Scott, alleging merely that he had died of disease. In the following summer these very same individuals visited this region in company with others and came suddenly upon the bones and skull of a human skeleton, which by certain signs some believed they recognized as the remains of Scott. This was sixty miles from the place where they had abandoned him. It appeared that the doomed man had crawled that distance before death put an end to his miseries; the picturesque bluffs, which became his lonely grave, have ever since borne his name.

Scott's Bluff is a large and isolated pile of sandcliffs and soft sandstone exhibiting all the architectural shapes of arch, pillar, dome, spire, minaret, temple, Gothic castle, and modern fortification. These, of course, are upon a scale surpassing the constructive efforts of human strength and energy. The tower of Babel, if its builders had been permitted to proceed in their ambitious undertaking, would have been but a feeble imitation of these stupendous structures of Nature.

The trail leaves the river as we approach these bluffs and runs through a smooth valley called Marshall's Pass in the rear of the Bluff seven or eight miles.[1] From this level plain we ascended some distance and found a faint spring of water near the summit of the ridge as cold as melted ice. I need not say that we refreshed ourselves from this gift of Nature to the weary and thirsty traveler. We reached the extreme height of the dividing ridge about three o'clock P.M., and from it we

[1] Gering, Neb.

had the first view of the peaks of the Rocky Mountains, especially of Laramie's Peak and several other elevations possibly
a hundred or a hundred and fifty miles distant.   The more
sanguine regaled us with the information that they could see
Pikes Peak three hundred miles to the southwest!

This first view of the Rockies [1] greatly impresses every soul
among these marching thousands — coming, as it does, in the
midst of extremely dusty and taxing day's journeys.   But that

Platte nearly crush the spirit of adventure, up loom the wild
turrets and spires of Court House and Chimney Rocks to revive
again our sinking zeal.   And now from the defiles of Scott's
Bluff we mount to view the long talked-of, much dreamed-of,
Rocky Mountains!

My doleful day dream was here happily broken by Uncle
Bob's enthusiastic invitation to the train to toast the Rockies
with appropriate ceremony.   The occasion took on an added
gala color because his robust summons to all "friends, Romans,
and countrymen" included not only Boardy's long lost brethren
of the Platte River voyage, Brown, Jingo, and Jeremiah, but
also the enterprising ragtag Pickpan, who now is the proud
possessor of two wagons well filled with trail-plunder, although
he has not yet discarded his professional *costume de voyage*.

"Fort Bernard," stately name for a shack or small building
rudely constructed of logs, lies half a dozen miles east of Fort
Laramie.   On approaching it we saw a large herd of mules
grazing on the plain and guarded by Mexican Indians.   One
of these had a small looking-glass with which he shot the
reflected rays of the sun into our faces by way of a distant

[1] The Laramie Mountains, Wyo.

salutation. Traders from Taos, Santa Fé, and the headwaters of the Arkansas in New Mexico were collected here, to whom the herd of mules belonged. They had packed flour, some four hundred miles, for the purpose of trading emigrants and Indians. Piles of buffalo robes here reminded us of Eastern haystacks.

This is a point at which, as mentioned somewhere in my Diary, "Mormons" rob the migration by exchanging good stock for the footsore and maimed at a scandalous profit. "Mormons" prove to be Americans like Kit Carson and his partner, Tim Goodale, from Taos, Mexicans and half-breeds.[1] If you merely want to sell your exhausted stock, they give from four to ten dollars for cattle and one dollar for a sheep if fat. They shoe oxen for six dollars each, four cents apiece for the nails extra.

I gave *carte blanche* to my imagination as, on June 7, 1849, we drew near Fort Laramie, in view of the Black Hills (as they are called) at its back, seeing, in my mind's eye, a bold fortress, perched in stern, solitary grandeur on a beetling crag, with corbeled battlements bristling with cannon, encircled by chasms through which mountain torrents roared vengeance on any foe's unbidden approach. But, "like the baseless fabric of a vision," my glowing fancy vanished before the sombre reality : a tawdry cracked and dilapidated adobe quadrangular enclosure, three sides of which were shedded down as stores and workshops, the fourth or front having a two-story erection, with a projecting balcony for hurling projectiles or hot water on the foe, propped all around on the outside with beams of timber, which an enemy had only to kick away and down would come the whole structure. It stands, or rather leans, upon a naked plain by the side of a rapid little river, in which a Frenchman named La Ramée was drowned, yielding up his name both to the river and the fort. It is not a military station, but belongs to the American Fur Trading Company, who keep here a supply of trumpery merchandise to exchange with the Indian and trapper for such skins as they can procure. On its early

[1] Carson brought fifty head of mules and horses to Fort Laramie, May 5, 1850.

FORT LARAMIE

(By Major Osborne Cross, in C

establishment the beaver abounded in all the rivers of this
region, but now the trade is exclusively confined to buffalo
robes.   It turns out to be, however, a point of great importance
on the overland route to California, though in my opinion there
are other localities much more eligible as depots for the accommodation of travelers.

The entrance into the "court" is through a gate of sufficient
strength, perhaps, to resist the Indians, but of little account if

River, three fourths of a mile above the mouth of the Laramie,
and stands near the direct wagon-road.   It is situated in the
immediate vicinity of the Oglala and Brulé divisions of the
Sioux nation and but little remote from the Cheyennes and
Arapahoe tribes.   Its walls are "adobes" (sun-baked brick),
four feet thick of varying height — enclosing an area of two
hundred and fifty feet in length by two hundred broad.   At
the northwest and southwest corners are bastions which command its approaches in all directions.   Within the walls are
some twelve buildings in all, consisting as follows: office, store,
warehouse, meat-house, smith's shop, carpenter's shop, kitchen,
and five dwellings — so arranged as to form a yard and corral
sufficiently large for the accommodation and security of more
than two hundred head of animals.   The number of men usually employed about the establishment is some thirty, whose
chief duty it is to promote the interests of the trade, and
otherwise act as circumstances require.

The Fort is located in a level plain, fertile and interesting,
bounded upon all sides by hills, many of which present to view
the nodding forms of pines and cedars that cover their surface — while the river bottoms, at various points, are thickly

studded with proud growths of cottonwood, ash, willow, and box-elder, thus affording the needful supplies of timber and fuel. Around the Fort were many wagons, which had been sold or abandoned by emigrants. A strong, heavy wagon can be bought here for from five to fifteen dollars. In ordinary seasons the company was able to keep some small supplies for emigrants, but such was the rush now that scarcely anything can be obtained, even at the most exorbitant prices.

According to such records as are kept here, we estimate that some 10,000 persons are ahead of us. There are seldom less than ten oxen to each wagon, and more frequently twelve. Besides, there are the many outriders, as well as cattle which are driven along, so that the number of animals going to California cannot be less than 50,000. It is not difficult to calculate from this the number of emigrants en route to California. To this number add those who are taking the Santa Fé route, also those in rear of us, and the total will not fall short of 50,000 souls. These figures do not agree with those I gave in another place, which perfectly reflects the circumstances — for no one in the least knows the truth and no one's computation agrees with any other.

UP SOUTH PASS TO THE CONTINENTAL DIVIDE

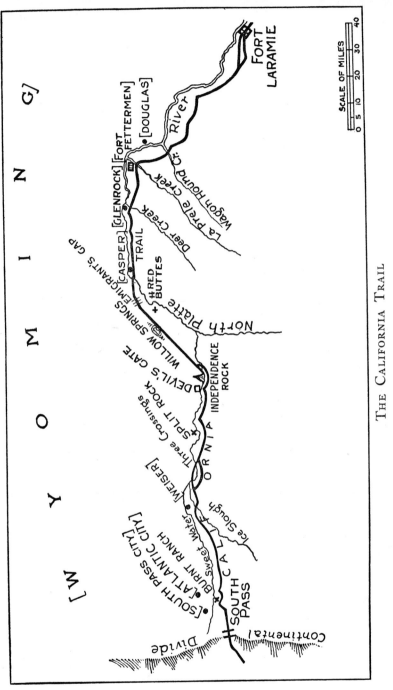

The California Trail

IV. FROM FORT LARAMIE TO THE SOUTH PASS OF THE CONTINENTAL DIVIDE

SECTION IV

UP SOUTH PASS TO THE CONTINENTAL DIVIDE

term and one quite significant), such as the axes, cleverly en-
sconced on the wagon-hounds, and the shovels and crowbars
in the tail of the wagons, bespoke seriously the promised heavy
going across the foothills of the Laramie Mountains, which are
here called the "Black Hills."

Our log, inserted later, for these thirteen days reads : —

June 8–10. Across the "Black Hills" [Laramie Mts., southwest
of Douglas, Wyo.].

June 11. Reach Platte River at Deer Creek [Glenrock, Wyo.].

June 12–13. Reach Platte northeast of Red Buttes [Casper, Wyo.].

June 14. Strike out for Sweetwater via Emigrant Gap route.

June 15. Willow Springs via the Poison Spider.

June 16. Independence Rock.

June 17. On by Devil's Gate.

June 18–20. On up the Sweetwater 95 miles via Split Rock, Three
Crossings, and Ice Slough.

June 21. Reach South Pass — summit of the Rockies and
Continental Divide.

The room devoted to games of chance is in the main building
of the Fort, and certainly no artist, with Boardy's eye for the
unique and eccentric, could have asked for a gathering of more

phizes significant of all for which the California Trail stands than were present, or accounted for, at or around the gaming table last night, the majority being our own gang or acquaintances — Uncle Bob, Wagonhound, Ox Bow, Brown, Jingo, Pickpan, Saddlebags, Carlo, and his usually distraught messmate "Picayune," so called.

An officer's servant volunteered, for a consideration, to play valet. Boardy was too busy with his notebook, and I roamed too much about the Fort and its environs meanwhile, to learn all the details of the battle. One thing Boardy swore to, which was that while Pickpan at the outset was a mere shadowy wraith in the background, before any cock crowed once he was resting easily from a monetary standpoint. We like Pickpan. As an example of what courage can do and how even in adversity everything is grist that comes to a determined man's will, he is a lesson to us all. Uncle Bob's only comment at breakfast this morning was that cards were invented to prove the exception to the Scripture which declares that "to him that hath shall be given."

PICKPAN SEEKING A CUSTOMER

Be all that as it may, I learned something of sporting life myself among the Indian lodges outside of Fort Laramie. Indian squaws engage in several gambling games which end in the loss of no little treasure to the defeated side. One of these is a ball game upon which heavy bets are sometimes made. The instrument used in this amusement consists of

"Phizes Signifi

(By W. R. Ryan, in "Perso.

two globular forms, about two inches each in diameter, which are attached by a short string. The playground is the open prairie in front of the Fort embracing an area of nearly a mile in extent.

Another game, still more extensively practised among them because it can be played indoors, is based somewhat on the principle of dice, though it differs in details. Six plum-stones, smoothly polished and marked with various parallel, triangular,

The loser, having paid the forfeit, next takes the basket and describes the same movements, receives her winnings in like manner, and passes it on to her opponent, and so on alternately. Much cheating and trickery are practised in this game.

Another similar amusement resembles our "Button, Button." This is a very common game among the mountain Indians. It is opened by one of the players who encloses a gravel-stone or a bullet in the curve of his two hands by placing the palms together, then, after sundry tosses and evolutions, suddenly parting them. If the opposing party is shrewd enough to guess in which hand the stone is retained, he wins; if not, he loses. Large amounts are often wagered upon the result of this play.

Before leaving Fort Laramie I must explain the confusion which exists, even among us Forty-Niners, with reference to the numerous routes which are known as the "Oregon" or "California" Trail; and I do this merely by passing on to you one of Guide Meek's little talks on western geography.

For if this is a matter of confusion to us, what must it be to you, who are far removed in space from us now, or those who may be far separated in time in later years?

The trail we have traveled from Independence, Missouri, was, back in 1832–1845, the main route to Oregon — and then acquired that name, the "Oregon Trail." As it is now used as far as Raft River beyond Fort Hall[1] by the gold-seekers of '49, it has taken on the new name "California Trail," as the name of those "California Crossings" on the South Platte indicated.

But long ago there were important branch trails or feeders of the main Oregon Trail; those who traveled over them thought and spoke of their route as the "Oregon Trail." There were four of these. When we reached Fort Laramie our route received the last of those four. We call our Independence–Fort Laramie road the main trail because all others flow into it, so to speak.

Meek drew a map in the sand to make plain to me this confusion in names. Here it is: —

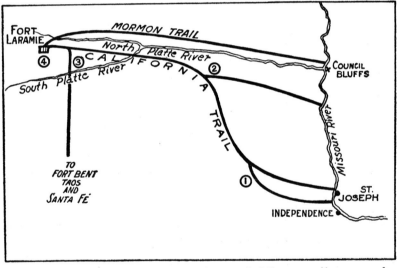

The four places where these four subsidiary trails enter the California Trail are numbered 1, 2, 3, and 4.

At No. 1 we met, at the crossing of the Big Blue,[2] the trail coming from St. Jo and Fort Leavenworth. You cannot com-

[1] Near Pocatello, Ida.   [2] At Marysville, Kan.

pare these routes from the standpoint of age; no one is older than another, although one may be shorter than another.

At No. 2, near Fort Kearny,[1] we met the trail (Brown and Jingo's) which ascends the south side of the Platte from its mouth, and is followed by all who cross the Missouri between St. Jo and Council Bluffs.[2]

At No. 3 we met a trail which came up at the foot of the frontal[3] wall of the Rockies from Taos and Santa Fé. Some

trail; in fact, over it came the first famous party of missionaries to Oregon — the Whitman-Spalding caravan of 1836.

You see plainly what these different connecting pathways mean, for instance, to persons going east over this route. You branch off at No. 4 for Council Bluffs; at No. 3 for Fort Bent, Taos, or Santa Fé; at No. 2 for the central Missouri Valley; and at No. 1 for St. Jo or Fort Leavenworth.

This does not include all the trails that focus here on this great trunk route at Fort Laramie; but the others contribute nothing to the rush to California except perhaps a few Indian traders turned gold-hunters and some gold-crazy Indians — a topic I must not forget to refer to later. Two trails from the north come in here; one from the headwaters of Cheyenne River up in the Dakota Bad Lands and the other from White River and Bad River — originating at Fort Pierre on the Missouri. This latter was the most important trail in the old West of fur-trapping days because it was the shortest from Fort Laramie to navigable water, Fort Pierre on the Missouri.

Now, as to these Indian Forty-Niners. No one knows how

[1] Opposite Kearny, Neb.   [2] Later Nebraska City, Fort Kearny Road.
[3] Rampart Range.   [4] Near La Junta, Colo.

many of the aborigines have joined in this wild race to California, but this much is certain: a week ago (near the "Forks of the Platte") we passed the encampment of a party of Cherokee Indians. It consisted, a few days ago, of fourteen persons; six had died with the cholera. One was dying at the time we visited them and the remainder were too ill to assist in burying the dead. Among the whole of this party there was but one man who was really able to render any assistance to the others. It was a sad spectacle to behold. These people had left homes where many of them were no doubt comparatively comfortable and happy, never, perhaps, having had to labor for their daily bread as hard as they had on this march. The gold mania was, however, spreading far and near, and, being seized with it, they had abandoned their homes, blinded with the belief that fortunes were soon to be realized, only to find their graves in a wild and lonely region. And this again reminds me that I have said little about the foreigners, individuals and in companies, who are found in this hurrying throng to California. The subject deserves a whole chapter of my diary; we think it brave and heroic for men to risk death in every form to make this journey from far-away Maine and Georgia. But what about those who are here rubbing shoulders with us, and dropping, like those Cherokees, into unknown and unmarked graves — those from Russia, Poland, Italy, Chili, Germany, France and Heaven knows how many other distant quarters of the globe?

June 8. — The California Road to the westward led over an interesting plateau between the North Platte on the right and Laramie River on the left. At the distance of ten miles from the fort, we entered the sandy bed of a creek, a kind of defile, shaded by precipitous rocks, down which we wound our way for several hundred yards to a place where, on the left bank, a very large spring gushes with considerable noise and force out of the limestone rock. It is called the "Warm Spring" and supplies the dry bed of the creek with water. On the opposite side, a little below the spring, is a lofty limestone escarpment, partially shaded by a grove of large trees whose green foliage, in contrast with the whiteness of the rock, renders this a picturesque locality.

With the change in the geological formation on leaving Fort Laramie the face of the country entirely alters its appearance. The Black Hills, so-called because the pine trees give them a sombre look against the parched face of the desert, form a rough country threaded by the southern tributaries of the

eight hundredweight of bacon, thrown away for want of horse-power to transport it farther.   Boxes, bonnets, trunks, wagon-wheels, whole wagon-bodies, cooking utensils, and in fact almost every article of household furniture, were found discarded for the same reason.   We covered twenty-five miles to-day.

June 9. — We followed up the dry bed of a fork of Bitter Cottonwood Creek over a high ridge and descended precipi-tously upon the head of Horseshoe Creek, a beautiful stream of running water, clear, soft, and very cool.   There are two tracks here, one crossing below the junction of the two forks, two hundred yards to the right, the other crossing both forks. The latter was taken, and, after crossing the western fork, we ascended its valley for a couple of miles over some very high, rolling country.   The road, as before, was strewn with frag-ments of broken and burnt wagons, trunks, and quantities of white beans, which seemed to have been thrown away by the sackful, their owners either having become tired of transporting them farther or loath to consume them for fear they carried cholera.   Guide Meek was certain that it was lack of horse-power, for he states that no deaths from cholera have been

known west of Big Muddy Creek, which we will pass in four
days. Stoves, gridirons, moulding-planes, and carpenters'
tools of all sorts were also to be had for the mere trouble of
picking them up!

Our course has been about parallel with the range of the Black
Hills, the base of which could frequently be seen from the more
elevated portions of the road. The valley of the Platte also
was to be seen far in the distance to the north. Crossing Big
Timber, or La Bonte, Creek, we encamped near a fine spring,
after a fatiguing march of twenty-three miles.

Except at some bad pinches, as O'Fallon's Bluffs, Ash Hollow,
and going down Scott's Bluffs, the emigration has not had much
experience with precipitous hills until now. Many are inexpe-
rienced even yet and have to learn that everything that is not
tied in the wagon falls out. It would have amused a disinterested person to stand to-day at the top with a spyglass and
witness the descent of a train down one of these terrible-looking
hills. You would see the women and children in advance seeking the best way, some of them slipping down, or holding on to
the rocks, now taking an "otter slide" and then a run, till some
natural obstacle presented itself to stop their accelerated
progress; those who get down safely without a hurt or a bruise
are fortunate indeed. Looking back to the train, you would see
some of the men holding on to the wagons, others slipping under
the oxen's feet, some throwing articles out of the way that had
fallen out; all have enough to do to keep them busily occupied.
Often the teams get going so fast downhill that it is difficult to
double-lock them, and if, at a still steeper place, there is no
stopping them at all, the driver jumps on the near wheel-ox
or mule and the whole concern goes down with a perfect rush
until a more level place is reached. Thus, you see the merry
gold-seekers have some "hairbreadth" escapes (even without
Indians with scalping knives), and a jolly time of it, if they
could only think so!

The emigrants find they have made a great mistake in over-
loading the teams, for as a rule, when making up their outfits,
they had but little idea what they needed. Hence, everything

that a man's wife or a boy's mother could think of was piled in the wagons — sheet-iron stoves, feather beds, pillows, pillow-slips, blankets, quilts and comforters, pots and kettles, dishes, cups, saucers, knives, and forks. Many of these things are about as much use to the emigrant as two tails to a dog. Talk about clothing! Some men had enough to last five years. Some had trunks full of white shirts and plug hats. To cap the climax, one man was hauling a great walnut bedstead!

spades, ploughs, large grindstones, baking-ovens, cooking-stoves without number, kegs, barrels, harness, clothing, bacon, and beans were found along the road in pretty much the order in which they are here enumerated.

You would not believe how suddenly what is called cholera can sweep a man off his feet and into his grave. Now that we are getting out of the region where it is fatal, I can write about it more freely. It is sometimes just a case of Death snapping his fingers at you and you are gone. Major Cross lost a man out of his company marching to Oregon that way to-day. "In the morning Miller was as well as any man belonging to the train," said the Major, "and had been sent out to help guard the mules. At sundown he was dead and buried." I wonder if it really is cholera?

June 10–11. — "Hear ye, hear ye," came the call from off the trail as we were drilling away into the setting sun last night. "Come to the wedding. Come kiss the bride, everybody."

The words, from out the stark dreariness of the tumbled hills, could not have provoked more surprise than the scene along the banks of a little arroyo which met our eyes. True, and true again! The blushing Lavina of Grant County, Wisconsin, could no longer withstand the importunities of insistent Isaac of Bodox County, Wisconsin.

Therefore this day of camping in this little brown valley; this bower of willows intertwined with grapevines; these old, greasy wagon-sheets spread out over the ground for table covers for a marriage feast; these bustlings of old ladies; these wild flowers uncounted; and this call from the roadside to the miraculous spectacle of a banquet — bread, beans, roast duck (providentially provided for Lavina and Isaac and sitting on fourteen eggs!), cake, and custard pie!

Before the ceremony was ready to be celebrated by a full-fledged Justice of the Peace, the company amounted to full two hundred people. At last came the bride from her tent, resplendent in a dress of dark brown figured nun's veiling, her hair combed over her head in coquettish curls. Under the bower she meets her lover. The words are spoken, and a salvo of cheers is reëchoed from the solemn-looking butte across the way, as though it had seen something too new even to talk about.

Forty of the bride and groom's immediate train sit down to that miraculous dinner of duck and custard pie — but not, bless their hearts, till Uncle Bob had ransacked the Ark and hurried to the table with wildly cheered materials for a royal toast, for which he received, and gallantly too, a smacking bride's kiss.

"That there marriage 'll take," soliloquized Ox Bow as we wound on, looking for a camp-site. "They would n't be half the weddin's they is if the parties o' the first end second parts hed to camp out on the California trail eight hundret miles together first."

The road these days passed over a rolling country, being more of the Black Hills. We crossed the dry beds of several small streams, skirted in some instances with willows, box-elder, wild-cherry bushes and occasionally with some large cotton-woods, until we reached the river La Prêle. At this spot the mules were watered only, it being impossible to procure a blade of grass for them all the day. Consequently, we were obliged to continue on some four miles farther, until we reached the Platte, where we encamped in a pretty little grove of large cottonwoods, with but a very scanty supply of grass. A distance of five miles up the Platte over a sandy soil brought us to Deer Creek, a bright clear stream, running pleasantly through a large grove of timber, principally cottonwood. Judging from appearances, this spot has been a favorite campground for the emigrants. Property of every description was strewn

hunting a little — and all the time studying the scores of ways by which this great straggling army is trying to throw itself across this everlasting Platte River. But that is libel, for, here [1] and now, we leave it once for all. It seems a far cry back to that day of "the Last Leaving of the Little Blue" and our first glimpse of the stern "Coast of Nebraska" and this Platte River. Only twenty-three days — but how many "years" of experiences!

At such a place as this you have a cross-section of all the world, so to speak, before your eyes, while the teams pile up here at the river's bank for twelve or fifteen miles and then filter out into every nook and cranny where grass is to be found. A sign we saw near the road read : — "LOOK AT THIS — LOOK AT THIS ! THE WATER HERE IS POISON AND WE HAVE LOST SIX OF OUR CATTLE. DO NOT LET YOUR CATTLE DRINK ON THIS BOTTOM." Put it down to the credit of the Forty-Niners that, whereas some were so ruthless as to burn property left behind lest others should use it, put sand in abandoned sugar and bacon, and so forth, someone here took the trouble to write and post this sign of warning.

[1] Casper, Wyo.

As mentioned heretofore, the Mormons early seized upon this one best ferrying-place. But they could not monopolize it. Three other ferries are now operating here. The charge is four dollars per wagon and fifty cents per mule. Partly to save expense, and partly to save time, — for only from one to two hundred wagons can be ferried each day, — hundreds are crossing elsewhere by one means or another. The commonest way is by constructing rude rafts of dry logs which are welded together by pieces pinned across to hold them. By placing two oars at the end, to be used as sweeps, these rafts are propelled to the opposite shore, falling downstream somewhat at the same time with the current. After reaching the opposite bank, a yoke of oxen are attached and the float is carried

UNCLE BOB DECIDES TO WALK AHEAD OF THE TRAIN FOR EXERCISE

high enough up the stream so that, when returning, it reaches the point from which it originally started, driven by the force of the current and the aid of the oars. The wagons have to be taken apart to be loaded on. It generally takes about three trips to carry over one wagon and its load. This, you see, is very slow work.

Not a few intrepid ignoramuses are tempted to flout this serious river's strength and subtlety. We saw a terrible case of this, that of a young man named Masters, who believed his bell-mare could swim across with him in the saddle. Contrary to a general remonstrance, he pushed the mare in and, with the mules following, got on very well for two thirds of the way across — to where the channel of the river ran with a seething sweep along the opposite shore. Here the mare, instinctively dreading the danger, turned round as she felt the power of the current.

FERRYING ACROSS THE NOR

(*By Charles Nahl, in A. Delano's "(*

Nearly all the mules, being close upon her haunches, were carried by their own impetus and that of the flood right against her, rolling her and her rider under the water and going clean over them. It was some moments after they had passed when the mare again appeared, but she came to the surface without a rider, swimming languidly, unable to stem the stream

AWAITS OUR COMING
WITH ANXIETY

life; for there was small chance, with so many hoofs passing over him, that he was not kicked in the head. The mare at length gained the other shore, fully a mile below, but instead of struggling up to dry land, she stood as though exhausted, with her head drooping, seemingly unable to move. Two men went down to where she was. Finding a weight attached to the bridle, they pulled at it and brought to the surface one of the boy's hands. That rein, firmly clutched in a death-grasp, was the cause of the bad landing made by the mare as well as of the tugging and jerking with her head that we noticed after her submersion.

An outfit at the ferry contributed a violinist of real merit to the evening's merriment of these waiting hundreds last night. Most popular of all — deservedly or no — was a queer little old man with a rather fetching voice who sang some songs which were being sung by returning Mormons and others from California; he had picked them up at Fort Laramie. The violinist accompanied him excellently, making generous allowance for the grimaces, antics, and gestures with which the singer grotesquely punctured his ballads, the first of which was "The Happy Miner," sung to the popular air "I Get in a Weaving Way."

"I am a happy miner,
    I love to sing and dance;
I wonder what my love would say
    If she could see my pants.
With canvas patches on the knee,
    And one upon the stern;
I 'll wear them while I 'm digging here,
    And home when I return.

Chorus
"So I get in a jovial way
    I spend my money free;
And I have got a-plenty,
    So come drink lager beer with me!

"My love writes about her poodle dog,
    But never thinks to say:
'Oh do come home, my honey, dear,
    I 'm pining all away.'
I 'll write her half a letter,
    Then give the ink a tip;
If that don't bring her to her milk
    I 'll coolly let her rip.

"They wish to know if I can cook,
    And what I have to eat;
And tell me, should I take a cold,
    Be sure to soak my feet.
But when they talk of cooking,
    I 'm mighty hard to beat;
I 've made ten thousand loaves of bread
    The Devil could n't eat."

As you can imagine, the "house rose to meet" the singer at the conclusion of these verses and clamored for more. The boisterousness of the applause touched something in the queer little man, and he and the violinist consulted a moment amid the hand-clapping and guffaws of the elders and the strident calls of the younger listeners. At length the singer disappeared, and the violinist stepped forward and stated that they were going to California to join a circus [1] which was being taken by boat around the Horn; he said that he, the speaker, was to direct the band or orchestra and that his friend, Denny, was to

of impromptu wit that Boardy or I have heard on this stormy voyage: —

"So we will see the Elephant, then?" piped up this unknown and uncrowned humorist.

The musician played a rollicking polka to fill in the time. When Denny appeared, the outskirts of the crowd heralded the fact with whoops of joy, for the comedian

DECIDES TO TAKE A NAP WHERE WE CAN'T MISS HIM

had, even in so short a time, metamorphosed himself into a very passable "John Chinaman," a part for which his own oddness of manner and eccentricities of pose and poise made him an instant and perfect success. I could not, of course, get the song while he sang it, but Uncle Bob (when told of the circumstance) wheedled it out of Denny later. The crowd did n't understand many of the allusions (maybe Denny

[1] A. Dressler, *California's Pioneer Circus.* "Rowe's Olympic Circus" opened at San Francisco Oct. 29, 1849. In its touring in later years it showed at Placerville, Georgetown, Michigan Bluffs, Nevada, Orleans Flat, Marysville, etc.

did n't either), but all understood, and got a good laugh out
of, the last verse : —

> "I started up to Hangtown, then,
>   But found I could n't stay there;
> Not even for poor Chinaman
>   The diggings would not pay there.
> So, I started there a washing shop,
>   And it was velly funny,
> The bummers all had dainty shirts
>   But nottee cent of money."

From what an emigrant was telling in camp the other night,
the one trouble in San Francisco is to find reasonable laundry-

SING & LEE, LTD., WORKING THE ROCKER[1]

men.   He said he had heard that washing by the hundreds of
dozens was being sent across the Pacific to be done in Canton,
China, rather than pay eight dollars per dozen at home.[2]   One
of the Indian tribes is said to call our emigrant wagons " Ric-ca-
chic-a-chic-a-ki-kosh."   This is supposed to represent the sound
of the wheels going through sage-brush and hitting a stone !

[1] From *The Miner's Own Book* (published in San Francisco).
[2] *Annals of Iowa*, XIII, 37.

June 12. — While our train was yet fifty miles away, the experienced Meek, out in advance, chose the ferryman having the strongest-looking ferryboat and went into negotiations for the passage of our wagons, which, for all the ferryman knew, were waiting then on the river bank. Making allowance for the number of outfits already contracted with, multiplied by the time in crossing which each would take, Meek planned for as brief a pause here in the congested area as was possible. His

shows, lie on the Platte, which curves sharply here. This curve explains why we leave it, to join its main tributary, the Sweetwater, to the west. The Buttes are composed of red sandstone, mixed with limestone, calcareous sandstone, and pudding stone.

Seen and overheard at Platte River Ferry [1] : —

Pack mules being repacked on north bank. They shift, sidle, plunge, and kick. Angered drivers try to bite their ears; get almost bitten in two themselves. Girth-straps and ropes drawn so tightly that it seems as though the hide would be cut. To counteract this "tight lacing" the beasts bray and squeal, hump their backs and swell out their bellies in order to burst the ligatures. Two succeed in doing this — and one prima donna accomplished it five times.

They say a "Mormon," supplied with a kit of tools for the purpose, including a long ladder, will carve your name high up on famous Independence Rock, just ahead, for five dollars — and will knock the letters off when you have driven by (all swelled up with pride) and insert another name for the same price. Typical case of prejudice!

[1] Casper, Wyo.

No case of death by cholera known west of this ferry.

An emigrant and the owner of a makeshift blacksmith's shop here have a row over the price of some repairing. An

BROWN AND JINGO: THE FINE ART OF PACKING MULES

innocent passer-by tries to smooth over the difficulty. His hand is broken by a blow administered by the angered smith. Man dazed by his suffering — his women hysterical.

The alkali on these flats is a devastating chemical. Men standing guard in it to drive back cattle have their shoes almost eaten off them while they wait.

SOMETHING DIFFERENT

Whoever said corn meal would not "travel well" on the plains never carried any — or else never aired out their stores regularly. Airing out carefully will let you bring any kind of flour and meal to California.

On a voyage like this men consume large quantities of sugar. One outfit started with 100 pounds for four men; it lasted ninety days only — about two pounds a week per man. Flour bought at Fort Bernard (from Santa Fé?) cost twelve cents per one hundred pounds. Worth thirty cents a hundred over on the Sweetwater.

Indians along the road gather vast quantities of discarded plunder. The sight of some of them "all dressed up" with

through to California — or, at least, say they are. They advertise to go through in ninety days. One owned by McPike and Strother went through here lately. The passengers were uneasy; doubted if the owners could fulfill their contract.

Everybody is guessing at how long it will take them to reach Hangtown and Sacramento from here. The optimists say forty-five days; some put it as high as sixty. The topic is in everyone's mouth.[1]

Experiments on the plains at agriculture have not succeeded. Corn, wheat, and potatoes tried at Fort Laramie either failed or prospered weakly or were destroyed by Indians who say they own the land and object to such experiments. Meek says they don't even own the dirt under their finger-nails.

Mexican mules and Indian horses do the best on these trails. I have heard it said that sheep do not sicken as easily as cattle. That is an error. They do not get footsore as easily; or, at least, they recuperate faster.

Everybody on the *qui vive* for the crossing of the Rockies at South Pass, the next lure on our California gold pathway.

---

[1] "Uncle Bob's" outfit took seventy-six, but, under pressure, could have made it in ten or twelve less.

Meek laughs at the fears expressed of steep and narrow passage-ways through and over terrific mountain cliffs. He says if any one of us knows and can tell when we pass from Atlantic to Pacific drainage he 'll give him any horse and saddle in camp, including his prize mule "Sacramento." By the way, I once asked the Captain about that name. He replied, laconically, "Mules have been called every other name, so I gave him that one."

We are told that no digging by these thousands who are so wild to dig will be seen till we get to Goose Creek, beyond Fort Hall. At intervals, when the road is clogged, or during the noon resting period, many have delved in the curious rock formations along our route for fossils. Some remains of encrinites[1] have been unearthed, as well as *Productus semireticularis*[2] and specimens of large oysters.

The Platte, to which we say good-bye here at Red Buttes, rises far to the south in a park, or "hole," as the French trappers called them ("glades," they would be termed in the Alleghenies), somewhere west of Pikes Peak. Cañons make the valley impassable for some distance south of Red Buttes.

Some parties cannot celebrate anything unless they roll out the keg. All hail John Palmer, in one Frazer's camp, who held a mighty celebration to-day by making doughnuts, Yankee style!

Altogether we know of six Forty-Niners who have been killed by lightning — one on a ferryboat crossing the Missouri. I tell Boardy he 'd better get religion right here with the conveniencies at hand before he goes any farther; for near us is a party of twenty-seven Mormon missionaries going across the sea to convert Europe.

The sheep drivers have a good time all the way trying to pick off wolves with their guns. Twenty-four hours of sport every day! But they say that even the large white prairie wolves, whose color makes them a good target night or day, are exceedingly hard to hit. Sheep outfits have made as high as twenty miles a day.

[1] Sea lilies.   [2] Leafy network.

The next Ohio beef you kill, Dad, will make you several pairs of good "mountain men's" shoes — if you follow directions. The mountain cobbler merely takes two pieces of buffalo skin (or any other hide), each being a little longer and wider than your foot, particularly towards the heel. Fold these separately, and lay them together parallel with the turned edges; then, rounding and trimming the sides to render them foot-shaped, with an awl and the sinew of buffalo or other animal, or small

Cross's men wandered out of camp one evening last week in pursuit of his horse, and, getting a little confused, with his whole mind filled with Indians and the thought of losing his scalp, he lost his self-possession. Supposing that he had been out longer, and had gone much farther than was really the case, he set up a yelling and made as much noise as if he had been attacked by a whole tribe of Indians. The guard found him in this condition, running about the hills, with but little knowledge of what he was doing and much less as to where he was going, and retrieved him. To his great surprise he found himself within a few hundred yards of camp. When the facts were known next morning the poor Dutchman, who had never dreamed of a prairie or an Indian until he came on this march, had but little rest the balance of the day.

Someone describing the perfect deluges of water which fall in these plains storms said: "You cannot see or feel the rain falling *in drops;* you seem to be in a river's tide."

Buffalo grass, "killed" by the frosts of winter, is resuscitated in the spring by becoming green from the root up without casing its stubble or emitting new shoots. It rarely ever exceeds two inches in height, and never four, and is green only about one month in the year — but is very nutritious at any time. It is cured "on the hoof."

June 13. — We have not yet gone through a prairie fire. But the Johnsons were caught in the track of one down near the Kaw and we heard the story the day we rode over to inspect Red Buttes.

"With a suddenness you'd never believe about mid-afternoon that day," Boo's father said, "we became conscious that what we were absent-mindedly thinking was dust in the air, or, at the worst, the hazy smoke of wayside camp-fires, was in fact a prairie fire rushing across our path from the southwest. My brother Henry, bred to plains life, met the danger like an old stager and to him we are much indebted for advice if not for all we own. He immediately ordered the prairie to leeward of us to be fired in several places and our bell-mare to be caught, which, with the loose animals, was betraying symptoms of alarm that threatened stampede. Meanwhile the fire came down upon us, roaring, extending north and south about three miles and presenting a grand but terrific spectacle. The next move was to get the wagons into the space cleared by the fire we had started and make the mules and horses firmly fast to the wheels. The smoke came drifting before the flames in dense hot wreaths as we securely tied the lariats — the animals snorting and shaking with dread. Some of them, rearing in affright, broke their tyings and bolted away wildly. I was for the moment concerned at their escape until quieted by Henry's laughing reassurance that they would come back as fast as they went. And sure enough they did. The fun was all over in a minute, and the calm way Henry took what we in Iowa had been taught to think was sure 'death and destruction' was a lesson to us greenhorns we haven't forgot yet."

Another young man, named Owen Powers, a strong, courageous swimmer, also attempted the feat which young Masters failed to accomplish — namely, to ride a swimming horse across the Platte here. When everything was ready, Powers stripped off and, mounting the horse he had selected, rode out into the stream. The other animals, forty-seven of them, followed, and, when a few feet from the shore, had to swim. Everything was going all right until Powers reached the middle of the river, when an undercurrent struck his horse, laying him over partly on his side. The young man leaned forward to encourage the horse when the animal suddenly threw up his head, striking him a terrific blow squarely in the face. Powers was stunned and fell off alongside the horse. It now seemed as though both

the shore for dear life. The men on the other side were ready to catch him when he landed, nearly exhausted by his struggles and the blow he had received. They carried him up the bank and leaned him against a tree, one man taking care of him while the others caught the animals, or rather corralled them, until the rest of us got across and went to their assistance. We brought the young man's clothes with us and fixed him up, washing him and staunching his bleeding nose and mouth. He had an awful-looking face; his eyes were blackened, nose flattened, and mouth split. However, he at last revived and was helped by a couple of the men down to his wagon.

Tell any friend of yours who is starting overland that the one thing everybody seemed to have forgotten to bring which is really necessary is horseshoe nails.

An emigrant came up from Fort Laramie on the north side of the river. He says a hundred dollars, judiciously expended, would make the road a good one. He says the ferry-owners at the crossing here pay men at Fort Laramie to urge everyone to come up on the south side and thus be compelled to ferry over — at four dollars each !

This Golden Army of ours contains, as you have guessed, every kind of mortal that goes under the species "human"; do not think, however, that it does not include very many of the devoted Christian type, even if one emigrant did say that he traveled a thousand miles on the plains before he had, knowingly, met one professing Christian.[1]   This is impressed upon one at hearing the hymns of faith drifting up from many a camp-fire at night along the trail.   Some of these are fine marching songs, fit to inspire the down-hearted to new and heroic struggles with the weary miles toward our "Promised Land."   The four most popular, of course, are "Coronation," "Old Hundred," "Windham," and "Wells."   The first you know too familiarly to require quoting; the others shall be written into my minutes : —

WINDHAM

Broad is the road that leads to death,
    And thousands walk together there;
But wisdom shows a narrow path,
    With here and there a traveller.

"Deny thyself and take thy cross"
    Is the Redeemer's great command :
Nature must count her gold but dross,
    If she would gain this heavenly land.

WELLS

When thickly beat the storms of life,
    And heavy is the chastening rod,
The soul, beyond the waves of strife,
    Views the eternal rock, her God.

What hope dispels the spirit's gloom,
    When sinking 'neath affliction's shock?
Faith, thro' the vista of the tomb,
    Points to the everlasting rock.

[1] B. N. Longsworth, *Diary*.

Windham. L. M.

D. READ

Wells. L. M.

HOLDROYD

Old Hundred

Be thou, O God, exalted high;
   And as thy glory fills the sky,
So let it be on earth displayed,
   Till thou art here as there obeyed.

From all that dwell below the skies,
   Let the Creator's praise arise;
Let the Redeemer's name be sung
   Thro' every land by every tongue.

Praise God from whom all blessings flow,
   Praise him all creatures here below;
Praise him above, ye heavenly host,
   Praise Father, Son and Holy Ghost.

And while I am on this topic it will interest some of you home-folks to know what the good brethren and others so inclined preach about at wayside services where tired and half-discouraged Christians of all brands meet to get moral help. The Bible seems full of just the texts the preachers need, and, so far as I have heard any of them, these are the favorite texts of this migration: —

Be thou faithful unto death, and I will give thee a crown of life.
And a highway shall be there, and a way, and it shall be called, The way of holiness.
Come unto me, all ye that labour and are heavy laden, and I will give you rest.
Now the king spake and said unto Daniel, Thy God whom thou servest continually, he will deliver thee.

One forgets to recount the common things, as, for instance, the almost continual singing of some members of some trains of the good old songs brought from every hearthstone in almost every county of every one of our States. Of these, as you would guess, the most popular are "Home, Sweet Home," "The Last Rose of Summer," "Ben Bolt," "Old Rosin the Beau," "Auld Lang Syne," "Arkansaw Traveler," "Annie Laurie," "Bonnie Charlie," "The Campbells Are Coming,"

"Eileen Aroon," "Flow Gently, Sweet Afton," "I Remember, I Remember," "O Charlie Is My Darling." I call these "popular" in the homey, hearthstone sense, in distinction from the popularity of the street songs that are on everybody's lips — like those Uncle Bob is collecting as we march along.

And by the way, we hear so much of our own hardships and of wishes expressed every day by somebody or other that they had made the journey by ship around the Horn, that the words

And a drunken mate a-cursing
    And a-damning you around,
And wishing that the boat would sink
    And everyone be drowned.

Chorus

Then come along, come along,
    You that want to go;
"The best accommodations,"
    And "the passage very low."
Our boats they "are large enough,"
    Don't be afraid,
The *Golden Gate* is going down
    To beat the *Yankee Blade*.

The Captain goes to dinner
    And begins to curse the waiter;
Knocks him out of hearing
    With a thundering big potater.
The cabin maid, half crazy, breaks
    The meat dish all to smash,
And the steward comes a-running
    With a plate of mouldy hash.

You are driven 'round the steerage
  Like a drove of hungry swine,
And kicked ashore at Panama
  By the Independent Line;
Your baggage it is thrown overboard,
  The like you never saw.
A trip or two will sicken you
  Of going by Panama.

June 14. — Looking back as we left the North Platte this morning, we had our last glimpse of that curious stream whose acquaintance we have tried to cultivate for 483 mortal miles without success. That final backward glance in parting awakened no regret, Heaven knows, in any breast; and yet, curiously enough, it brought to our eyes the one thing about the river that is always a pleasing memory — its vivid, green islands; one of those we now saw was heart-shaped and has been named by the emigration "Heart Island."

It was heavy going over the sandy uphill road through Emigrant's Gap, a depression in the bleak landscape, on our way to the Platte River's chief tributary, the Sweetwater; we follow that stream to the summit of the Rockies. Came eighteen miles. Here we pass more poison in the lonely alkali lakes, and more bones of animals who saw "the Elephant" — and are now his! "Mineral Springs" and "Mineral Lake" are names attached to this Poisonland.

Uncle Bob, who needed horseshoe nails, met a man to-day who had a half-bushel measure full for sale at the modest price of a "bit," or twelve and one-half cents, apiece. No amount of argument about taking advantage of a traveler's necessity could bring down the price; so Sir Robert paid him ten dollars in gold for eighty nails. Ox Bow (who if anyone, is to blame for our plight) said, "I really would like to be alone with that man for a while, I love him so."

Out by a bunch of sagebrush where we nooned to-day sat the largest jack-rabbit I ever saw. Wagonhound hit him squarely in the neck, killing him. He took him by the hind feet and slung him over his shoulder, and as he hung hold of his feet in

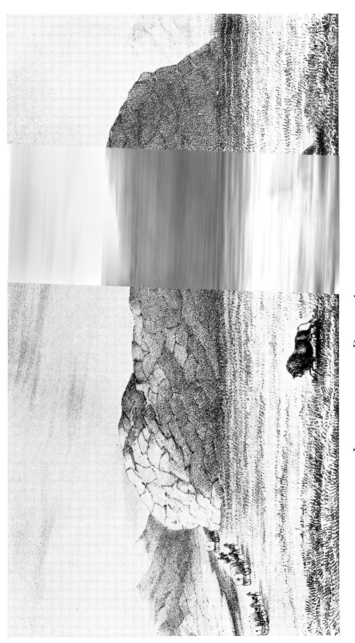

Independence Rock, A
(By Major Osborne Cross, in C

front the wounded neck came down to his heels. That rabbit's ears were as long as a mule's! Cook dressed it and made it into rabbit stew by putting into the kettle first a layer of bacon and then one of rabbit and then a layer of dumpling which we made from flour and water. Layer after layer followed until our four camp-kettles were filled. We had a late supper that night at Willow Springs, where the water was good.

Boardy wonders just how clear an idea the world really gets of it. As to height, the guesses vary as follows: 120 feet; 60–70 feet; 100 feet; 500 feet; 80 feet; 75 feet; 300 feet. As to length, which can be paced off, the variations are smaller, with 600 yards being about the average.[1] As to area, the guesses run from half an acre to over four acres. Supposing 120 feet by 600 yards to be nearly correct, a lump of granite that size, rising alone on a plain, would be significant anywhere. A solitary dwarf pine relieves the contour of the mass from absolute bareness; it and a few shrubs are kept alive by water which rains furnish to a tiny reservoir, or depression, on the summit. The slope on the northeast side is sufficiently gradual to admit easy ascent. "Mound" and "lump" are words most frequently used to describe this curio of the desert. "It looks," said C. Putnam of Kentucky, "like an Indian Mound about the size of some three or four squares of buildings in Lexington." The rocky mountain range of which this rock is a sentinel lies six miles away on one side, to the right, and three miles away on the left.

[1] The U. S. Geological and Geographical Survey in 1870 found the rock to have a circumference of 1550 yards and to be 193 feet high at the north end and 167 at the south.

The origin of the name "Independence" is lost in a maze of tradition; the story most often quoted, and as reliable as any, is that a party of John Jacob Astor's Oregonians, fur-trappers, passing this way to the discovery of famous South Pass in 1810 or 1811, spent the Fourth of July here, and named the rock from the day. R. B. Sage states that the leader's name was Tharp.

It is as a "Register" that Independence Rock attracts longest attention. For you must realize, and the map will show this, that not once from the Missouri River to this point has the California Trail been a single road with no alternative to be chosen. Indeed, from the last Platte Crossing to here several tracks offer passageway, as via Red Buttes to the southward of the track we traveled via Emigrant's Gap. But every Forty-Niner by the California Trail passes Independence Rock and ascends the Sweetwater to South Pass. This rock, therefore, is the only one of the billions of rocks we have passed which everyone has seen. This fact, and the surface afforded for writing by the great flat faces flanking the northeast side, have encouraged passers-by to carve, chisel, or paint (daub) their names from the "beginning of time."

"Independence" was inscribed on it, report says, by the original party. But scores of names have since been superimposed and subsequently erased by hand or by sand-storms. Among those on record as having been inscribed here are Frémont (in 1842), the two Sublette brothers (Milton and William), Bonneville, Fontenelle, Cicero Dowd, William Palmer, Henry Seamon, R. B. Sage, and J. Ralston. Fifteen years ago Townsend wrote that the "Register" contained "most of the names" of the plainsmen and trappers of the day. In the eager competition to inscribe a name highest on the Rock, Cicero Dowd of Ohio holds the palm.

Boardy and I sketched the Rock from different angles and distances. We both felt an unforgettable sense of eternity as we slept in the lee of this sombre pile, while the companies and regiments of our great army of a Good-Time-Come-At-

Last deployed on this most famous of camping-ground of the California Trail all through the night.

June 17. — Our train came up late yesterday after seventeen miles of dusty "rolling on," crossed the Sweetwater here at the Rock, and made camp. The name of this Platte tributary we are now following has caused much discussion. It undoubtedly intends to live up to its name and be "Sweet." When alkali lakes drain into it, it is decidedly bitter. Two or

sketch the Gate this morning. The near-by mountains of granite shine so brightly that many debated whether they were snow-covered. But they were.

On the front of the southern wall the face and body of a venerable man are clearly delineated by Nature's plastic hand. A round cap or bonnet bearing a resemblance to that worn by the Covenanters adorns the head and almost conceals the brow. The nose is prominent, but corresponds with the remainder of the figure; in that particular it might be Boardy himself.

As we have seen, newcomers into the wilds have a passion for writing their names where posterity shall see them and bend its back to do so. About two yards from where the Sweetwater enters the cañon, a vein of black granite is seen running from the summit of the south wall to its base almost perpendicularly.

Last year a California party was passing through the Gate when one member, E. E. Brock by name, conceived the ambition of carving his name forevermore just below the summit of the cliff on the black vein of rock. "He would have done it, too," said our informer, "for with the presence of mind of a skilled circus performer he reached the point he chose for his patronymic when the twitch of a muscle, perhaps, or the yielding of a crumb of rock caused him to drop his writing material." [1] The speaker added that, disgusted with his failure, the young man determined to baulk Fate to the limit by descending the face of the precipice. "We watched him from below," said the spokesman, "with painful anxiety; after an hour's struggle he accomplished the descent somewhat mollified by our applause for the failure of his mission." If friend Dowd of Ohio still holds the palm at Independence Rock, the intrepidity of young Brock — maybe, who knows, a relative of the British hero of the Niagara frontier? — deserves that we fancy his name sky-high here on Devil's Gate.

June 18–20. — Boardy affirms in language I will not repeat that "Sweetwater" ought to be the name of a Shakespearean tragedy, enlivened with comic interludes, and divided into three acts entitled, "Split Rock," "Three Crossings," and "Ice Slough." The first act would show us trying to cross a level plain a thousand miles wide by nine hundred long through a rocky crevice an inch wider than a wagon's tread. The second test of sanity is to cross the same zigzag stream three times every four rods without allowing the lead mules to walk through a King Richard's Ark that brings up the rear of the train. The final mental hazard to overcome is to dig ice calmly on a blistering desert of sand and build an ice palace without succumbing to sunstroke or allowing the ice to boil over and drown you.

This flippant description of these three days' grind up the Sweetwater has the merit, at least, of depicting three memorable scenes, one of which borders so closely on the fantastic as to relieve somewhat the strain of the cruel difficulties imposed by the other two. Split Rock is another Devil's Gate where the tortuous Sweetwater has pounded its way through another mountain ridge. Our road, now congested as never before, clings to the river here and strikes five and six miles inland there. If the former alternative is chosen, you may be driven into the river frequently, which is the case at Three Crossings,

[1] C. McPherson, *Diary.*

DEVIL'S GATE

(*Sketches by Frederick Piercy, in "Route from Liverpool to Great Salt Valley"*)

where you splash through the swift, cold current three times in the space of a few hundred yards.

Ice Slough is one of the Seven Wonders of our hot, desert World. It lies in what we call a low, boggy valley, or morass, a mile in length and half as wide. As one of our fellow travelers, A. Delano, well said, "From its peculiar situation in this dry, barren, sandy plain, this natural ice-house is entitled to be called the 'Diamond of the Desert.'" Meek explained to

the ice to a degree from the burning sun; what between the natural coolness of the nights in this altitude (6000 feet), and the protection given to the Slough by its thatched roof, ice is found here in diminishing thickness until late summer. Meek said that the thousands of cattle accompanying this Golden Army will destroy this thatched roof, and travelers in other years will brand the story of this "ice-house" as a tale of persons rendered mentally unsound by the tortuous Sweet-water or the alkali pools near its banks.[1]

At "Burnt Ranch," the junction of the Sweetwater and its chief tributary, Strawberry Creek, we leave (June 20) the former and strike up the winding course of the latter with a renewed zeal inspired by the prospect of conquering the Rockies on the morrow. I have said somewhere that this California Trail spreads its lures along the way with great cunning, and if you had seen what we have in the rough, winding, hot Sweet-water valley these last three days you would believe me when I say that anything less than the prospect of gaining the Summit of the Continental Divide on top of the Rockies would not have

[1] R. H. Hewitt in his book, *Across the Plains* (pp. 202–203), ridicules the finding of ice here. He made the trip in 1862.

sufficed — and chaos would have been the result. But the less strong, the less well-prepared, the less hardy have fallen by the way before this — and by hook and crook, with wagons discarded at many points, with such piles of stores thrown away as would have made those on the Platte seem insignificant, up, up we climb.

The world-famous Pass now began to be distinguishable, widely differing from what we had pictured in our glowing fancies. The names Rocky Mountains and South Pass awaken a chain of mental associations that foreshadow stupendous crags and beetling cliffs on the peaked summits of which the fleecy clouds perpetually nestled on spotless beds of everlasting snow, as well as narrow chinks and black chasms through which the trembling traveler hurries, fearing to pause and contemplate the sublime creations of Nature lest the dripping crags should close and shunt him into eternity. How widely different was the reality! A range of rounded mountains, without cone or peak, with a sloping gap some thirty miles wide, was approached so gradually that only by the temperature at night could you conceive that you were on the summit of one of the ranges which, in our geographical lessons, we were accustomed to consider one of the great marvels of creation.

In a sense we have been in South Pass (so-called because it lies far south of the Pass in the Bitterroots crossed by Lewis and Clark nearly fifty years ago) all the way up the Sweetwater. So gradual is the rise and descent at the apex that it once took Kit Carson the best part of an hour to locate it for Captain Frémont. The culminating point is between two low hills, rising on either hand fifty or sixty feet high. From the impression made on my mind at the time, and Boardy agreed with me, I should compare the elevation which we surmounted immediately at the Pass to the ascent of Capitol Hill from Pennsylvania Avenue in Washington. It is difficult for me to fix positively the breadth of this Pass. Its height is conservatively estimated at 6500 to 7500 feet. It will be seen that it in no manner resembles the places to which the term is commonly applied — has, in fact, nothing of the gorge-like character and winding ascents of the Allegheny passes and nothing of the characteristics of the great St. Bernard and Simplon passes in Europe. By the route we had traveled, its distance from Fort Laramie is three hundred and twenty miles, or nine hundred and fifty from our starting point, Independence, Missouri.

Our train came to the summit the day after Boardy and I

boys."

Our own elation — Boardy's and mine — on crossing the Great Divide was sincere and deep. But I cannot describe to you the curious little grip at the throat that came to me as a result of two or three seemingly casually spoken words, meant for my ears alone, as we jogged down South Pass. They came from Meek — of all men!

"Those songs and stuff," he said, almost sheepishly, "you've gotten for Uncle Bob . . . and been singing some. Get 'em out; we'll need 'em." Then with a curious, almost fatherly, affection, he spread both hands out to the mêlée and wreckage of the Crusaders on both sides of the trail. I got the point all right. There was rough going ahead!

And for the only time in 2100 miles I saw Guide Meek whip old "Sacramento," mule-of-iron, as he rode away to the front — quite abashed!

Section V

From South Pass to Fort Hall

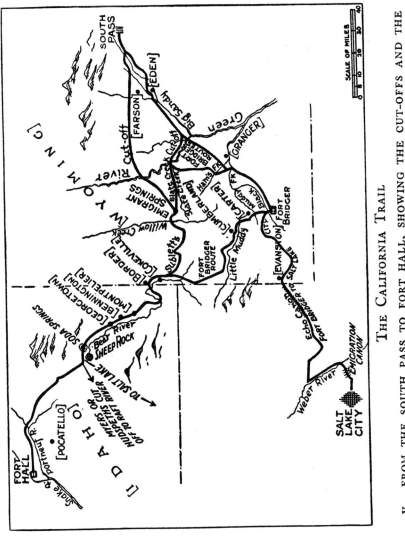

The California Trail

v. FROM THE SOUTH PASS TO FORT HALL, SHOWING THE CUT-OFFS AND THE
MORMON ROUTE TO SALT LAKE CITY

SECTION V

FROM SOUTH PASS TO FORT HALL

June 24. Forty-four miles of desert to Green River.
June 25. Across Grand River to Fontenelle Creek.
June 26. Spring on Sublette's Cut-off.
June 27. Across Ham's Fork.
June 28. To Bear River.
June 29. In camp.
June 30. Across Smith's Fork of Bear River to Thomas's Fork.
July 1. Over mountain to Bear River.
July 2. Along Bear River.
July 3. By Soda Springs and Sheep Rock.
July 4. Through pass in the divide between Great Salt Lake drainage and Snake River drainage.
July 5. On Portneuf River.
July 6. To Fort Hall.

June 21. — The view descending South Pass on the west shows the glittering snow peaks of the Rockies (of Colorado) on the south and southwest and the bleak and broken jumble of Wind River Mountains on the right — bringing back to us Meek's geography lesson of some weeks ago which pointed out the ease of the route across this summit, because here the highest mountains and the Continental Divide do not coincide.

Straight ahead of us lay a bare basin, surrounded by cones of sand and gravel. Here runs a brooklet from "Pacific Spring," as it is called, and we raise a shout at first sight of a Pacific Ocean waterway. Beside it we make camp — along with more hundreds of people in all known frames of mind and flavors of disposition than I shall ever expect to see on this earth again. As two poisons are said to counteract one another, so here surely the most amiable were those who had stifled fatigue, anxiety, and discouragement with a hip-pocket celebration of the conquest of the continent's summit.

Here, luckily, we found the Johnsons, and with "Boo's" help quite a big campfire sing was organized; for something had to be done after Captain Meek's request for song. And, later on, it required no great amount of encouragement (with the Johnson girl's help) to induce our worthy warbler Carlo, the teamster whom I have often mentioned, to get up a series of pantomimes at an impromptu camp show. Inveigling his fellow "geehawer," Picayune, into acting certain scenes representing a California miner in his ups and downs, Carlo dressed him up as a fine counterpart of friend Pickpan and read the verses of a popular song to accompany each individual pose. This is a fair sample of the theatrical performances presented along the trail.

The curtain (a piece of ragged canvas) is now pulled aside, and our hero from Maine is poised on his pick handle, supposedly gazing on a tear suspended from a finger; from the wings Carlo recites, as soon as the bedlam raised by our crew subsides sufficiently so that his voice can be heard: —

> "A Pilgrim from Maine's rocky Shore
>   Surveyed old Hangtown's strand;
> A tear was in his hither eye,
>   A pickaxe in his hand.
> A tear was in his hither eye —
>   And in his left to match,
> There would have been another tear,
>   But for a healing patch." [1]

[1] From *The Miner's Progress.*

A TEAR WAS IN HIS EYE

THE BOOTS WERE WEAR-
ING OUT

Applause, jeers, groans — curtain.

Second scene follows, with Picayune engaged in looking for game well-known to this migration : —

> "The Pilgrim Father looking down,
>   As one who is in doubt,
> He sighed to see how fast that pair
>   Of boots was wearing out.
> And while he filled an ancient pipe
>   His wretchedness to cheer,
> He stopped, with hurried hand, to pick
>   A flea from out his ear."

Carlo's rowdy critics are now drowned out by the general applause, or maybe the drops of honest sweat from Picayune's brow — he never having succumbed to the footlights — drew pity from his companions' calloused souls.

Scene three was a reminder of our dusty roadway : —

SO HERE CONDEMNED

"Thrice have I left this cursed
    spot,
    But mine it was to learn
The fatal truth, that 'dust
    we are,
    To dust we shall return.'
So, here condemned, by
    Fates unkind,
    I rock illusive sand,
And dream of wailing babes
    at home,
    Unrocked, an orphan
    band."

The remarks of Carlo's
messmates which greeted
this sad reference to the
fatherless babes at home
reflected in a perfectly un-
prejudiced way upon both parents alike, and I save the
censor's anxiety by deleting them at once.

Scene four would alone have made Carlo famous : —

"Once more returned, at
    close of day,
    To a cheerless, dismal
    home,
He vows, if he was back
    in Maine,
    He never more would
    roam.
Now hunger makes 'his
    bowels yearn,'
    For 'yams' or 'Irish
    roots,'
But these he looks in
    vain to find —
    Then tries to fry his
    boots."

TRIES TO FRY HIS BOOTS

The last two scenes of Carlo's triumph touched the hearts of his audience who so dream and dream of gold. Even Picayune's perspiration stopped flowing (at least in torrential currents) in Scene five — although he was now, for the first time, carrying a burden.

He leaves the diggings far behind,
His purse he holds with iron gripe.
Resolved to dig and toil no more,
Nor more in dreams to trust,
His well filled bag upon his back,
Of pure and shining dust."

HIS BAG UPON HIS
BACK

The climax was unusual in more respects than I can enumerate, not yet having consulted all the witnesses. The last picture was a home scene, including the Pilgrim's "wife" and "children." Evidently Picayune, in getting "set" for the last scene, thought it highly desirable that his "wife" ("Boo" Johnson) sit in his lap; he and Carlo and the parental Johnsons had a "run in," as the boys say, and a substitute was installed in "Pic's" place.

Scene six : —

"His wardrobe changed, behold him now,
   In affluence and pride,
Surrounded by the forms he loves,
   With joy on every side!
Pressed closely to his heart he holds
   His wife and children dear,
The latter shouting madly, while
   The former drops a tear."

HIS WIFE AND FAMILY DEAR

I gather that when the reconciliation occurred between Carlo and Picayune somewhat later in the night (and stimulants seem to have been required to bring it about), the two tried to raise the camp to see the last act revived — and had to be silenced by the butt of the guard's gun.

Aroused by the commotion, and feeling somewhat responsible for the entire episode, I went out as peacemaker. The men went to bed "like good boys" and left me to a moment's night-dream that lives long in memory. The Wind River

Mountains lifted their hoary, tower-shaped pinnacles to the north. To the south were the shining Colorado Rockies. The scene was one of sublime and solemn desolation. No wonder the resolution of these hundreds of prostrate men and women all but faints in contemplation of the uncounted desert miles yet to be covered, and knowing, if they had never realized it before, that it is now too late to turn back. *No one unable to go forward could hope to get back!*

creek of pure, sweet water. Here at the end of a twenty-mile march we camped the night of the twenty-second. To-day we parted with all and sundry whose destination is either Fort Bridger or the Mormon Paradise, Salt Lake City; or with such as William Kelly, an interesting Englishman with a sound outfit whose acquaintance we have lately made and who wishes to go to California by way of Great Salt Lake and see the Mormons in their last "new" home. Dead oxen and other evidences of the breakdown of outfits line our sandy road to-day; croaking ravens literally blacken the animals' carcasses and scream at us as we approach. Camp to-night is half nightmare — getting ready for an early push across the six parched miles to the Big Sandy, where good grass is fortunately found and where we bait our stock until four in the afternoon; then for the forty-four-mile dash by night for Green River.

The contradictions of this desert are a part of its intriguing mystery. Just as we complete the hectic task (because of the crowding and confusion) of filling every convenient receptacle with water for this savage march in a cloud of stifling dust, a storm strikes us, handsomely cooling the plains for a start, but giving us a thirty-mile contest with a handicap never dreamed of — mud! At daybreak we watered our animals and let them graze two hours, and then entrained again. We reached the Green at about four o'clock in the afternoon at the end of a ten-mile drive ankle deep in dust, with a savage gale whipping it into our faces, making us look as though we had been rolling in dry ashes.

Wonderful Green River! The migration has devoured all grass along its banks, but the coolness of the water makes temporary amends. Take it all in all, Providence has dealt lavishly with this Golden Army in this usually sterile world between South Pass and Bear River. Meek tells us that the season is very unusual; more and later rains than have ever been known here have made grass cover hills that in other years have as a rule been parched and brown. Cold night! Half an inch of ice in our buckets.

The rains have given this truly *green* river an abundance of water. Many look down its emerald course longingly — knowing that it leads to California, Southern California. It intrigues one, that cool pathway, when you think of the deserts which we must travel! An army officer says that Major Cross, coming in our rear, has a party named Manly who, with some adventurous companions, avow that they will rig out a boat here on Green River and set sail for the Gulf of California! They will certainly see some rough rapids on the way, if the current rumor is to be credited! I am going to leave a letter with a ferryman here for Manly, asking him to write a curious inquirer when he reaches California how he stood the trip by the Green River route.

Our Green River trip is not long in miles, but when you have crossed this ferry with fourteen wagons each weighing from 1200 to 1500 weight you have done a big day's work! Two ferries operate here, but charge the same price, $5.00 per wagon; it takes upwards of an hour for each to get across. Meek will send half ours over one route and half over the other, to-morrow, thus saving some time.

Here, with the Johnsons again, "Boo" and I exchanged diaries as once we agreed to do, and with the privilege of copying anything significant which was not too personal. Sisters, if you read this you will appreciate some touches that "Boo" Johnson has given her pages unlike anything you will find in mine. As, for instance: —

Tell Aunty I am becoming quite a good cook on the prairies. I wish she could take a peep at us while we are sitting at some of our meals. Our table is, of course, the ground, our table cloth an India rubber cloth, used when it rains as a cloak! Our dishes are made of

Uncle Henry taught us that there is a different way for cooking each cut of buffalo meat and the rule must be observed. We found it very awkward at first to bake out of doors but now it seems easy.

We have found no berries; neither have I found any of Aunty's bread. Girls, do not waste bread; if you knew how well I would relish even the dryest morsel you would save every piece carefully. "Mountain" bread is simply coarse flour and water mixed and roasted or fried in buffalo grease. Tonight we had a present of fried cakes. Girls, if you wish to know how they taste you can have that pleasure by taking a little flour and water and make dough; roll it thin, cut it into squares and fry in beef fat. Do not put either salt or pearlash in your dough.

You cannot believe the affection the plains give us for some of these simple things we've brought from "Home, Sweet Home." Among the things you girls gave me this little trunk has been such a blessing. Back on the Sweetwater Dad began to say that everything of any bulk had got to go — be thrown away. I expected every minute to be told to make some bundles of the things in the trunk and hand it over to the alkali desert. I was just ready to write here: "Goodbye, dear little trunk I have loved you but now I must say goodbye to you, Poor little trunk. I am sorry to leave thee all alone and not have you to remind me of my dear cousins at home. Farewell, little trunk, I thank thee for thy services and for having been cheered by thy presence so long." And then Dad said that if I thought so much of it I could keep it!!

June 24. — We cross safely, but the operation consumes most of the day; during the remainder we drive across to Fontenelle Creek, six miles, to good grass. Boardy gets out his hooks and lines to provide our stomachs with a surprise. The surprise was all his. He found no fish in the Green! For your benefit (supposing you are bothered by these various pathways of our dust-covered regiments) I give you here two keys to the main routes. They present, also, a sample of our guidebook information, such as it is: —

From South Pass to Salt Lake City by Way of Fort Bridger

Miles

$20\frac{1}{4}$ South Pass. Road crosses the dividing ridge, and strikes the Pacific Spring, where there are excellent water and good grass if many cattle have not passed, in which event the traveler had better continue on down the creek which issues from the spring. Sage for fuel; no wood.

$15\frac{3}{4}$ Dry Sandy Creek. Grass scarce; no wood; some sage and greasewood; water brackish, but drinkable; road good. Here the traveler should send ahead and have the best spots of grass found, as it is very scarce throughout this section. Sublette's Cut-off turns off here for Soda Springs and Fort Hall. Take the left for Fort Bridger and Salt Lake City.

15 Little Sandy Creek. Grass in spots along the creek bottom, and some fuel.

18 Big Sandy Creek. Grass in detached spots on the creek, and little fuel.

$21\frac{1}{2}$ Green River, Upper Ford. Grass and fuel on river.

7 Green River, at the Lower Ford. Good grass and fuel below the ford. Ferry in time of high water.

16 Black's Fork. Good grass and fuel.

7 Ham's Fork. Good grass and fuel.

12 Black's Fork. Road forks at the crossing of Black's Fork. Take left-hand road.

13 Smith's Fork. Wood, water, and grass.

18¼ Fort Bridger. Good camps above and below.

?   Muddy Creek. Good grass, wood, and water. Grass short after many trains have passed.

19   Bear River. Good camps.

19   Red Fork. In "Echo Cañon," two miles below Cashe Cave. Good grass and fuel. Water plenty.

19¼ Weber River. Good grass, wood, and water.

5¼ Spring Branch. Good camp. Road leaves the river and takes

best for those who encamp to cross the Jordan River or stay in the cañon before entering the city.

FROM THE BIG SANDY TO SODA SPRINGS (SUBLETTE'S CUT-OFF)

Miles

7   Big Sandy.

44   Green River. From the Big Sandy to Green River (upper road) there is an abundance of grass in places along the road, but no water.

6   Small [Fontenelle] Creek. The road runs up the creek. Good grass.

4   On the creek. Good grass and water.

12   Small spring. The spring is on the left of the road. Good grass.

9   Ham's Fork. Good wood, water, and grass.

6   Spring. On the summit of a mountain. Good grass.

6   Muddy Creek. Wood, water, and grass.

10   Spring. In Bear River Valley. Good wood, water, and grass.

10   Tomaus' [Thomas's] Fork. Road runs down Bear River. Good wood, water, and grass.

7   Spring Creek. Wood, water, and grass.

7   Smith's Ford. Road crosses over a spur of the mountain. Long and gradual ascent. Descent rather abrupt. Good wood, water, and grass.

8   Telleck's Fork. Road runs down Bear River. Good camp.

4   Small creek. Good camp.

4   Small creek. Good camp.

7   Small creek. Good camp.

12   Soda Springs. Left side of the road, among some cedars, is a good camp.

As it has been the general rule that no one we have known or heard about has had any real trouble so far this year with the Indians, we were all rather shocked over on our side of the fire, where Boardy and I were talking, to hear from a brusque old duffer who would n't be bluffed what had happened to him back down the road apiece.

"I was out ahead that day looking for a deer we had sighted," the speaker began, "and coming back over a little elevation I caught a glimpse of a party of Indians moving through a patch of willow bushes not quite as high as their heads.   In an instant and all together they dropped out of sight.   There was time, however, to see that they were moving camp, and Indians, squaws, and papooses did not make a rustle even.   I remained at my point of observation, thinking they would emerge from the brush which came up to the road.   The squaws and young ones did not show up, but I think slipped away down the bed of a small stream which was close by.

"Presently an old one-eyed mean-looking cuss of an Indian with a boy of fifteen or sixteen years came up on horseback from quite a different direction from where I had discovered them at first, and took positions each side of me — the boy calling the old one Captain with a motion of his hand towards me as if by way of an introduction. The Captain was armed with a flintlock old English musket and the young one with bow and arrows. The Captain, pointing to my Navy pistol, said, 'Pop, pop, pop.' I nodded in the affirmative. I knew the advantage was on my side with a six-shooter and double-barreled gun and percussion caps. The young scamp com-

menced to draw up his bow with an arrow intimidatingly —
each time a little stronger, until I thought it was high time it
was stopped lest he might let fly at me. I was more afraid of
the arrow than of the musket — therefore mentally decided
that if the motion was again made I would shoot him, but made
no demonstration or motion to use my revolver, whereupon
the boy meekly dropped his bow and arrow down by his side.
Th. .ld Indian moved a little higher up the hill and, holding

seen and stop for the arrival of the rest of the men with the
sheep. Soon after halting, a half dozen Indians bounced out
of the brush and commenced to pillage the wagons.

"My three teamsters were scared out of their wits and offered
no resistance, but the wife of one of them went after their hands
with a hatchet when they went to help themselves to things in
her wagon.

"I found it was necessary for me to put on airs, so went to
the wagons, scolding the teamsters and ordering the Indians
by signs to put everything back they had taken from the wagons. They were sulky, and one of them, taking an ox-yoke
bow he had taken by the ends, made a motion to strike me with
it, whereupon I brought my pistol to bear upon him with the
intention of shooting, when he dropped the bow and every one
of them got off to the opposite side of their horses. Then I
knew that I was master of the situation. Furthermore I knew
they were not prepared for a fight, as if they were, they would
not have their squaws and papooses along with them. We
waited until the men with the sheep came up to us and got all
of us around, for it being a warm day, the men had put their
weapons into the wagons, excepting Ben and Lewell, who from
my signals surmised something was wrong; when my first two

Indians approached them they put their pistols under their clothing with just a little of them in sight. The other men did the same with their clothing but had no weapons, yet the Indians supposed they had, probably.

"After we were all armed I felt better able to manage affairs, though I knew by experience that four of our party could not be depended upon in a fight.

"Two more Indians joined those already present — one of them with a certificate that they were 'Good Indians.' It was written in faultless penmanship, expressing the hope we would treat them well, so we gave them some hardtack and a sheep that was lame.[1] They did not seem satisfied.

"After we had got our train in close order we told the boys to start ahead; as they moved, the old one-eyed Captain said to his Indians in Spanish that they would not let us go until they had the black cow and the sheep that had bells on, and told his boy to go ahead and stop us. The boy started, and when nearly ahead we told him in Spanish to come back. As he started to obey the command, the old one-eyed Captain called him derisively a boy, and said he would stop the train until they had what they wanted. He started, and when part way round we leveled our rifles on him and told him to come back; he hesitated a little, but came back to where the other Indians were.

"As we were moving on, the old Captain got down on one knee and leveled his gun at us, which frightened two of our men so they ran for shelter, much to the delight of the Indians. Just at that time a report came that the black cow was missing. Supposing the Indians had slipped out of the brush and cut her out, we made a rush for the Indians, when they rushed into the brush for shelter. Then it was our turn to laugh, as the cow was only a little way off when found browsing. The Indians were very greatly surprised when they found we could use the Spanish language."

"Well, what kind o' Indians were them?" broke out a lis-

---

[1] Indians with good reputations on the plains were often given such certificates by Government Indian Agents. Doubtless some, however, carried forgeries.

tener, voicing the question that lay on threescore lips and had
brought concern to as many faces.

"And that's the funny thing about it," concluded the
speaker; "they did n't act like these-here northern Indians
that are supposed to be so fierce but are n't! By gum, they
were a maurading pack of Arapahoes from Texas up here looking over the gold rush to see how much they wanted of it!" [1]

— and the slow time made on it allowed us to push ahead and
have parts of two days here. The week's trip from the oasis
of Green River to the royal camping grounds of splendid grass
and water on the Bear was made bearable by the unusual
weather of this memorable year of '49. If in one place we had
to ascend a ridge on the worst road Providence ever kept a
wagon from falling out of, in another our spirits were enlivened
to find on a veritable mountain-top (where we might have
expected any disaster in the catalogue) a beautiful grove of fir
trees through the cooling shadows of which, *in the heart of a
desert*, our road wound most alluringly for nearly a mile — the
only grove of timber we have passed through since "the last
leaving of the Little Blue." The hard grind of these hot
days has been enlivened by singing songs, some of which we
have learned on our camp-grounds and now began to sing on
the march to relieve the monotony. I believe our singing has
been a real factor in cheering on many who are discouraged.

I wonder if I am putting it too strongly to say that we American people never really got together until now? Surely there
was never such a wide representation as is now seen on these

[1] Thomas Flint, *Diary*.   [2] Present Soda Springs, Idaho.

California trails, for here are thousands from perhaps every state. You notice this, for instance, by the curiosity with which Yankees watch and listen to Southerners, or as both of these watch and listen to Missourians and the hill folks of Arkansas. Strange worlds — customs, dress, dialect, and manners — here meet together. While travelers from both North and South have visited beyond the Mason and Dixon line, and while minstrel troupes have carried darkey songs far and wide, I think negro melodies never acquired the popularity which is accorded to them here and now. It is not real "darkey" music exactly, I admit; but certainly plantation songs, as written, for instance, by Stephen Foster, are the most popular of all songs among us. Has that been true in the North or West before? The three sung oftenest are "Oh! Susanna," by Foster, "Dearest Mae," by James Power, and "Mary Blane," by an unknown writer. Perhaps Power's song is the most popular. We learned it first and sing it over and over. I give Power's masterpiece: —

DEAREST MAE

Now, niggers listen to me,
    A story I 'll relate;
It happened in de valley,
    In de old Carlina State:
Way down in de meadow,
    'T was dere I mow'd de hay;
I always work de harder
    When I think ob lubly Mae.

Chorus

Oh, dearest Mae, you 're lubly as the day;
    Your eyes are bright, dey shine at night,
When de moon am gone away.

Old Massa gib me holiday,
    An' say he gib me more,
I thank'd him bery kindly,
    An' shoved my boat from shore;

Dearest Mae

James Power

So down de river I glides along,
  Wid my heart so light and free,
To de cottage ob my lubly Mae,
  I long'd so much to see.

It is plain why this song is popular among these regiments who are leaving home — the note of lonesomeness — of affection for those far away. The same is true of Foster's

OH! SUSANNA

I came to Alabama wid
  My banjo on my knee,
I 'm gwine to Louisiana,
  My true love for to see.
It rain'd all night de day I left,
  De weather it was dry,
De sun so hot I froze to death;
  Susanna, don't you cry.

Chorus

Oh, Susanna, oh, don't you cry for me,
I've come from Alabama, wid my banjo on my knee.

I jumped aboard de telegraph,
  And trabeled down de riber,
De 'lectric fluid magnified,
  And killed five hundred niggers.
De bull-gine bust, de horse runs off,
  I really thought I 'd die;
I shut my eyes to hold my breath;
  Susanna, don't you cry.

The third song we learned was also a "farewell" song in every line, namely,

MARY BLANE

I once did love a yellow gal,
  I 'll tell you what 's her name;
She came from old Virginia,
  And they call her Mary Blane.

Oh! Susanna

STEPHEN C. FOSTER

Chorus

Den farewell, den farewell,
 Den farewell, Mary Blane,
O do take care yourself, my dear,
 I 'm coming back again.

They 've sang of charming Lucy Neale,
 They 've sang of pretty Jane,
But I will sing of one more fair,
 My own sweet Mary Blane.

Noted Soda Springs, or Beer Springs as the trappers usually called them, are better described by pen than crayon — for our expectation of making sketches to portray them proves an illusion. The first things you see are two conical mounds, twenty feet high, with a base of more than a hundred feet in diameter, which was formed by the deposit of lime from the water. These are rather more than half a mile north of the road, and near them is a fine brook, lined with cedars, which runs into the river a mile or two below. These springs are one of the greatest luxuries on the whole route. They are highly charged with carbonic-acid gas, and are as delicious as they are refreshing. They are equal to any soda water in the world, and, though good without any additional flavoring, with lemon syrup or sugar they are delicious. Two miles below are a dozen more, near the brink of the river, some of which are even stronger than the upper ones. On the opposite bank of the river are numerous cones formed by the deposit from springs, but the incrustation has completely prevented the water from flowing. A spring on the right bank, near the Soda Springs, through which much gas is discharged with a loud noise, resembling the ejection of steam from a boiler, is, in consequence, called "Steamboat Spring." The following is an analysis of the water of these springs according to Frémont : —

Carbonate of lime	92.55
Carbonate of magnesia	42
Oxide of iron	1.05
Silica, alumina, water, and loss . .	5.98
	100.00

The surrounding country is one of barren mountains, romantic and peculiar, filled with evidences of volcanic action. With the abundance of travelers' comforts which this site offered, and the wayworn and weary condition in which we were, we felt a strong desire to linger a week amid the curiosities of this place; but our anxiety to reach the end of our journey led us on.

About three miles below the Soda Springs the river makes a

the country, to avoid Fort Hall, and saving ninety miles of travel; but the first twenty-five miles is without water. This will become the principal road; but as it is not marked now, we take the old road to Fort Hall and turn north around the point of a rocky spur at the extremity of the Bear Valley.[1]

"Now is the time for you boys to look the other way," said Wagonhound this morning suddenly, as Boardy and I were riding with him at the head of the column. We had just rounded a butte and the trail ahead was a straightaway disclosing one of those [strange un-American wilderness-flotillas[2] that thrived so uproariously by breaking every golden rule and could not have been more distinctly heralded if the vanguard had borne the sign, "Whore, Rogue, Robber and Co." About fifty people and all of one hundred horses made up the company of hunters, trappers, thieves, and murderers, and every mixture of cross-breeding known to man or god was there to be seen, no two in the whole crowd being able, according to

---

[1] In early August Myer's or Hudspeth's Cut-off was said by Major Cross, U. S. A., to be open and in use by many California-bound trains. It is on record, however, that the difficulties of the route counterbalanced the saving in miles.

[2] A. W. Harlan, *Journal.*

Wagonhound, to give the same account of themselves. Americans, half-Americans, Indians, half-Indians, French, half-French, Spanish, half-Spanish, — and then the combinations to the third and fourth generation, till legitimacy and consanguinity shrieked for mercy, — were what you saw in the faces as they passed.

Not to be outdone by their (spare the mark!) betters, horses, ponies, jinnies, cayuses, mules, cows, dogs, and cats had also intermingled to such an extent that if one of the half-wolf canines had heehawed at the sight of us no surprise would have been felt by anyone.

Devilishly attractive in their barbaric clothing and trappings were the white women in the company who, said Meek, were used as bait to draw in weak-minded swains who were later robbed and made away with. The brazen devilishness of these in exposing physical charms to our wagoners down the line — so we heard and quite believe — was more than many a love-lorn emigrant boy in the Golden Army will be able, judging from the past, to resist. This is a "golden year" for these gypsies, too. As to their physical prowess in the way of banditry, we noticed some government wagons in the caravan and Wagonhound saw a traveling government forge.

July 4. — Bear River may be put down by future historians as one of the absolute necessities of the march of the Argonauts of 1849 to California by this line of communications. I do not believe any outfit less strongly fortified against disaster than ours could have made Fort Hall in good condition to go on with the journey without the water, grass, wood, and shade afforded by Bear River to tide them over — and nine of our horses and six of our mules were traveling loose because of galls, sore feet, inflammations due either to insect bites or to bruises from bad falls.

Do not think that Uncle Bob allowed breakfast to pass without commanding all and sundry to remember this was the Great and Glorious Day of Independence and ordering Guide Meek to pitch camp at the first pleasant and convenient site. We cov-

EXTERIOR OF FORT HALL, 1849

INTERIOR OF FORT HALL, 1849

(Sketches by Major Osborne Cross, in Congressional Report)

ered fifteen miles to the summit of the pass or divide between Great Salt Lake waters and those of the Snake–Columbia drainage, where a fine stream, capable of turning a mill, offered a celebration-ground worthy of the day. Happily a score of outfits were on the ground, or were hailed in passing to adjourn the day's labors, or came into camp in time at least to join in the big campfire sing and share with us a great kettle of "flip," as Uncle Bob dubbed it. New songs, old songs, songs good and

large and beautiful springs which fed the Neuf; and then on into a great, barren bayou which led through vales of excellent grass (surmounted by an army of mosquitoes that would have put to flight any but hard-shelled emigrants) to the Snake River, a main tributary of the world-famous Oregon or Columbia.

Fort Hall, where we arrived July 6, resembles in form Fort Laramie, although it is much smaller. It belongs to the Hudson's Bay Company, who, by treaty at the cession of Oregon to the United States by England, was allowed to retain possession nineteen years in order to close its affairs. Three of these have expired. We had hoped to obtain some supplies here, but were disappointed. The fur company was even purchasing bacon and flour from the emigrants who were overloaded. The fort stands on the left bank of the American Fork of the Columbia, sometimes called Snake, and formerly Lewis and Clark's River, which is here perhaps five hundred feet broad. On the west, nothing is seen but a vast barren plain, as far as the eye can extend. On the north, at an apparent distance of thirty or forty miles, high buttes and mountains rise to the clouds, with nothing in the view to cheer the traveler; and this we felt more keenly after having passed through the fine fertile valley of Bear River.

On applying at the fort, we were courteously told that we could leave our letters and they would be forwarded by way of Oregon at the first opportunity, but that there was no certain communication with the states, and our surest way was to take them ourselves to California! Nothing has made us feel so far away from home as those words!

July 7. — At Fort Hall. The talk in camp to-day always seemed to come around to the history and future of this "fort," so odd in its origin and so dubious as to future outlook; for there is no doubt that all California-bound caravans will take Hudspeth's Cut-off from Sheep Rock after this year. A man in a company near us hails from Boston. He told us the strange story of how this post was planted fifteen years ago by the Cambridge iceman, N. J. Wyeth, who planned a fur-trading company with the idea of exchanging furs for salmon on the Columbia River and shipping the fish around the Horn to be sold at a big profit in New England.

He went on to add a juicy bit of scandal to the tale to explain why Wyeth did not happen to get the credit he ought to have had among his home-folks. As a favor, Wyeth brought with him a nephew. This boy did not enjoy frontiering and sided with a clique in Wyeth's party which lost heart and turned tail and went home. The boy kept a diary which was full of the nagging, critical spirit of the band of quitters of which he was one; this fell into the hands of a literary free lance who rewrote it. Thus a book on Wyeth's Expedition appeared, known as John B. Wyeth's *Oregon*, by a writer who never went there, and which N. J. Wyeth has mildly described as filled with "little lies." But as it was the only book resulting from a most extraordinary expedition, an unthinking public got only a negative and pessimistic picture which in nowise correctly represented the strong and soldierly qualities of the unlucky founder of the first inland post beyond the Rockies to fly the American flag, Fort Hall.

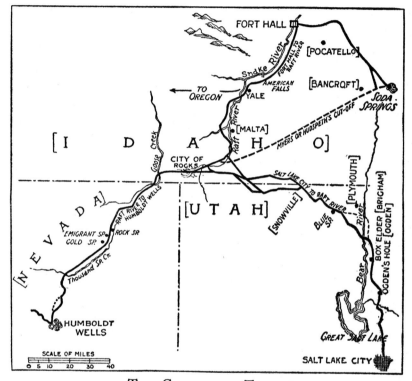

THE CALIFORNIA TRAIL

VI.   MAIN ROUTES FROM FORT HALL AND SALT LAKE CITY TO
HUMBOLDT WELLS

SECTION VI

FROM FORT HALL TO HUMBOLDT WELLS

will insert, if I can get them, logs of the other two routes that run into ours on Raft River — namely, the new cut-off from Soda Springs to Raft River, and the Salt Lake City route to Raft River (see map).

FORT HALL TO HUMBOLDT WELLS

July 8. Across Panack [Bannock] River to camp near American Falls, Snake River.

July 9. By American Falls, 18 miles.

July 10. To Raft River [Yale, Ida.].

July 11. Up Raft River, 16 miles.

July 12. To head of Raft River and the City of Rocks, passing entrance of Salt Lake City Road.

July 13. On Goose Creek.

July 14. Down Hot Springs Valley.

July 15. Over divide by poison wells.

July 16. To Humboldt tributary.

July 17. To Humboldt Wells.

SODA SPRINGS TO RAFT RIVER: SALT LAKE CITY TO RAFT RIVER

"HUDSPETH'S" OR "MYERS'S   [EXPLORED 1849]
CUT-OFF" [EXPLORED 1849]

Miles   *Miles*

Miles		Miles	
20	To Bear River. Good Camp.	18	Hait's Ranch.
10	Portner [Portneuf].	17½	Ford [Weber] River.
12	Fork of Portner [Portneuf].	15	Point of Mountain Spring Water.
15	Panack [Bannock] Creek. Road crosses summit.	12¾	Box Elder Creek.
12	Snake Spring.	23	Bear River [ferry].
12	Utha [Utah] Spring.	6	Small Spring.
15	Decassure [Cassia or Raft] River.	17½	Blue Springs. Water and grass scarce.
18	City of Rocks. Junction of Salt Lake Road.	21¼	Deep Creek. Heavy sage, but good grass.
114		20½	Cedar Springs. Water, wood, grass.
		10	Rock Creek.
		14½	Raft River: Fort Hall and
		176	Soda Springs Roads.

July 8. — As we pulled out from Fort Hall into the dust for the Panack or Bannock River crossing, six miles away, Boardy and I both commented on the fact that no one of us had given this mighty Columbia or Snake River its proper attention, save as we had done justice to two messes of fish some Snake Indians had brought in. What a river — broad, cold, fast-flowing! We agreed that to our old-timers it was no novelty; for our part we had been interested in the so-called Fort; as for our fellow emigrants, their lack of interest was due to something more ominous, more insidious. I think these last dusty days from Sheep Rock — and perhaps a disappointment at not finding Fort Hall to be the sort of "City of Refuge" which the migration begins to need now sorely — have told on these toiling thousands more than any similar number of miles. Or is it that no one of our guides or leaders now holds out any of the "lures" which have beguiled our fancies heretofore and aroused flagging enthusiasm?

My partner and I mulled this over as we outrode the train to have a longer visit with the Snake River at its only "show point" that we shall be privileged to see — American Falls.   I prowled around this delightfully huge rapid while Boardy regaled himself by catching salmon; and the two of us in our camp alone by the river held high carnival at our fish dinner of which the last dessert course was — guess!   The finest red currants you ever saw!   Picked beside us, right on the river's

and scattered about the falls in fragments.   The inner sides of these basins seem entirely glazed, as if submitted to the action of very strong heat, while others resemble very much the appearance of a surface polished by water.   Many small pieces of stone were lying about which were evidently volcanic productions.   I obtained several specimens of the rock and some large pieces of obsidian; the latter seemed to be scattered in small fragments for miles around on the plain, as it could be picked up wherever you went.

Before I say good-night — and while I think of it — they had a shooting match at Fort Hall lately and a number of "mountain men" took part.   The gun belonging to one of them burst. They carried the mangled victim of the accident into the fort, but he soon came around, saying, in a disgruntled tone, "No damn gun can kill me."

July 9. — The train caught up with us this morning. Crossed Fall River, which Boardy and I explored for a mile or two to see the "petrified beaver dams" — *i.e.* the pretty succession of cascades which give the stream its name.   We decided that if these are petrified beaver dams, Niagara Falls is a petrified Icthyosaurus dam. Met a caravan of mules in this desert to-day that seemed to have stepped right out of a page of the *Arabian Nights* (if they had only had a hump or two each) — five hundred Hudson's Bay Company mules bringing supplies to Fort Hall.

Skip the following, for you will think I have been "seeing things" along this broiling road far stranger than any dream of Araby. Passed to-day a singular vehicle drawn by two horses which belonged to an inventor from Milwaukee, Wisconsin, who, in company with two men, was traveling with it to California. It was a cart having tires a foot wide and two sets of spokes to each wheel. The bed was an immense tin box made water-tight, having a framework upon the inside to strengthen it. The owner was writing a guidebook for the use of future travelers, and within the huge tin box was a roadometer of ingenious construction. When they started on this journey the carriage had six wheels, all of the same construction, and it was drawn by six horses; the cart also contained a curious piece of machinery for the purpose of propelling it by hand in case the horses should fail. Six men had originally agreed to take passage on board this carriage, but three of them had backed out before starting. By this time the owner had lost four of his horses and had been compelled to cut down the ponderous chariot to the mere cart for two horses which we saw. He had expended near two thousand dollars to put his experiment to the test and now seemed to be in somewhat reduced circumstances. He was evidently the author of an unprofitable invention, although a man of extensive scientific knowledge and mechanical ingenuity. His horses were now low in flesh and his cart was already quite too heavy a load for them to draw. Eighteen miles of dust to-day.

When I left home everyone who was starting for California took, as a first precaution, serious thought about arming himself with gun, pistol, and bowie-knife and having also on his person various incidental daggers, stilettos, and dirks as handy as might be, or handier. When we first crossed into the Indian territory every man displayed his arms in the most approved

WAGON TRAIN CROSSING SAGE PLAIN ———— LLEY, 1849

(*By Major Osborne Cross, in C*

desperado style and rarely thought of stirring from the train without his trusty rifle; accidents and deaths were recorded almost every day.   But no enemies were ever seen.   By degrees these arms were laid aside and by the time we reached Fort Laramie all were abandoned except a knife and sometimes a pistol which might be seen peeping from a pocket.   Since leaving Green River we had heard of scarcely an accident from firearms   As to danger from Indians, thus far any of twenty foes,

There was a general distribution of property, but only a few passengers could secure a beast of burden; the rest had to take such supplies as they could get (and could carry on their backs!) in return for the two hundred dollars passenger money they had paid.   Many became dependent on the migration; such was the case of one of the ill-starred "passengers" whom we overtook to-day.   He had become very efficient in one of the arts in which, I must admit, the emigration highly excels— that of profanity.   Profane language is the common dialect of a great majority of the emigrants.   The poor Indians apply the most-frequently-heard words to us.   On one occasion a party was inquiring for a good camp-ground of an aborigine and was assured that there was "plenty of grass ahead for the 'whoa haws,' but no water for the 'G–d d—ns.'"

July 10. — Another day in a cloud of dust across deserts of sage to Ogden's River, Cassia Creek, or Raft River — whichever name you please.   Few streams on our whole 2100–mile jaunt are more strategic to this Golden Army, and few, perhaps, will be more quickly forgotten by us and the nation at large.

1. All Argonauts who come by Fort Hall leave the old Oregon trail on Raft River.[1]

2. All who take Hudspeth's or Myers's Cut-off from Soda Springs strike the "main trail" on upper Raft River.

3. All who come by way of Fort Bridger and Salt Lake City hit the "main trail" on upper Raft River.

Here, Meek tells us, all of the Forty-Niners are once more on a single track (as we were on the Sweetwater), stretching along Raft River, Goose Creek, and Thousand Springs Creek to the Humboldt River; beyond, on the Humboldt, there are parallel routes uniting here, separating there. Raft River was doubtless so named, Boardy says, because a raft of any kind will reach across it.

July 11. — We forge on up this stream to-day, crossing it at least three times. It is a parched, desert country with this thin thread of green winding willy-nilly through it; the brook seems as careless of where it rises, flows, and ends as we are anxious. For I might as well confess that this our once valiant and bumptious, if not bold, army of crusaders begins to look frayed and battered — whether you examine equipment or faces. Formerly, on the Platte, we met individuals glibly walking "to California"; on the Sweetwater, in turn, we met dozens of such walking delegates — somewhat subdued, it is true, but yet determined. Now we find the route fairly well lined with them in some places and more of them begging their way along than we had ever thought to see at any time.

As usual our pathway is along the bottom lands of the stream; on either hand high hills rise abruptly, with black trap-rocks protruding; the hills are quite destitute of vegetation except now and then a cluster of fir or cedar trees and odd tufts of bunch-grass growing on the summits. Perhaps it is the despondency of some at seeing things going to pieces; perhaps it is the monotonously drear landscape on a part of the road far from any centre of human knowledge or interest; perhaps it is the absence of those insidious lures toward a welcome, or

[1] Present-day Yale, Ida.

intriguing, objective such as we have had so often — at any
rate, Raft River is not gaining a good reputation these days.
Thieving by sullen and surly vagabonds among us is becoming
common, and we are warned again to place guards at night to
watch the horses lest white "Indians" make away with them.
One entire train, captained by S. N. Harriman of Howard
County, Missouri, was surrounded here by ruffians who took
it bodily from the owners at the point of guns and drove onward

their importunities hardly tends to restoring our
gaiety and song.   The singing at our evening camps is not what
it was.   We have trudged so long now in a column of dust, and
the days are so hot, that men eat supper and throw themselves
prostrate, almost too tired to attend to the wants of nature.
Yes, Raft River may be forgotten, but you can put it down as
marking a turning-point in the life of this strange, great beast
— this unkempt army.   The strongest outfits are now to be
tested; the weakest will surely crack.

July 12. — On the head of Raft River all the divergent tracks
of this Road to Gold converge; first we pass the junction of the
Myers's or Hudspeth's Cut-off from Soda Springs, which is said
to save ninety miles.   Farther on we pass the junction with
the road that comes up from Salt Lake City.   Both roads,
especially the latter, add numerous trains to our moving, dust-
covered line.   From such as William Kelly, and others, we hear
the news from the Mormon Haven of Bliss — with still more
promised in camp to-night.

This camp was pitched in a unique spot between Independence and Hangtown, one to be remembered along with Ash
Hollow and Independence Rock for genuine singularity.   A

spectre came down the trail, one might suppose, and gave us the keys to this strange "City of Rocks" or "Pyramid Circle," as it is variously called. Into this odd, five-mile-long Temple of the Druids (as I would dub it) an inlet fifty yards wide admits us at the east, and on the west an outlet not half as wide points the road to the Humboldt and California. These gateways are pierced through the towering wall which surrounds the level amphitheatre I have described. This contains some twenty-five square miles. All about it are curious altars of white and green stones rising to from sixty to one hundred and fifty feet in height and sometimes very pointed at the top. Around about this vast, lost temple of the West rise high mountains whose peaks, also, pierce the sky like pointed Gothic arches. From near the centre, tower two colossal columns of solid rock, one hundred to two hundred feet high; in outline they perfectly resemble church steeples. From the base of these great turrets, allowing the eyes to follow the circular mountains, we could see a striking resemblance to a city in ruins. Tall columns rose with broad façades and colossal archings over the broad entrances and seemed to lead into those great temples of Nature. Many of the formations strongly resembled huge lions crouched and guarding the passageways. Altogether the spot was one of intense interest, and stood as strong evidence that

> The manuscript of God remains
> Writ large in waves and woods and rocks.

From the human standpoint, this Pyramid Circle is of greater interest because here we have another registration book of transcontinental travel. Rocks, walls, and monuments are covered with thousands of names and dates, and bear, as well, messages to on-coming friends and acquaintances. Some names date back to the earliest explorers who passed through its portals, perhaps with the Hudson Bay pioneer, Peter Skeen Ogden, who was here a generation ago. The road from the Missouri River westward is lined with penciled messages or names and dates of passage, and every smooth-faced cliff or bluff is so utilized; but Pyramid Circle is the volume *de luxe*, in both the quantity and the quality of its records.[1]   Some of the more ambitious registrants, like our Ohio friend Cicero Dowd at Independence Rock, must have been shot up out of a gun or cannon, or have had themselves suspended by ropes from the tops of the cliffs, to enable them to record their names at a point so much higher than their less aerially inclined rivals.

song I have mentioned heretofore innumerable parodies and burlesques are already heard — these drift along the trail eastward with returning miners, Mormons, trappers, and traders, as sung last winter in San Francisco, Sacramento, and all the mining camps.   The lingo of the mines is fascinating to newcomers when they hear it, and mere boys on the trail talk airily about "long toms," "Bogus Thunder," and "Hangtown Jail" as if these were old acquaintances.

The commonest of these parodies you have surely heard : —

> Oh! Susanna, don't you cry for me,
> I 'm gone to California with my washbowl on my knee.

Tunes known to everybody are the ones to which the doggerels attach themselves — like the following, sung lustily to the music of "Old Rosin, the Beau."   On these hot deserts the cooling effect of its illusion doubtless makes it doubly popular!

> I 've traveled the mountains all over,
> And now to the valleys I 'll go,
> And live like a pig in the clover
> In sight of huge mountains of snow.

[1] V. A. Williams, *Diary.*

Chorus

In sight of huge mountains of snow,
In sight of huge mountains of snow,
And live like a pig in the clover,
In sight of huge mountains of snow.

I 'm greatly in favor of mining,
With me, though, it does not agree;
I 'd rather be gently reclining
With Beauty upon a settee.

Chorus

With Beauty upon a settee etc., etc.

I 'm not much in favor of thieving,
At all events, just as I feel;
But I never will work for a living
So long as I 'm able to steal.

Chorus

So long as I 'm able to steal, etc., etc.

A parody on the likewise popular "Lucy Long" celebrates "Miss Ella," a "gallus nag": —

Miss Ella she is twenty-nine,
    Has taken two degrees;
And torn her shirt tail off behind
    So she can show her knees.

Chorus

So take your time, Miss Ella,
    Take your time, Miss Ella, do;
And I will rock the cradle,
    Give the *oro* all to you.

Miss Ella is a gallus nag,
    Miss Ella she is neat;
Her eyes look like a saffron bag,
    And, Lord, what awful feet.

I saw Miss Ella on the Platte,
  Where she got alkalied;
Her jackass he was rolling fat
  And straddle she would ride.

She 's from Lumpkin County, Georgia;
  I know her like a book.
I used to see her wash her feet
  In Johnson's sawmill brook.

Warn All You Darkies Not to Love Her."

Joaquin to the mountains was advancing
  When he saw Lola Montez a-dancing;
When she danced the Spider dance, he was bound to run her off,
  And he 'd feed her eggs and chickens, make her cackle, crow, and
    cough.

Chorus

Now I warn everybody not to ramble,
  Never drink, never fight, never gamble;
For you 'll never have a cent, all your money will be spent,
  And to Sacramento, to the prison brig, be sent.

Joaquin, just before he was taken,
  Killed a Chinaman and then stole his bacon;
Then he went to Sonora, where he killed eleven more-a,
  And a big Digger Indian, which made the twenty-four-a.

Chorus

You have heard of the steel he wore round him,
  I will tell you what it was when they found him;
'T was a long tom iron, to protect him in his crimes,
  And they swore by the holes he 'd been shot a thousand times.

The "long tom," as our illustration shows, was an artificial wooden sluice for washing "pay dirt"; the lining, if the poet is to be believed, was our hero's coat of mail.

Here at the "City of Rocks" we met several parties who had come by way of Salt Lake City, and around the fires, after supper, we got from them fresh news and new opinions of the much-married Mormons in the new home of the Saints.

MINING WITH THE LONG TOM
(*From "The Miner's Own Book"*)

The barren wilderness through which Green River runs changed, they said, into a beautifully wooded and watered region on Black's Fork where Fort Bridger is located — much like the Bear River country. From there some difficult climbing to Bear River to the north was necessary; then the route led through Echo Cañon. The Weber River was ascended and Salt Lake City was reached by way of Emigration Cañon. The route has been pretty well broken open by the Mormons; they use the last few miles from the mountains daily as a wood-road.

The plan of Salt Lake City covers an area of four square miles. The streets are to be laid out at right angles, and the principal business street will run due north and south. A delicious stream of water flows through the centre of the city and this is to be subdivided into rivulets on either side of all the streets. The water, coming directly from the mountains, always pure and fresh, will thus be within reach of everyone. Cottonwood trees grow on the main stream, and saplings had just been planted, while our friends were there, on the sides of the streets. Most of the dwelling-houses are built a little distance from the sidewalk, and to each dwelling is appropriated an acre and a quarter of ground for gardening purposes.

"The masses," said one of our educated emigrants, "are sin-

served no Catholic proselytes. The people have been induced to emigrate by the offers of the Mormon missionaries to transport them free of expense to a land 'flowing with milk and honey,' where, they are told, the Protestant Christian religion is inculcated in all its purity and where a farm and house will be given to each family. Seduced by this promise of independence from the state of poverty which surrounds them at home, they have taken advantage of the opportunity and are baptized into the faith of the 'Latter Day Saints,' and it is only after their arrival in the Valley that the spiritual wife system is even mentioned to them. Thousands of families are now in Utah who are as much horrified at the name of polygamy as the most carefully educated in the enlightened circles of Europe and America. More than two thirds of this population (at least, this is the ratio of my experience) cannot read or write, and they place implicit faith in their leaders, who, from a pecuniary point of view, have fulfilled their promise; each and all are comfortably provided with land and tenements. The first year, of course, they suffer privations until they build their houses and reap their crops; yet all their necessities in the meantime are provided for by the church, and, from a social point of view, they are much happier than they could ever hope to have been at their native homes."

One of the recent comers from the Mormon Paradise described a public baptism he had witnessed. Seeing a crowd assembled, he joined it and found twelve persons, some of whom had already undergone the ceremony of baptism, and others patiently awaiting. The first immersion was of a lady about eighteen years of age. The priest who officiated was standing up to his waist in the stream with his coat off and his sleeves rolled up to his elbows. The lady was handed in and the shock to her system of the plunge into freezing-cold water was evident. The baptizer, placing one hand on her back and the other on her head, repeated the following words: "I am commissioned by Jesus Christ to baptize you, in the name of the Father, and Son, and of the Holy Ghost. Amen." He then pushed her over on her back, allowing the water to cover her. She struggled to get out of the water, but her husband remarked that the whole of her head had not been submerged and insisted that "his wife should be properly baptized." She was consequently ducked effectually a second time and the poor woman finally made her escape, almost frozen.

The next subject was an old lady of seventy-five years. She tottered into the stream by the aid of her crutch and underwent the same ceremony. Would persons submit to those extraordinary tests if they did not possess real faith?

The third person was a young man of about twenty years, with a calm, placid countenance, and he underwent the operation without flinching. His face was the impersonation of faith and purity. "I should have liked to paint him as a study for a Saint John," said the narrator.

"When we entered the city," said Thissell, "there were but few places of interest to visit except the Tabernacle. It resembled a large kettle turned bottom upwards. Near by was Brigham's residence, known as the Beehive. Here lived his 'twenty-five' wives and 'one hundred' concubines. Some of these were old, while others were very young. As for beauty, they compared with the rest of his flock. Many of them were foreigners. Now and then there were lively times at the Bee-hive. Over one hundred children called him 'papa.'

While in the city, I had the pleasure of an introduction to Brigham Young — a man of medium height, thickset, with a short neck, his face full and round. He wore a dark suit of homespun goods, and was a man of fine appearance. Every word that fell from his lips was law and gospel to his followers.

the day of rest. All labor was suspended. The men, women, and children put on their best to attend preaching in the Tabernacle, conducted by Brigham Young. The road was lined with wagons. I shall never forget that Sabbath. In every wagon (they had no carts or carriages) were one man to five women, and children by the dozen. At an early hour the Tabernacle was filled to overflowing.

"Salt Lake Valley is one of the garden spots of the earth. All kinds of produce were cheap, contrary to what we had heard. The Mormons did not care for our money, as pumpkins were legal tender. Spices of all kinds were high. Cinnamon, cloves, ginger, nutmeg, and allspice, sugar, tea, coffee, and rice were five dollars per pound, while we could buy a fresh-made cheese as large as a small washtub for one dollar. Butter ten cents per pound. And we could get a cartload of eggs for a pound of tea. As a class, the Mormons were sober, clean, and industrious, also ignorant and happy. They had no commu-nication with the outside world. They knew but little about the discovery of gold in California and nothing about the roads.

"After eight days' feasting, recreation, and rest, we bade adieu to these kind and hospitable people and took the trail that led to the north of the lake. This trail also led to Oregon by the way of Fort Hall. We crossed Weber Creek and Bear River. About halfway between Weber Creek and Bear River we passed a boiling sulphur spring. The Indians and Mormons used this water as a panacea for all kinds of disease. There is also another spring near by that is icy cold."

A man by the name of Stuart added a little color to the story, as follows : —

"Our horses were greatly in need of rest, so we stayed with the Latter Day Saints, as the Mormons called themselves, for several weeks and were very kindly treated by them. In fact, I here got into better society than I have been in since, for I lived a month with one of the Twelve Apostles and his family. It was Apostle John Taylor, a pleasant old gentleman. He wore a snuff-colored suit and a rather rusty old plug hat. He owned a whole block and had an adobe house on each of the three corners, in which lived his three wives, each in her own house. I had the honor of living with the Apostle and wife No. 1, in a house on the fourth corner. She was a most amiable woman, a good cook and a good housekeeper. She kept everything nice and clean but the confounded bedbugs ran us out of the beds in the house and we all slept out in the yard. Luckily it never rained. Mrs. Taylor felt greatly mortified about the bedbugs and said that she just could n't keep them out although she fought them all the time, and when one day I pulled a piece of bark off a fir pole on a near-by fence and found innumerable bedbugs under it I knew why Mrs. Taylor could not keep them out of the house. The entire Valley swarmed with them.

"When we camped on Weber River on our way up here, the sagebrush, just after sundown, swarmed with skunks and I felt certain that Great Salt Lake could beat the world for bedbugs and skunks. At this place I was stricken with a severe attack of mountain fever which laid me on my back in the wagon On Bear River, at the Mormon ferry, we found the mosquitoes were terrible. 'How on earth will you be able to live here during the summer months?' I said to one of the men, seeing him tearing them from his cheeks with both hands. 'Well,' the captain of the party replied, 'they are purty damn bad here, I admit, but when you get over yonder they 'll give you particular hell.' And maybe he did n't tell the truth!"

To state the simple fact: we of the migration who do not come from the States where the Mormons have had their principal settlements neither bring with us nor acquire by expe-

the value and amount of the testimony.

3. That citizens of the United States have been sentenced to labor in the chain-gang, without having committed a crime, and without having a legal trial. They had spoken against the Prophet.

4. That liberty of speech has been destroyed in the Valley, so that a man while there hazards his life by speaking against the proceedings of the Mormons.

5. That they break open letters sent by emigrants to their friends.

6. That all their pretended courts of law are a cruel mockery of justice, the story of a Mormon who is a party in the suit far outweighing the disinterested testimony of emigrants under oath.

7. That bigamy and incest are sanctioned by the united voice of the Mormon church and government.

8. That they entertain treasonable designs against the United States, pretending to be independent and defying the Government.

9. That the Mormon church is nothing but an organization of banditti, with Brigham Young the captain.

10. That their government and laws are but a cloak under cover of which many emigrants have been robbed, the officers of the courts sharing the booty with the plunderers.

11. That citizens of the United States have been murdered at Salt Lake, and Mormon courts have discharged the murderers with honor.

12. That the Mormon rulers will trample all justice and liberty under their feet, and American citizenship will be no protection among them.

We have no means of knowing the justice or injustice of these numerous accusations. There is not the slightest doubt that they are believed sincerely by hundreds, if not thousands. Our experience, as my diary entries will show, is that numerous instances of rascality and crookedness have been attributed to Mormons which we found — so far as any were found — being practised by others than Mormons. The worst true things we have heard about them were the allegations of Brigham Young in his sermon. But the "crimes" he denounced are common to all emigrants. In the Salt Lake City courts the Gentile may get as crooked a deal as most of us outsiders think the Mormons got in Illinois or Missouri courts. If so, God help him.

As a matter of fact, the hostile things you hear against the Mormons are vague and indefinite — so far as finding anyone at your elbow to substantiate them goes. Whereas the things which are creditable are to be heard frequently from living witnesses who speak by word of mouth. We met one of these only yesterday. This party had come through Salt Lake City with a drove of sheep. Speaking of arriving at Salt Lake City from Fort Bridger, he said that up on the mountain beyond Emigration Cañon, before the travelers could see the city, two men came along and said, "Are you Saints or sinners?" This man replied that it all depended on how you looked at the thing. "Are you Mormons or are you not?" was the disgruntled, testy reply. The emigrant said he was not. The Mormons then asked what train it was and were told.

[1] F. Langworthy, *Scenery of the Plains.*

Whereupon the riders whirled about and trotted back to the city. Later on two other men were seen approaching from the same direction. Meeting the now somewhat alarmed sheepherder, they said:

"We know who you are. You are the ones that assisted some of our people on the plains who had been robbed by the Indians. You may turn off to the left and go down the hill to the church gardens and camp there until you hear from us again — but

us to come to a certain house in the city where we should be repaid in kind for all we had given away to the bereft Mormons on the plains. And we were — with interest."[1]

July 13. — We ascend to the rim of the basin watered by Raft River through a narrow ravine full of steep, sidling passes through a volcanic country which begets volcanic language, especially as we drop down into a branch of romantic little Goose Creek from a cliff the wagons let down with ropes. After nooning, and a climb to a hilltop, wild Goose Creek Valley came into view, looking like the breaking up of a world — a world no one wanted. As far as the eye could reach,

UNCLE BOB DREAMS OF GOLD ON GOOSIE GOOSIE GANDER CREEK

¹ Thomas Flint, *Diary.*

cones, tables, and nebulæ, peculiar to the country, extended in a confused mass; many hills looked white with lime and melted quartz, some presenting a combination of lime and sandstone which you might call volcanic grit. Other heights exhibited, with surprising regularity, those varied colors of the rainbow which broken hills are known to show in parallel lines — white,

HE HEARS THAT HIS DREAM
HAS COME TRUE

red, brown, pink, green, and yellow, and sometimes a blending of these. A mountaintop or table-land within sight seemed covered with débris such as I have seen on the cinder pile of a blast furnace.

Do you know, I have a feeling that when you put your finger on the map on the precipice over which we had to lower wagons by ropes to-day you absolutely mark the spot where our Golden Army began to bend, if not break, psychologically. The brain can stand just about so much, but some are more rugged or tenacious or something than others.

Boardy and I feel as though we were sort of looking on at an operation, so to speak. It is exceptionally interesting. If we are right in our analysis, it is something for the records. These are the reasons why we think the famous California migration of 1849 really began to waver on the Goose Creek Mountains: —

1. Men by the dozens now begin to unload wagons and pile what they could on animals and try to "pack" through to the Diggings.

2. Horses, mules, and oxen now really begin to show signs of "breaking" themselves.   Dogs, for instance, frighten animals now that would never have noticed them a hundred miles back on this road.   They are killing the dogs in every outfit.   Too much alkali dust, too many long miles to water, too uncertain grazing since South Pass, are beginning to show their effects.

3. Responsible leaders, like Meek and Wagonhound, try to take people's minds off their troubles by artifice.   If one of

> In the shadow of the temple
> Close by its 'holy gate.' "

If you don't appreciate this attempt of the wagon-driver to do his noble best to bring smiles to faces, you should have seen Meek scratch his chin on his beard !

> "That I might see the Prophet pass,
>   That good and gracious man;
> More wondrous than false Mahomet,
>   Tamerlane or Ghengis Khan.
>
> "I'd like to be a Deacon bold,
>   They lead such pious lives,
> With lots of 'tin' and real estate,
>   And half a hundred wives.
>
> "If one, with us, you consider right,
>   Then no one can deny,
> That fifty wives are just the thing,
>   The flesh to mortify.
>
> "I don't know how they manage there,
>   But I'd like to see the man
> Who'd bring another woman home
>   To my wife, Sarah Ann.

> "There'd be the tallest kind of row
> That ever you heard tell;
> The other gal would have to clear
> Or else be sent to ——— Well!"

Surly as this driver-artist was (a natural reaction from his flippant outbreak) when I found him down near the head of the train later on, his laconic explanation touched me: "Ye see," he said, "some boys in that other train beside us had the old folks worried because of talk about quittin' California fur good and striking back the Salt Lake trail fur Mormontown to live. I was jes' tryin t' create a little anti-Mormon diversion, see? Don't hold it agin' me."

But on getting down on Goose Creek a real diversion came. Where could the rumors have originated that credited Goose Creek with possessing gold? Yet, along with everyone else who had nothing to do, Uncle Bob and the rest of us streamed out with pick and pan (and with many a brave huzza) to look into the limpid water and see its bottom speckled with shining yellow particles, the

WITH A LOUD HUZZA HE JOINS
THE FOOL'S GOLD BRIGADE

very image of gold! We soon found that the "gold" that glistened in the sands of Goose Creek was only deceptive mica. You should have seen the elongated jaws of some of the sanguine, ignorant ones when that fact was ascertained; but, though sad the disappointment, it afforded fine food for fun and kept us joking all the evening, with every now and then an ironical cheer for Goose Creek.

July 14-16. — You see from the map what our business is for these four days until we shall view the strange, welcome-unwelcome objective toward which we are heading, the arid four-hundred-mile Humboldt Valley.

Our road, dusty, congested with ox-teams in the narrow pinches, and showing at every step the breaking-up of outfits, leads from Goose Creek through hills of sand covered with sage and greasewood (named thus because it makes so bright a

foot and on half-rations. These hungry ones become "wolfish," as the expression goes, as is proved by the case of a man from Salt Lake who overtook us with twenty-five head of fat cattle. One party of hungry emigrants offered him two hundred dollars for one ox. AND NO ONE GETS A The owner refused to sell at any BIGGER "PILE" THAN price. Later in the day twenty- HIS — THAT IS, NOTHING five half-starving men, with rifles in hand, walked into his little herd and killed the best ox they could find. Then the Shylock offered to take one hundred dollars for the ox, but it was too late. He had played the wrong card.

When we arrived at Thousand Spring Valley we found many bottomless wells on a great plateau; the water flowed out and formed a beautiful meadow, a real oasis, in this barren and sterile land. These were life-savers, and many camped here several days to rest their cattle. It seems strange that so beautiful a meadow can be surrounded by one vast desert of sand-hills. Fortunately we found here, next camp to ours, old Denny and his rare fiddler-friend; and, with Carlo's help, we managed to put on quite a little show that night. Wagon-hound engineered it — with the rather ominous statement to me and Boardy that "we'd better do it while we can; a little later nobody will even want to try." As on that other occasion at North Platte ferry, Denny was, again, the hero of the hour. His masterpiece took the form of a ballad-résumé of the overland trip. Recalling, as it did, to all of us the old land-marks of our journey, as well as many of our exact experiences, and sung to the notes of a good accompanist, it made me feel that hearts were really healed by Denny that night on that wide meadow. The song was entitled "The Arrival of the Green-horn," and it was sung to the air, "Jeanette and Jeanot."

> "I 've just got across the Plains,
>   I 'm poorer than a snail;
> My mules all died but poor old 'Clip,'
>   Who I pulled in by the tail.
> I fed him last at Chimney Rock —
>   That 's where the grass gave out;
> I 'm proud to tell we stood it well
>   Along the Truckee route.
> But I am very weak and lean,
>   Though I started plump and fat;
> How I wish I had the gold machine
>   I left back on the Platte.
> And a pair of striped bed-tick pants
>   My Sally made for me,
> To wear while digging after gold;
>   And when I left says she:
> 'Here, take the laudanum with you, Sam,
>   To check the misiree.'"

The laughter that greeted the little old singer will not be explained by your merely reading his song. For his antics and grimaces — his pulling "Clip" over the Sierras by the tail — his feeling in his pocket with quick, horrified anxiety for the laudanum — well, it was n't worth going to the Thousand Springs to see, but it was something we who did go will never forget. As the crowd yelled I was a good deal impressed with old Wagonhound's repeated "Good for Denny!"

"When I left Missouri River
    With my California rig,
I had a shovel, pick, and pan,
    The tools they used to dig.
My mules gave out along the Platte
    Where they got alkalied,

And a flintlock musket loaded full
    To shoot the Digger Tribe.
But I left them all on Goose Creek
    Where I freely did imbibe.

"I joined in a train from Pike
    At Independence Rock;
The Indians came in that night,
    Stampeded all the stock.
They laughed at me, said 'Go afoot,'
    But soon they stopped their fun,
For my old mule was left behind,
    So poor he could not run.
So I packed my fancy nag,
    For the rest I could not wait,[1]
And I traveled up Sweetwater
    Till I came to Devil's Gate.
I 'd have given all my boots and shoes
    If I had not been born;
Next time I 'll strip at New Orleans and,
    By God, swim around the Horn."

[1] Meaning that the *raconteur* swapped a poor mule for a fancy nag and took French leave.

Boardy found on a camp-ground on Hot Springs Creek or Thousand Springs a company of Mexicans among whom was a Chilean, on his way to meet countrymen of his in Pleasant Valley, California, who had a clipping from a Chilean newspaper which was creating a good deal of merriment. He secured a copy of it and brought it to camp and posted it where it would be seen by all — an encouragement to every would-be Californian. It read : —

Ojo Al Aviso

Un comerciaciante respétable cuyo nombre no podemos decir por ahora, nos encarga hacer el signiente aviso en castellano.

Ce necesitaran docientas jovenes, blancas, pobres i de conducta intachable, que no sean del todo destituidas de gracia i beldad, para embarcarlas para California i procularles enlaces honrosos, con los millares de norteamericanos i bestranjeros que han adquirido una fortuna en las minas, i desean establecerse. Un anciano sacerdote las acompana, para responder de su conducta. — Los padres de familia que quieran acompanar a sus hijas, pagaran sol lo mitad del pasaje, de un buque fletado es profeso para este objecto, i donde no se recibiran otra clase de pasajeros.

Si la empresa se realiza, el empresario recibira en Valparaiso a bordo a las personas admitidas, la vispera del embarque. No se anticipa dinero alguno; ni se admitira mas equipaje que un baul por persona.

La mantencion desde el momento del embarque corre de cuenta de la empresa. — Dos meses permansera el buque en San Francio, obligandose por este tiempo, i durante la vuelta a Valparaiso a sostener a las personas que hubieren de regresar.

No se recibiran propuestas hasta el 15 de Marzo proximo.

The combined linguistic talent of our camp and several neighbors resulted in the following translation, which we also posted : —

From the Santiago de Chile "La Cronica"

Your Eye to This Notice !

A respectable merchant, whose name we cannot at present give, requests us to insert, in Spanish, the following notice : —

WANTED.—Two hundred young girls, white, poor, and of irre-
proachable conduct, not altogether destitute of grace and beauty,
to be shipped to CALIFORNIA, and to be there honorably married to
the thousands of North Americans and other foreigners who have
made their fortunes in the mines, and desire to get married. An
aged priest accompanies them, to answer for their good conduct.
Fathers of families who may wish to accompany their daughters
will be admitted at half the usual passage in vessels chartered expressly
old . . . and which will not receive any other class of passengers.

No application will be received until the 15th of March next.

As you can imagine, I saw, thereafter, a fresh explanation of
everything in Boardy that smacked of optimism and undue
haste to be on the way; and I greet him nowadays frequently
in my best Spanish whenever things go amiss and delays ensue:
"Alégrate! Amiguito! Acuérdate, son blancas, pobres y no
del todo destituidas de gracia y beldad!" (Cheer up, comrade!
Remember they are white, poor, and not destitute of grace and
beauty!)

The Hot Springs (which we pass on the fourteenth) are close
to the road on the left and are a curiosity indeed. From perhaps three quarters of an acre of low, marshy land hot water
flows constantly, forming a creek from six to eight feet wide;
it is from one to two feet in depth and has a very rapid current.
At the points where the water issues from the ground it is nearly
boiling hot. Clouds of steam rise from the surface like the
steam from boiling water and this is seen some distance before
you reach the springs. The water is strongly impregnated with

[1] Printed under date of February 11, 1849. A party of Chilean miners in Pleasant
Valley were met by some of the first Americans of 1849 to cross the Sierras by the
Truckee route. W. Kelly, *An Excursion to California.*

alkali; where the water is not flowing it looks as if strong lye had been standing there. The creek is said to run about two miles and lose itself in the sand; I did not trace it out, but as another creek runs near, it probably receives a large portion of the waters from the springs through some unseen channel. Immediately after passing the springs the water in the creek is much sweeter and better than it was below.

In such a vast, wild army as ours there are people capable of committing any indiscretion; this came forcibly to our attention here. After leaving the hot springs we heard a noise in an outfit near by that appeared to proceed from a person in great distress. It seems that one of the party, soon after leaving the springs, suddenly became quite frantic, as if temporarily insane, a condition brought on by fatigue and hardship and from drinking the impure hot water. The men of the train were compelled to place the invalid in one of the wagons and confine him there. When, early the next morning, the train pulled out, this veritable madman leaped from the wagon, under the influence of a paroxysm of insanity, uttering loud cries and shrieks. After describing a circle several times by his movements, he announced that the destiny of Providence, so far as he was concerned, was accomplished; that nothing more was to be expected of him or could be demanded from him in this life and that he was willing to submit to his fate and die on that spot and be buried within that circle. It took some time and the united strength of two or three men to get the lunatic back again into his wagon.[1]

In these last days we have had more than one case of dementia — the most gruesome and certain evidence of the psychological "breaking" I have feared. In one instance a woman, whose husband had refused her impossible request to turn about and start back home, began setting fire to their camp. In her first attempt their wagon was saved by the intervention of a passer-by. And, though watched carefully, the poor woman did succeed at last in destroying their tent, bedding, and some baggage. If I were to name the most horrible phase

[1] W. Kelly, *An Excursion to California.*

of this whole gold-rush episode across the Plains it is that —
insanity. We had passed a number of lone individuals going
homeward down the trail before Meek pointed out that these,
in most instances, were demented emigrants whose minds had
given way through fear, worry, or lonesomeness, or because of
poor food or water, overwork, sleeplessness, disease, or family
disputes, or all or any of these combined. He warned me to be
careful about attempting to argue with, or to try to thwart,

true that they are paying up for the abuse they received at
the start. Many of them have undoubtedly been maltreated,
cursed, and hallooed at most of the way. If so, they now have
their innings, for the men dare not speak loud to them, they are
so easily frightened. Some emigrants do not care to ride in
the wagons now, for their cattle are perfectly wild — and many
cannot milk their cows any more than they could milk so many
untamed antelopes. Perhaps the cows smell the wild animals
or scent the Indians, though the dogs frightened them in the
first place. Men, women, and children now either precede the
teams or stay far behind them, so as not to frighten the cattle.
Many outfits have killed all their dogs.

To-day at daybreak I was awakened by a disturbance
among a neighboring outfit's cattle, which had got frightened
at the barking of a dog. They ran against the wagons, broke
the wheels and tongue, and bawled and pitched around till
they finally got loose and ran off in a stampede. For a while
all was confusion in the camp. The runaways kept on going
until something in the distance frightened them back again,
and they returned as furious as they went. The men with
great difficulty managed to stop them. The boss of the train

ordered all the dogs to be killed. By mistake Picayune's "Tray" was shot. Some of the company were not disposed to comply with this sanguinary (but seemingly necessary) decision of the captain's, and threatened retaliation in case their dogs should be killed. But the row ended there — and Picayune is a bereft soul.

Speaking of dogs, I remember seeing one run up to a hot spring as if to lap the water, and as he did so his feet slipped into the edge of the pool. He gave one yelp of pain and jumped into the middle of the spring, stretched out his legs, and never gave another kick. In a short time the hair was all scalded off him. This, again, reminds me of a Dutchman who, 't is said, came to his first hot spring and at once ordered his teamster to drive on, as "Hell could not be more than a mile away." But the dog I saw knew it was nearer than that.

July 17. — Boardy and I will be old men before we forget our first view of the Humboldt, or Saint Mary's River, as the trappers used to call it. The climb over the last divide was on by far the roughest track we had yet met with, being, in great part, a road in the bed of a mountain torrent so narrow, in many places, that the wagon-wheels were working upon the edges with the mules endeavoring to work below in the bottom. Since this was too much for a single team to master, Wagonhound took up two wagons at a time, using the teams of that four; and in getting round the mountain's summit he took all out but the wheel-span, as it required the greatest precaution and precision in driving, there not being six inches to spare from the edge of a deep precipice. It was a nerve-test with your foot hanging out over a thousand feet of fresh air; and only one teamster in twenty was game enough to sit in the saddle and pilot all in safety over the dangerous place. We had this grinning precipice disagreeably contiguous for more than a mile, till we got to the western side of the range and started down the valley of Bishop's Creek.

From there the valley of the notorious Humboldt lay exposed to view. Contrary to our expectations, it was a perfect match

for the barren leagues we had been traveling since saying good-
bye to Bear River, except for a narrow margin that runs along
it like a shelf, marking, I should suppose, the high-water line
when the river is augmented by the thaws of the adjacent
mountains.   Its course was perceptibly marked by dense lines
of willows.

THROUGH THE VALLEY OF THE SHADOW AND THE
SINK OF THE HUMBOLDT

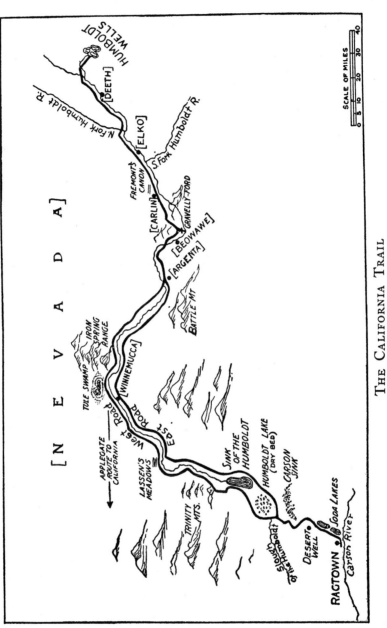

THE CALIFORNIA TRAIL

VII. FROM HUMBOLDT WELLS TO THE CARSON RIVER

THROUGH THE VALLEY OF THE SHADOW AND

July 19. Off and on the river. Rough going.   22 miles.

July 20. Over mountain [east of Elko, Nev.].   16 miles.

July 21. Off and on river. Rough road.   25 miles.

July 22. Around Frémont's cañon to Gravelly Ford. 34 miles.

July 23. Sandy road [north of Battle Mountain]. 29 miles.

July 24. More sand.   30 miles.

July 25. Across sloughs [Iron Spring Range]. 23 miles.

July 26. Grass in sloughs [Tule Swamp near Winne-mucca]. 21 miles.

July 27. Desert Road.   25 miles.

July 28. To Cold Springs [Eugene Mountains]. 34 miles.

July 29. [Lassen's Meadows].   12 miles.

July 30–*August* 1. In camp.

August 2. To Sink of Humboldt.   20 miles.

August 3. To end of Sink [Humboldt Slough].   8 miles.

August 4. Across Desert to Carson River [Ragtown]. 40 miles.

    364 miles.

July 18. — All the world has been hearing of this Humboldt River since Frémont came this way six or seven years ago; and will hear a lot more of it when this and the next year's migrations go through. You ask, "What is it like?" Well, take it from Meek: no description describes it, for it is a differ-

ent river in almost all of its 364 miles from these Wells to the
dreaded Sink; and in any one of those miles it is a different
thing in a wet season from what it is in a dry; and a different
thing when used by many emigrants from what it was in a
"state of nature," so to speak.

No river, from what we see and hear, could run through
a more barren wilderness of great rocky peaks and ridges.
Denny sang us another song last night which I may quote later,
but one verse correctly explains (we think) the stark and
abandoned look of this country : —

> "I crawled out and started on,
>   And managed very well,
> Until I struck the Humboldt
>   Which I thought was nearly Hell.
> I traveled till I struck the Sink,
>   Where outlet can't be found;
> The Lord got through late Saturday night —
>   He 'd finished all around,
> But would not work on Sunday,
>   So he run it in the ground."

And that 's the Humboldt Valley — the Creator never went
back on the job Monday morning. Someone said that the
Humboldt was filled with what the Lord had left over when
He made the world and what the Devil would n't take to fix up
Hell.

The plan of our "deepway" or "roughway" (certainly not
highway) in negotiating this valley, Meek says, is to try to
make a straight line from "point to point." The river zigzags,
and at every "zig" a height of ground is passed through which
the river has bored its way. The "zags" are the intervening
level stretches. We cross these often at from two to five or
even ten miles' distance from the river; then again, to show that
no rule here holds true, we go far back from the river, sometimes to get around these "points" where the river, like as not,
cañons its way through. That 's the general scheme. At the
"zigs" the road is too rocky for words; and in the "zags" you
would not believe sand and lava dust could be hub deep, but it

can and is. As a result, the passing trains leave a wall-like wake of dust that at times just about smothers both man and beast.

Boardy is fascinated by the spectacle about us. Down come these hundreds, if not thousands, from off that high Goose Creek Mountain country to the eastern tip of this valley — to these "wells" (half full of stagnant water) which pit the plain for miles about like a tan-yard; they are all of such a uniform size and are laid out as regularly as though planted by a land-

Of course this is all

early in the season; the thousands behind us will not find the grass and tule which *we* take; nor find untarnished water in pools where *our* oxen fall and putrefy in the sun!

We are agreeably surprised at the bright side of to-day's march of twenty-five miles down what is really the Cañon, or East,[1] Fork of the Humboldt. Good grass is to be had near the water, though because in some places the sand is deep (or, if wet, boggy), we go and bring it to the animals. Game is ours in plenty — sage hens, ducks, geese, and cranes are numerous. How we all — the emigration — eat! Have I told you of the quantities a single one of us — take Carlo for example — can down at a meal? Four slabs of ham and half a gallon of coffee! If Uncle Bob had not followed Meek's advice and laid in a goodly supply of vinegar and acid we would have been troubled, as so many of our fellows are, with scurvy. When walking in this dust, scurvy in the mouth renders a man a pitiful object.

July 19. — If it was possible for anything to have broken our rest last night, it would have been the constant creak and

[1] Now Bishop's Fork.

crunch and clangor of trains passing us, or the blood-curdling dreams which followed Meek's stern admonition to us regarding the native denizens of this valley — these Humboldt Ghouls, the Digger Indians. Night traveling is advocated here by many; and if an outfit does miss the path at times, and overlook good grass in the dark, it certainly also misses this frightful cloud of alkali dust we get during the day in trying to worm by, through, or around ox-trains. As to the Diggers; that I fear will be a long story — time will tell. We have surely been unmolested thus far by all Indians whose hostility went beyond the thieving point. So far as our actual knowledge goes, we know of no emigrant who was shot by an Indian, except one; he was shot, scalped, skinned, and dismembered with no one to raise a finger or utter a word of protest. By hook or crook, gewgaw or tin whistle, that party lured an Indian girl off the road and ravished her. Taken red-handed by the girl's relatives, he was brought to his train and his life demanded. No voice was raised in protest; and the result was as described. I do not recall the particulars, but I have a hazy impression that the Indian executors had the assistance of some men from the train to which the victim belonged.

Road rough and hilly to-day. We of '49 are as lucky here as we were back there between Fontenelle Creek and Bear River; there is more grass here than has been known in the memory of the oldest old-timer we have with us or have met. Heavy winter rain or snow may or may not bring this salutary miracle to pass; if too hot a spring ensues, it matters little what provision of moisture was laid up — it gets boiled out by the heat, and the summer grazing is then poor. You must have just this year's condition — plenty of winter deposit, and a cool, wet spring. We came twenty-two miles. Stopping to cut grass shortens our day's runs in this valley.

July 20 *and* 21. — Rough road again to the mountain east of a river [1] where the road forked. Most trains were following each other inland, and no questions asked, over the mountain.

[1] North Fork of the Humboldt.

Meek took ours straight into the river cañon road, which we found level and good and supplied with plenty of grass. A. Delano, mentioned elsewhere in this record, in passing here went up the mountain road; becoming very thirsty, he clambered down the mountainside to the river and was amazed to find that the ignored road was 100 per cent the best. The mountain route was dubbed "the Greenhorn Cut-off," which was funny on two counts: first, its truth; second, as a play

method of stealing

crawl up to your stock noiselessly in the dark, and the silent discharge of bows and arrows arouses no alarm. There you are in the morning — with a wounded animal you must kill, the large part of which you are compelled to leave to the enemy.

Of the real unfortunates that almost line our road you do not know which to pity the most. Of course women and children are given a ride by the stronger outfits; but the aid thus furnished, which takes them onward, separates them from friends and kin. I think Boardy and I are most affected by the sight of the undying loyalty of women to their men who are half killing themselves to get their stock through alive. The battles we see fought here in clouds of alkali dust to drive half-crazed cattle back from "poison water"! The river water is comparatively safe if it is flowing; when stagnant, it is dangerous. You can let stock drink a little; but when you try to draw the line between a little and more, and then to beat the dumb beasts back from a bog they can hardly get to and you can hardly get out of — well, that's a story of which no one will ever tell the half. By the way, — this will be so useful to you, Dad! — if your cows get alkalied give them a nicotine sandwich — *i.e.*, a plug of tobacco between two slices of bacon.

You can spell "dust," and you think you know what it is. Well, if so, what is this brand that we call dust: as fine as the finest flour, and yet which envelops the traveler as in a cloud; so light that the least wind can raise it and yet so dense that you cannot see through it to a wagon ten feet ahead of you — and so chemically charged that it blotches and blisters the lips of nearly everyone as though they had touched poison ivy?

I once studied algebra, but here in this land, which was ruined because Saturday night once came so soon, we see problems worked out in queer ways. Let A stand for an Ohio outfit in need of flour. They offer B's outfit $1.00 a pound for some, but the offer is refused through lack of supply left. By night the only camp-ground to be had affords no grass which cattle can get to without miring. B outfit have lost, or been robbed of, their scythes. They are compelled to ask A to sell them one. A refuses to take money, but offers to sell one for twenty pounds of flour. B is compelled to agree, each wagon in the outfit "whacking up" its share! Let C represent the row that followed in outfit B, and D–D stand for what was said when the train broke apart as a result.

I have mentioned trail quarrels before. If they are more frequent as we scramble along by this Humboldt River, they are at least more quickly settled. Nerves are getting too taut to permit much debate; the overt word and act follow quick and fast — and partnerships, hallowed by long friendship and a hundred self-sacrifices in the mud of the Little Blue, in night storms on the Platte, in the hot sands of Ash Hollow, and by the poison water in the ghostly Goose Creek Mountains, crack, like that, in this Humboldt dust.

And, oh! but we met an old hero to-day — speaking of disputes. Outfits differ on no topic oftener or more radically than on whether to march ahead or lay by a day. This old man, who somehow has acquired the name of "Indiana," belonged to a company which had bickered over this subject, but had reached a healthy agreement to banish it as a cause for quarreling. "Indiana" had fallen behind, but, knowing that some of his company that morning would want to forge ahead and

not wait for him, he had sent word to his folks to "Go on."
When we overtook him, and offered him a ride, he answered us
pluckily through the dust: "Go on, partners — Go on.   I 've
sent on my vote for to march ahead *whether I ever catch up or
not.*" [1]   You should have seen Uncle Bob literally haul old
"Indiana" aboard his Ark!

These smiles along the road go further to help these days than
you can dream.   If you saw the faces of these sick people who

and his companion quickly spread

all the water it caught would not run together.   "The darned
fool," said scoffer March, one of the party, "he might just as
well have prayed for a barrel full, for he got ten times what he
asked for."

You must not think of me any longer as a gay outriding
Lothario on pleasure bent.   No one in his right mind to-day
can travel this road and not put a shoulder to the wheel.
To-day, as usual, Boardy and I cut and carried grass, often
sinking to our middles in the mire and water.   This soil has a
large percentage of alkali; when the river overflows (as it
often does), the whole bottom becomes very strongly impregnated with it, and as a consequence the water is poisonous to
our animals and ourselves; yet it is our only supply.   Wading
in the filthy alkaline mire and water produces nausea and
sometimes vomiting, but this is the only means the emigration
has of procuring food for its animals.   They are beginning to
fail with surprising rapidity on the scant and filthy fare and
poisonous water, and many men begin to feel apprehensive that
they will not get their stock off the Humboldt River alive.
This water is also extremely weakening on animals, acting with

[1] L. Sawyer, *Way Sketches.*

great power on the kidneys and producing inordinate secretions of the fluids depending upon those organs.

To-day was harder than any day yet, because the grass we went to get was thin and grew in water from six to twelve inches deep. A scythe is nearly useless under such conditions, and we had to do our "haying" with pocket knives. We both have been nauseated, but neither of us has handed over any of our dearly bought meals to the Great God Alkali who rules here where the South Fork of the Humboldt enters the main stream.

Speaking of incidental humor amid circumstances of acrid stringency like these — sometimes the very measure of the suffering or privation being endured makes a thing funny which otherwise would be silly or worse. Just that combination to-day created a ripple of laughter up and down the whole line. It was nothing more than a loony clown of an emigrant dragging a battered handcart behind him. When he came up to any outfit he would whinny like a horse and ask if he would find grass further on. Do you know, down here, where the Humboldt runs so close to Hell, it actually saves lives for people to meet those who can grin their way along — who are big enough to realize the futility of being discouraged?

Gave a meal to a man who lost his all crossing Green River. He had lived two weeks on four pounds of hard-tack, or pilot bread, they call it here. They tell of a train's captain who gambles with Fate along here as follows: he picks up likely-looking stranded men and gives them food and transportation to California in return for half the gold they find during the first two years in the Diggings! A new type of redemption-eering! I made the same offer to Boardy, if he'd carry me through on his back, agreeing to keep chanting "De gracia y beldad" all the way, and got only a ruffian's reply.

July 22. — To-day brings a long, weary detour inland from a cañon [1] and over a range of mountains to a gravelly crossing-place.[2] Boardy and I ride ahead looking for grass with Meek.

[1] Frémont's Cañon, near Carlin, Nev.
[2] Across the Tuscarora Range to present-day Gravelly Ford.

Found a fine river bottom six miles down the river from the ford,[1] which, by the way, we did not cross. This mountain climbing gives a new cross-section view of this army that seemed to be cracking away back there on Goose Mountains. True, the numbers that discarded their wagons there in order to "pack" through changed, to a degree, the aspect of our column. But "we" are so many; a large part are strong, self-reliant, resourceful men: they could not have come as far as Goose

just that much more exultingly! It is the frantic turmoil of this element in our army that engrosses the centre of the lime-light and creates the illusion that we are "breaking." So far as they are concerned, we were broken on the Kaw or Little Blue.

You would think that none but the very fit — I mean those who have cream of tartar to make this alkali water palatable, and the alum that will keep the blisters on their horses' noses from turning into glanders — could take these days of furnace dust "standing," as they do. But there is here, too, a lure, almost equally devastating in its power of magic beyond anything heretofore presented to us by the will-o'-the-wisps that have drawn this army forward thus far. They feel that this is the last; this is the end; this is "the Elephant"! If you can stand this you are victor! Beyond is California and its gold. Hang on now and see the thing through the Humboldt Valley and you have won!

You must get that view of it. The finding of gold is luck; you will not be held blamable if you are unlucky. But making the journey — overcoming obstacles — fighting your way

[1] Four miles north of Beowawe, Nev.

through — that is a matter of grit, not luck. Do that, get there, and you are absolved, you have filled the bill, eaten the "Elephant's ears," mastered the part of the game that depended on you. Whether the god, Luck, will give you gold or not is another question and out of your control. If you see this view of it, Dad, you will know how thousands endure these days in this Valley of the Alkali Shadow of Death.

Interesting beyond words to Boardy and me are the sly ruses adopted by our old-timers to ease folks along through these hot ways and days. Last night Meek threw himself into a perfectly strange rôle — for him — of public lecturer; but he drew a crowd and accomplished his purpose of making at least a hundred emigrants think we were having a nice, easy time of it! That he had "laid himself out" to do this thoroughly was proven by the fact that he had a chart to illustrate his speech already drawn in charcoal on a piece of a canvas wagon-sheet. The map (which I have copied for your information, see next page) shows Great Salt Lake and the terrible Great Salt Desert in which so much suffering has been experienced by those who have attempted cut-offs from Salt Lake City to the Humboldt River. I wish I could paint the picture of the gray old plainsman, pointing to his map and telling a hundred or so faces — tired faces, exhausted faces, scared faces, tear-stained faces, brave faces — of trials such as they will never know.

I will not be able to give Meek's talk with a hundredth part of the thrill that he, in those circumstances, put into it; but it ran something as follows. I will insert figures to indicate the points he mentioned in describing the Donner party route.

"There were eighty-five of them, about half of them women and children. They had been following Lansford W. Hastings's advice all the way from Fort Bridger to make the short cut which became the Mormon Trail from Fort Bridger to Great Salt Lake, then across the Great Salt Desert to this Fort Hall Road we are on. Hastings was ahead of them with another party. He was too impetuous and sanguine a man to guide folks, but he had some real good points at that.

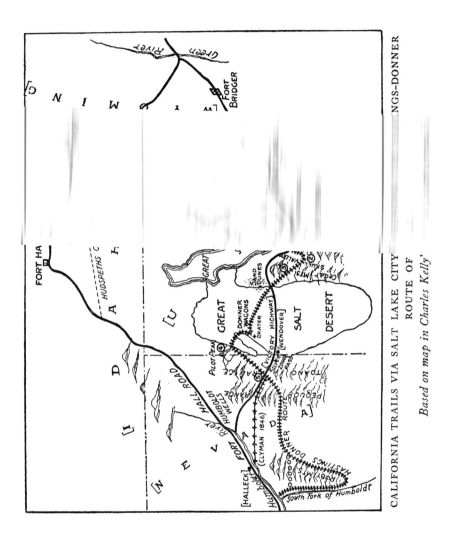

CALIFORNIA TRAILS VIA SALT LAKE CITY

ROUTE OF

Based on map in Charles Kelly'

"Trailing out from what is now Salt Lake City on September 3 or 4, they reached 'Twenty Wells' [1] right there (Fig. 1) September 6. Rolled on next day to more springs, maybe Burnt Spring there (Fig. 2), and someone found on the ground some pieces of paper that the birds had picked nearly to pieces. Puttin' it together, it read: 'Two days — two nights — hard driving — cross desert — reach water.'

"You 've had enough experience with travelin' to know that for anybody to go back on the track even a mile to tell anybody anything is mighty accommodatin' and mighty unusual. But what did that birdpecked note mean? That somebody (we don't know who) crossed a ninety-mile desert without a well on it and, knowin' that the folks behind had n't an idea that it was so wide and terrible, went back over it to pin up that notice and cross it all again — *a hundred-and-eighty-mile mission o'mercy* that I bet will hold the record for many a day.

"Well, filling every bag and cask with water, the party took up the dim tracks of the Hastings outfit across the Salt Desert which Hastings had said (?) was thirty miles across but, by that heroic messenger, had sent word was fifty, although time proved it was ninety. At the foot of Cedar Mountain, there (Fig. 3), no sign of the damp ground where Bryant found water by digging in '46 was visible; sand storms had buried it. Crossing the mountain that night, all day and night of the tenth, all day and night of the eleventh, and until ten o'clock of the night of the twelfth had passed before the springs at Pilot Peak (Fig. 4) were reached by the first wagons. When about thirty miles from the Peak, Jim Read, realizing that the oxen were about to go crazy and everybody might follow suit, rode ahead to bring back water. He went to the Peak and back while the folks behind were abandoning wagons and staggering onward ten miles. While his family had been without water thirty-six hours longer than he had, he had been constantly on the move without sleep for five days and nights; yet he shouldered the children who could walk no longer and came on through 'anyhow'!

[1] Grantsville, Utah.

Remains of Wagons Abandoned in the Salt [...] Party in 1846. In the Foreground Are the Bones of an Ox [...]istance and Beyond Are the Remains of Other Wagons. Note the [...]ower Right Corner, Running toward Cr[...]

(From Charles Kelly's "Salt Desert Trai[...] author)

"One of the terrible events of those terrible hours was the attack on the train by a crazy ox in the middle of one night.

"At Pilot Peak, after several days' rest, the party followed on the Hastings trail to Silver Zone Pass (Fig. 5). Here Hastings, for some unknown reason, left the trail he had followed when he came eastward[1] which was the short cut to our road along this river. Perhaps Hastings thought wagons could n't get through Humboldt Pass.[2] This long track down

Those in the rear never expected to see the unmarried man, Stanton, again. But the other, McCutcheon, got sick and stayed at Sutter's, and Stanton came back and froze to death. Forty-four out of the eighty-five survived the Desert and the snow (where so many died near Donner Lake) and reached California. Some are said to have existed, after the ox-hides had all been eaten up, on their dead companions. If so, the regrettable thing is, not that they did this, but that that horrible necessity ever arose."

We went to bed a pretty thoughtful crowd that night and very much less inclined to complain of our lot after hearing the story of the Donners in the Desert; for that part of their journey is usually forgotten in view of what happened by Donner Lake.

Carlo had his introduction to Digger diplomacy to-day while out on leave hunting ducks, and it is a lesson to us all. Reaching the point where I am now, a mile or so from the trail, and coming where he expected to find game, he was crawling cautiously around a clump of willows when he noticed something white on the dead grass, which, upon investigation, proved to

[1] Marked "Clyman 1846" on map.   [2] Frémont's Cañon.

be a human skeleton in a perfect state of preservation. He picked up the skull, looked it over, and took off the under jaw, which was filled with beautiful teeth. Putting these in his pocket and replacing the skull, he moved carefully forward, expecting soon to see the geese. Striking some stiff mud, he saw several moccasin tracks. When on the point of turning back he saw the head of an Indian to his left, within easy range of his rifle. Looking hurriedly about him, he saw another at his right and quite a distance to the rear. In a second the Diggers drew their heads down into the grass. Carlo immediately realized the danger of retreating back into open ground, so he plunged forward into the wild rice, gripping his rifle with one hand and making a path through the rice with the other. He ran along in this way until his strength was nearly gone and the hand with which he worked the rice lacerated and bleeding. Then he faced about, dropped to his knees, and, with rifle cocked, awaited developments.

After resting a few minutes and getting over his scare, he started in the direction of our trail, hoping to get out of the rice and willows into the open. Again he had to rest. His hands and arms were now both so lame and sore that he could scarcely use them. When he finally got out of the rice he straightened up and ran like a deer, expecting at every jump to be pursued and shot — making straight for a bend in the slough which was partly filled with water. The opposite bank was lined with willows; some of them began to move a little, and Carlo concluded that someone was coming through. Leveling his rifle, with an itching finger on the trigger, he was nonplused to hear someone shout, "Don't shoot." It was a white man looking for strayed cattle and trying to cross that slough! He ran pell-mell into the water and mud far enough so that Carlo could reach him and pull him on to the bank. He, too, had encountered the Indians in the rice and willows. For a time he was unable to stand, being completely exhausted with fear and his efforts to escape. As soon as he could walk the two made their way into camp — thinner, wetter, wiser.

Boardy and I are quick enough, I feel sure, to give way to our elders in plainsmanship on almost any topic. But we cannot imbibe the traditional hatred of the migration for Mormons — never having yet found them guilty of a "crime" of which others were innocent. And while we find nothing desirable in these Diggers — although, like most others, we make it a point to treat those who come to camp kindly — we cannot sympathize with the rabid denunciation of them which you

the game to be found. For catching with willow seines all the fish. For burning every scrap of fuel to be found within three miles of the trail. For exhausting every good well and spring, cutting all the grass mortal man can carry, leaving a thousand oxen's bodies to putrefy in the alkaline pools and ten thousand such carcasses in the river and along the roadside (so thick in places that the route of the road has had to be altered), creating such a stench of putridity that hundreds of us have been made nauseated and several, 't is said, have been rendered insane! And yet the damned, tanned banditti take pot shots at us!

I have made, a few lines back, a sort of classification of our trudging host — the broad line of demarcation between the real and the spurious, just as you find them on your sidewalks at home. But what you do not get there as a daily diet is the tragic testing — the taking the cover off a man, so to speak, and saying right out loud, "My God, the man's a beast!" Well, we do that — in this alkali hell. Listen. Riding down a steep, narrow place yesterday, Wagonhound heard loud screaming for help. At first he could see no one, but coming closer to the Humboldt he soon saw a man in the river struggling with a span of horses to which was still attached the running gear of a wagon. A few rods below him were his wife and two children about five and three years old — floating down the strong current in the wagon-bed.

Wagonhound stopped the train, but before he could unlimber his legs Picayune was scrambling downstream over the rocks after the woman and children, who were screaming at the top of their voices. The river here made a short bend around some rocks and on the point Picayune was able to grab the corner of the wagon-bed as it came along — already well filled with water. He held to it, and the current swung it ashore. The woman handed her children out to other emigrants who had rushed down, and then climbed out herself. When all were safe the woman, hugging her children with one arm, knelt at Picayune's feet and, clasping his knees, sobbed as though her heart would break, repeating over and over that he had saved their lives.[1]

By this time no less than fifty men who had seen the rescue crowded the rocks where the man and his horses had gotten safely out. This alkali, you know, works into the nerves and leaves them pretty taut. This crowd "knew" that the man had deliberately let wife and children go in order to save his team. Quicker than I can tell it the tongue of the man's wagon was set up and hasty preparations were being made to hang him from the end of it. Almost frantic at this demonstration, the wife again threw herself at Picayune's feet and begged him to save her husband, also! Her tears and entreaties, more than anything Picayune said, quieted the men, although a good many were still in favor of throwing the scoundrel into the river. But we helped them get their wagon together and then moved on.

July 23. — Sand and poor grass. Not much to do to-day as haymakers. Boardy and I rode ahead and spent some time having a good swim at a willow bend. Looked back through my notebook — at dozens of notes for entries that I have never written into this record. For instance, are you at all interested in the type of "joke" that gets a laugh at our camp-ground performances? Here are some of them : —

G. L. Cole, *In Early Days.*

Why do teeth resemble verbs? Because they are regular, irregular, and defective.

Why are kisses like rumors? They pass from lip to lip.

When is a baby like a cannibal? When it eats its "pap."

Why will Ireland become the richest land in the world? Because its capital is always Dublin.

Why were the Jews of old like bad debts? Because they killed the Prophets.

What is smaller than a mosquito's mouth? What he puts into it.

approach to real success was when he hit the nail terribly on the head with a take-off of a Down-East Yankee miner. He got the yap and the drawl fine as he spoke (supposedly) by the Humboldt Wells: —

"I oncet lived in peace and prosperity, away deown in the State of Maine, and owned ten cows, tew oxens, ten chickens, and three goats, besides dear Polly and Ike, and Jake and Tabitha, and Sarah Ann and Eliza Jane, together with the darling babe that was named Rachel because she lifted up her voice and wept when I kissed her and departed for Californy. Y-a-s, 't is even I, old Zenas, that 's now at the Humboldt Hells and did n't strike a single *pocket* nor *crevice* on Goose Creek, and I 've traveled e'en a'most as fur as 't is tew hum; and here the road forks — wonder which of these onlikely roads nears off tu Hangtown? Hello! I 'm blazed if here ain't jist the sarcumstance I 'm looking arter! By golly! A guide-board! Sartin as preachin'! Ah! Oh! By God-lings the finger is pintin' *up* and it reads 'The Elephant'!"

By the way, speaking of bathing in the Humboldt; it is not deep, but (if you have time and are arrow-proof) you can swim it by the mile if you want to emulate six boys in a train

right behind us — one of them being the famous Cicero Dowd
of Ohio whose name was written highest on Independence
Rock.

As the sun rose one morning hereabouts, and promised
another blistering day, these youths bethought themselves of
swimming down the cool river while the train pushed on with
its pillar of cloud-dust. Accordingly Ike and Sam Harris,
Green Teas, Cicero Dowd, Silvester Jones, and G. W. Thissell
put their clothes in a wagon and took to the water. The river is
crooked and the road leads, as I have said, from bend to bend
or from "point" to "point." This made many cut-offs, but
as they splashed gaily on they omitted to notice that the train
was leaving the river, and had gotten out of sight before they
knew it.

On and on they went, at times leaving the water and running
through on the hot sand and gravel. "Soon the fun began to
grow serious," said one of them afterwards, recounting the
escapade; "the train had taken a cut-off, and left the river.
The heat was intense. The sun was almost blistering our backs,
which were now as red as lobsters. It was ten o'clock and no
train could be seen. We left the water and heeled it down the
river through the willows, like so many wild men. One o'clock
and the train came in sight, but many miles away. In the
willows we came upon a band of friendly Indians who gave us
old moccasins to put on our feet. At two o'clock, when the
train came back to the river and camped, we were still two
miles away. Two of our company on horseback brought us
our clothes. Our backs were so blistered we could scarcely
wear our shirts. At six o'clock we were only twelve hours
older, but many years wiser."

Their train had traveled only twelve miles while they had
covered — who knows how many thousand? If they had been
near the road they could have clothed themselves a dozen
times. It is well-lined with cast-off garments. All day long
and all the way along you see the foot travelers examining
garments to ascertain whether they are preferable to those they
have on. If so, they make a change.

Passed yesterday [1] a field of red-top grass three feet high so much like an Eastern field of the same that every Yankee felt like taking his hat off to it.

July 24–27. — For variation and, perhaps, vividness, let me put side by side what the country looks like for a day or two and what we see through the dust as we grind along — describing the two columns as : —

Monotonous sage plain.

Among things thrown away are many books. From this traveling library Boardy and I now and then draw books, returning them later at the same counter.
The man with handcart who whinnied for grass to cause a diversion has been joined by one with a wheelbarrow ! [2]

River several miles to right.

The Diggers tip their arrows with either iron or glass. Their bows are not over a yard long; the arrows are almost as long. They can get much power into their shots. We have seen oxen with arrows buried to a depth of ten inches. It is said they can shoot an arrow through a man's body.

Hills ahead. Prospect of river going into cañon.

A train traveling all night early this morning found an emigrant

[1] Near present-day Argenta, Nev.

[2] L. Sawyer, *Way Sketches*.

WHAT WE SEE

While everybody has an instinctive dread of this desert, it is curious how its varying appearances in different lights and different times of day affect different persons. To some it is always and forever utterly forbidding; no alteration in its appearance can presage anything but some fatality more awful than history until now records. But oh, not so to Boardy, who has the gift of taking a thing out of the clouds and putting it into words and phrases: —

"What did I tell you — look there! This Desert is our continent's one great and unperturbable Humorist! You must come here well-prepared to see it; otherwise you find it only a Ghoul thirsting for your life. But once enter its portals fitted to enjoy it — and its playful antics, its sleight-of-hand performances, its tricky mirages, playing possum, hide-and-seek, make-believe, the necromancy of its lightning

¹ Lassen's Meadows.

WHAT WE HEAR AND THINK

by the road shot through the heart. The body had been drawn along in the sand to void the blood before the clothes had been removed. He had been scalped, and had died slowly. His agony in his last hours was graphically written on the ground, so to speak. The hole which his heels had dug in the soil was nearly a foot deep. His fingers had scratched up the earth as far as his arms would reach all around. Papers found on or near him showed that he was a German hailing from St. Louis.

Friend A. Delano, now ahead of us, is quite determined with others to take the new "Applegate" cut-off from the Meadows ¹ to Sacramento. It runs north of the Humboldt Desert and Sink and comes into California by one of the northern Sacramento River tributaries. A branch turning north from this route goes to Oregon and was blazed by the famous Applegate who commanded the Cow Column of the 1843 Oregon migration.

WHAT WE SEE

WHAT WE HEAR AND THINK

changes, all defy the eye of any but a trained prestidigitator. It gives you a day so hot that your ox's breath feels like an arctic wind — and then a night cold enough to freeze water — and it laughs! It introduces you to

a *good horse* helps one to do those things!

An ox train which we passed reported finding an emigrant and a Digger near the road — both dead. Men of the train had been delayed by sending a party after Indians who had purloined five of their cattle. Followed the thieves' trail twenty-five mortal miles; found them in the midst of a feast — all the cattle slaughtered.

High bench of rocky land [2] with mountain range to north.[3]

Guide walking ahead of some wagons on the night drive went to sleep on his feet and walked spang into the river. Came up "all standing" and got out all right except for leaving the bark of his nose on the bark of the willows.

The river changing in appearance. Only river in the world that gets

[1] Golconda Hot Springs Range.

[2] Iron Point.   [3] Iron Spring Range.

What We See

smaller the farther it flows. Fortunately for us it becomes brackish very slowly. Still palatable and harmless if flowing.

Bluffs of white marl somewhat resembling those Black Hills east of South Pass.

July 26-27. — River takes great bend to north. Wide valley. Then it turns south where a stream [1] comes in from the north through a six-mile-wide tule swamp.[2] Valley more rolling and broken. Queer, huge masses of vegetable matter with appearance of petrified fungi; seem odd in a volcanic region.

[1] The Little Humboldt.

What We Hear and Think

Visited the country-seat of a Digger King. It is a cleft in the rocks, strewn with wild grass.

Wagons are now our principal fuel. Every other outfit seems to abandon one about every other night. Many are trying to get through to the Meadows with as many as possible in order to transport grass in them to feed animals at the Sink and on the night run across the Desert. Others hope to pack grass muleback or oxback and also to feed gruel to the teams during the Desert run.

The dust seems to be leagued with Death to keep these exhausted thousands from even trying to cross the Desert! The most smothering drives we have had come here. The light ashy dust, mixed with white powder, drifts like a volatile composition that, once stirred up, only goes to rest with the sun, filling the air with all sorts — or was *I* going a little crazy? — of prismatic hues. At times these clouds seem to gather in waves like a frozen ocean, reaching the mules' bellies as they pelt along at a snail's pace.

[2] North of Winnemucca, Nev.

WHAT WE SEE

River shrinking — more alkalied. Dust terrible. Some wear green goggles; some with bandages on the mouth or little aprons covering nose and mouth.

River drops about 4 feet 4 inches to the mile. In dry places it lies in pools which are joined only by trickling rivulets. Here the water fairly stagnates.

Strange kind of static wall, this make-believe river seems to be. A whirlwind on one side — not many feet away — was watched by all of us as it sucked sage and sand up into clouds and wheeled

WHAT WE HEAR AND THINK

I was not wholly flippant when I mentioned insanity above. To show how close it comes home, one of our own men (well supplied with vinegar if he needed it) turned right around out of the blue at sight of a vinegar jug in

on a wagon where he can be watched. None of us are wholly safe, except those immune by experience.

It is certainly a commentary on what we are going through that, at a noontide's council of war between Meek, Uncle Bob, Wagonhound, and Ox Bow, it was agreed that five hundred weight from each of our fourteen wagons should be discarded. We had started from Independence with two thousand weight in each; it was now reduced to twelve hundred. We spent an afternoon at this — making it a memorable half-day for hundreds to whom I suppose it actually meant life. We had been generous everywhere, but we could not become known as a traveling

WHAT WE SEE

them on in mazy gyrations, without a *breath of air stirring where we were.*

Mountain range [1] to the south.

Crossed a saline plain on which the incrustation was so hard that no wagon-wheel cut its marble-like surface!

July 28. — A mountain range [2] appears north of the river which marks the site of Cold Springs — only twelve miles distant from the beginning of the long-looked-

[1] Sonoma Range.

WHAT WE HEAR AND THINK

supply train — we would have been mobbed. Most of the provision discarded was flour, biscuit, dried peas, beans, raw coffee, and bacon. It was given to those who were needy within reach; the rest was left by the roadway, covered from the sun with rushes and willows, for those who came after. With studied care our loads (mostly powder, shot, caps, and lead, as profitable a cargo as could be carried to the California mines, according to best advice) were now distributed evenly among the wagons. In fact some of this freight was discarded also — but it was thrown into the river, lest Digger sharpshooters should acquire it.

These last days have shown a new form of disintegration of our once grand — but still brave — Golden Army. The terrific drain on stores in these last two hundred miles has warned many scattered outfits to make the last momentous cast of the dice for safety — *i.e.,* to unite forces and then send a fast, able-bodied relief squad ahead to obtain food and bring it back to the rest. As succor is now known to be not over 250 miles away (Sacramento), such parties, traveling light across the Desert and the mountains, can

[2] Eugene Range.

WHAT WE SEE	WHAT WE HEAR AND THINK
for Meadows. The river gives indication near here of something new by breaking up into numerous little channels.	hope to buy supplies and get back to their trains before the latter attempt the ascent of the Sierras.

As I read these entries of fact and incident, with their running obbligato of geographical information, it comes home to

o' sun,' the lame, the sober, the drunk, the hopeful, the hopeless. It can never happen just this way again. Other human rushes will come overland as long as the gold lasts, but there is only one Forty-Niner." I am just going to describe a few moments of one day and let my pen "go it"; these things did not come to pass so instantaneously as I imply, or in just this order; but it is all "true" in the real sense. And worse may happen any minute! Excuse the torrid language; remember we are chewing the "Elephant's ears" along here. Fit the words to the various mouths the best you can, for in the mêlée the actors themselves are not always sure who is doing the talking : —

Two parallel roadways near a bend of the Humboldt. No water running. Just alkali pools. Dead cattle line the edges. The two roads converge in the neck of the bend and there merge into one track. Dust in the air so thick that those in wagons on one track can only now and then see into the wagons on the other. Everything at a standstill along the line, while the teams alternately move into the single track ahead. Sun. Dust.

"For Christ's sake let 's go to California," somebody says, looking ahead to see the cause of delay. "You 'll never go

far till you soak that hind wheel o' yourn," said a gaunt man
on foot, loaded with a bedroll and a combination tin pot-and-
pan dish, and all but blowing rings with the dust he was inhal-
ing. Those on foot can always filter by. "I soaked that this
morning."

An ailing boy, too big to ride, too sick to walk, lies on the
ground in the shade of one of the wagons. A woman sits in a
chair in the rear of a covered wagon, across from a built-on
privy. Sick child in her lap. Her face is bandaged. The
child moans and the woman moistens its lips, turning her face
so as not to smell the damp rag. "Where did yer git yer
water," says the boy on the ground. "My man walked out
on ox carcasses on the edge of the last pond and sloshed a
blanket around and we wrung out a pailful. My God, how it
smells, but it is wet." "Here, wet your lips, but if you 've
got any food in you don't drink a drop." A cow from nowhere
breaks in among the wagons between tracks. Somebody waves
a sudden shirt in its face. It bolts and knocks the boy uncon-
scious. "Hey, whoever owns that cow 's got a boy to carry
now." "Who owns the cow?" goes down the line. The
wagons ahead start. The woman screams. Men pull the
boy from the wheels. "All aboard for Ragtown, Hangtown,
Hell's Delight, and Groundhog Glory," calls out "Crazy
Ann."

"Sure you can see it," a dust-enshrouded plodder argues
with a companion, referring to his view of a mirage to the left;
"see that cow standin' in the corn and the big red Pennsylvania
Dutch barn." "Seen a cow in among these wagons?" "No,
but there 's a boy o' yourn in that Iowa outfit's travelin'
bunk-house."

"Oh! Susanna,
   Go to Hell for all of me;
We 're all a livin' dead
   In Californ-ee!"

came from beside the road. "They say there 's a man ahead
in a big palace car giving away bacon and beans and biscuit."
"Christ, that 's nothin'; yesterday a cock-eyed Digger Indian

on Stony Point was givin' away little white angels; you jest hopped on its back and flew to California."

"What the hell 's the use of trying to swell a felloe to fit a tire that 's worn through?" Grave beside the road; paper in forked stick states that man below was killed by Diggers and that he hailed from Keokuk, Iowa. Man sitting on a driver's seat, mouth open, drooling; scurvy in the mouth. Line stops. "Meeting a party going east," is the word that goes along the

Brigham found his virgin dears,
Had all been Mormons thirteen years."

So many dead oxen lie around a wagon on the left that the last two to die had climbed up, one at each end, and gotten their heads and fore feet in under the cover of the wagon out of the pitiless rays of the sun and died there, half in, half out. The place smelt like a tanyard.

"One stormy night when winds blew hard
　　Around an old tent door,
A '49er sat on a three-legg'd stool
　　Because it had n't four."

Where the grass has been eaten out the willows are the emigration's only supply. Fortunately the cattle can keep going on it. Camps all along that have been abandoned or whose owners died while off looking for grass. Folks everywhere visiting all such, peering here and there, wondering if owners are near by or gone to their long home. "Pardon!" "Pardon hell! Get out or I 'll pardon you with lead!" Teams standing in the dust-cloud. Line starts. One driver begins sneezing and cannot stop. Irate wife takes the reins.

> "And thus he spake, while from his eye
>   A tear rolled down his cheek;
> 'Oh, give me back my little home
>   For that is all I seek.' "

"Would n't you think even a sot like that song-bird of a driver could leave the old bumblings alone till he got out o' this hell?" "No use; it 's for sale even here." "No?" "Yes. Yes, at that last slough yesterday; under that little white tent a man was drunk, but not too drunk to sell a quart for five dollars." "Ain't it hot enough here without puttin' fire-water in yer mouth?" "They don't put it in straight. They make coffee. Filled six little canteens and divided the quart equally with the coffee and sipped it all day long."

> "The wind is howling worse and worse,
>   I don't know what it means;
> Nor do I give a big black damn,
>   For I 've burned up all my beans."

Around the Point — a camp; cattle lying down; men asleep under wagon. Out in front the brave sentry, face to the foe, gun resting on knee, is snoring the loudest of all. Someone throws a chunk of clay at him. Pass "friendly" Indians going up the river to fresh water to fish. Have bunches of angle-worms wrapped in bags made of handkerchiefs.

> "Hangtown gals are plump and rosy,
>   Hair in ringlets mighty cosy;
> Painted cheeks and gassy bonnets,
>   Touch them and they 'll sting like hornets."

Men in a well-supplied outfit are eating near the road where our train is delayed. A Digger Indian, so famished that he is just a bag of bones, sits near on his haunches. A wager is made as to how much he would eat if given the chance. A biscuit is thrown to him and it disappears. A cut of bacon follows it. The game goes forward; gets exciting. All the cooked meat that can be spared is devoured. A big greasy wedge of raw flitch of bacon is then attacked with unflagging zeal and is nearly consumed before anything happens. The swollen bone-bag, now suddenly stuffed to suffocation, finally seems to choke. He then passes into something like a swoon; he lies on his back, his stomach puffed out to a pregnant rotundity that threatens explosion. The "cruel men" settle their wager and come with us as the train moves along. But before we are out of sight Sir Digger rises, slowly; he finally walks away at a queer, toddling gait, stopping every twenty-five yards or so,

My lousy shirt crawled off one day,
When I went off to prospect."

July 28. — The arrival at Cold Springs, only six miles from the far-famed Meadows, heartens everyone. You could feel it in the air; every outfit that had made any real semblance of hanging together pulled in here elated, although elation and exhaustion came hand in hand. Good water, such as few had had for three weeks, was a boon not soon forgotten. Our run to-day of thirty-four miles was hard on every man, beast, and wagon-spoke, but the good water made amends. We now take practically four days' rest — in preparation for that Desert run. Boardy and I agreed on one thing: tremendous as the stress and strain of the Humboldt days are on everyone, the hardships have had one effect that no one could anticipate: they have robbed the long hard days preceding of much or all they contained (in memory) of the bitter. As a result, nothing we suffered east of the Humboldt is remembered as very difficult; the days by the Blue, along the Platte, by the Bear and Snake, have already acquired quite a halo of romance. Ash Hollow, of course, remains Ash Hollow; the Goose Mountain precipice was a real jump-off, it is true.　But we are inclined to think of them as childish bugaboos, something to smile over, after these near-four-hundred Humboldt miles.

July 29–*August* 1. — We reach the Meadows early in the day (July 29) and plan to spend three and a half days resting, airing out, grazing the mules, and "putting up" hay for the Desert run (August 2 and 3).　As our wagoners are a sufficient force as haymakers, Boardy and I are free to examine this strange phenomenon of a lush meadowland of a thousand acres set fair and square in the very bottom of this great Valley of the Shadow of Death.　Among other things, I have time to go back in this record and insert in longhand what, for lack of time, I then entered in a kind of shorthand.

As all descriptions of this section are somewhat confusing, Boardy and I determined to start out unprejudiced and, if necessary, give fresh names to distinguish the various phenomena of local geography.　This we classify with the distances as follows : —

The Meadows[1] extend in a wide sweep southward.　Evidently there is, at times, enough water to cover all this region and justify calling it — as travelers do — Humboldt Lake. It is really a great morass, pitted with water holes, bottomless and otherwise.　The firm ground, where cattle can graze and where grass can be gathered without wading, is, as stated, about one thousand acres.　In about thirty miles the Humboldt enters Humboldt Sink,[2] about six miles long.[3]

Five miles west of the end of the Sink lies the head of the Dry Bed of Humboldt Lake, stretching southward about ten miles.　Two roads lead from the Meadows to this Dry Bed; they are the "east" and "west" roads, one on one side of the Sink, the other on the other.　These meet at the foot of the Dry Bed, where the Humboldt Slough flows in from the south. This offers the last water before you enter the Desert for the

---

[1] Lassen's Meadows lie in west half of Township 33 North Range 33 East.
[2] In Township 26 North Ranges 31 East and 32 East on the line.
[3] Ending in Township 25 North Range 31 East.

forty-mile dash to Ragtown on the Carson River. The worst
part of this run is met with twelve or fifteen miles south of the
Slough, where you have about four or five miles over the western
tip of what we call the Carson Sink.[1]

The Meadows seem placed by Providence just where emigration needs them. We do not see how Forty-Niners in any
numbers could have reached Carson River with stock but for
them. They supply the needed forage for as arid a hundred-

Where there is dry ground the mules are grazing; in places
the grass and rushes are as high as a man's head. You cannot
be sure of your footing anywhere. Charles Durham, of another
outfit, fell in a hole and was glad to get out even without his
gun. These holes are natural wells; some are said to be
bottomless. Camps are pitched everywhere; old trail cronies
and companions pull in every day; some are always pulling
out for the break across to the Carson. We air the stores; we
wash our clothes; we mend bends and cracks and breaks. But
we do not sing at night as of yore. No one needs any particular encouragement to herculean struggles — for it's death
if you waver now. It is mighty fine to see the courage these
thousands show here when face to face with "the Elephant."

"Talk about giants in the old days," says Boardy. "California ought to have the race *par excellence* when this is over!"

Rare dinner in this Grass Kingdom to-day (July 31)! Venison, upon my honor. Last night a panther or mountain lion
chased a deer almost into our camp — the poor bleating thing
making for the bright camp-fire light as the beast caught it.
The growl the beast emitted with its last pounce sent a chill

[1] Carson Sink: Truckee-Carson Irrigation Project.

through every mother's son of us. He feasted on the head and neck and buried the body under grass and leaves. We recovered it and oh, what a change from bacon![1]

To-night we fill our buckets and casks and in the morning we tackle the Desert with a supply of grass and water sufficient for ourselves and some to spare.

August 2. — Even the very wagons seem to know that we are off to-day for the great adventure — in sand, volcanic ash, alkali, furnace heat, and the stench of putrid flesh! As we pass along through the Slough, members of other outfits everywhere wave to us and halloo "Good luck!" One company, which was short-handed for the "haying season," had broken in some Diggers who applied to it for food; we had heard of this experiment and watched the Indians at work; the latter seemed to think it great fun and cavorted about as though the idea of working was an invention of their own!

We crossed along the edge of an immense baked plain with the fœtid, stinking slough for a guide, although the wreckage along the way almost paved our route, proving how many had undertaken this drive with light-heartedness, entirely oblivious of the fact which underlay Wagonhound's sage advice to an inquiring emigrant: "Brother, the great difficulty about crossing that Desert is getting to it in a condition to cross it." The nearest to a real desert any of us had yet experienced was on that night run from Big Sandy to Green River, and that was more plain than desert. Here, for instance, we were surprised to find that our way was far from level, for we were constantly going up and down hillocks of sand. Farther on there were great, still billows of ashy earth in which (partly because of the dust raised) the mules seemed to be wallowing belly deep. We had about three miles of this in one place. It was the worst three miles in all our 2100 so far. The mules were in a tremble of lather most of the time — as though they smelled "the Elephant"! Probably it was the stench of dead cattle which so affected them. It must have been here that one

[1] G. W. Thissell, *Crossing the Plains.*

emigrant said he counted a dead animal every 106 feet. The count seems reasonable — if not the counting!

We went into camp by one of the sloughs of the Sink, selected, Boardy affirmed, by Meek's successful exploration with a "scentometer"; because, for some reason, the air was comparatively free from putridity, owing, no doubt, to underground drainage. Twenty miles on this Road Paved with Good

than death — no wonder that we never spoke!

August 3–4. — We break away early. Our method of attack is, first, to gain the Slough of the Humboldt. Rest the mules and refill empty canteens. Then to strike into the Desert at 4 P.M. and make half the forty-odd miles by midnight. Boardy and I talk as we swing along beside the teams down the parched dry Bed of Humboldt Lake — of what do you think? Of these men, Meek, Wagonhound, and Ox Bow. They are grim past-masters of wilderness clairvoyancy, Doctors of Foresight, undisturbed by anything that happens, undismayed at any rumor, unannoyed by dust-cloud, storm-cloud, stink, or stench; but best of all, instantaneous to solve the exigencies of the hour on this trail, to shoulder the responsibilities that accompany the possession of strength and resourcefulness in a frightful charnelhouse of weakness, unpreparedness, poverty, sloth, irresponsibility, sickness, death. No company, however strong, could pull the whole migration through this hell. But Uncle Bob's, well-manned by many men, led by these three superb commanders, can help whom they will, put anybody on their feet, pull anybody through, save any lives they wish — and yet, by a nod, let any sinking outfit die and rot right there. Their use of this power of life and death, their swift systems of judgment, lightning-like decisions in the face of agonizing appeals, their bursts of sympathy for one party, icy coldness for another — what psychologist could fathom it?

At the Slough, before we jump, these three concern themselves with the eleventh-hour exigencies; one superintends the dismounting and soaking of every wagon-wheel, with a checking of all the main wagon-parts, especially tongues, axles, brakes, and hounds; one attends to the watering, feeding, and conditioning of the animals, testing all harnessing and filling all empty casks; one visits every man in our caravan, prescribing a bandage here, blue mass there, or laudanum somewhere else.

We pull out about 4 P.M. for "the Elephant's" lair, after a final moment's consultation by our strategists at the head of the line; and to Uncle Bob's credit be it said that, on the moment of departure, his one order to his field marshals is: "If it is only a matter of delaying us, Meek, help all these poor devils you can."

From the Slough of the Humboldt (as you see by the map) a space intervenes before we cross the Carson Sink.[1] These miles were smooth and plain, with some sand and clay mounds at the end — the old shore, perhaps, of what may have been a "Carson Lake" before dinosaurs were supplanted by "elephants" here. Then came the miles of heavy sand.[2] I may get the things which follow in the wrong order, Dad, and my account will have its weak points; but it is mighty true in one respect: I will not curdle your blood with a lot of things I saw. Keep the two sand areas in mind, this one between the Humboldt and Desert Wells and the other on the "Carson side," as they say, or across the Humboldt-Carson Divide and ten or fifteen miles this (north) side of Carson River. Those who leave the Slough in late afternoon take the first of these by night and the second by day. Those leaving the Slough in the morning take them vice versa. Meek chose the former and safer course; for by so doing you cross the first desert after

---

[1] Present-day Carson Sink.
[2] In Township 22 North overlapping into both Range 28 East and 29 East.

dark, and, if you get stuck in the second, water can be fetched to you from the Carson in a pinch. The water at the Desert Wells, by the way, is very bad, while that of the Carson is excellent.

The darkness hid much from our sight. What seemed to be a pile of wikiups ahead in the heavy sand proved to be a veritable ghost village; it was scores of abandoned wagons. You

had now and then been pulled loose from tops; and, in order to clear a track, some had been overturned and many burned. It was said that we were early, and that the bulk of the Golden Army was behind us; that we, therefore, would not see "the worst." Well and good; but the wiseacres who thus forecast the situation ignored the fact that the migration had to learn much from the experience of others; they overlooked the fact that many of the first-comers were as rash, perhaps, as they were early — inclined, so to speak, to rush in where later comers, seeing what "the Elephant" did to those who preceded them, were more filled with a holy "fear to tread."

Ox Bow pioneered our caravan with six mules in harness, unattached. He outstepped us enough to cause an unexpected delay, for, as it happened, an outfit or two fell in between. Ox Bow's mission was to remove from the path any abandoned wagons, or, in case of blockade, to drag aside wagons or carcasses which would block any detour that he chose for us. The outfits that crept in between were those which, so to speak, came to life or revived between the time of his passing and our arrival. One of these got stuck in one of the detours which he opened for us. But why try to tell even the fraction? The big thing for Boardy and me was that we were here — to see, hear, and smell it — the tragedy and the heroism. "Look," said Boardy, "we 're seeing something men will never forget — Crossing the Red Sea, the Moscow retreat, The March of the Ten Thousand, all rolled in one."

At the Desert Wells, dug, it is said, by emigrants, but doubtless opened by hands long stilled before the emigration of whites was dreamed of, twelve or fifteen outfits in every condition of existence — strong, broken down, absolutely defunct — were found, bailing bad water out of shallow holes. Giving much-needed assistance to two crews, former friends on the trail, and taking on board two families which were completely stranded, we pushed on, after feeding and watering our animals. Not far from those "Wells" a branch road which enters California by the "Truckee Route" leaves ours, which is the "Carson Route." Two half-demoralized outfits, which had been trail companions for goodness knows how long, had broken into a violent quarrel over which path to take. Meek, finding the men had been drinking, left them in anger to solve their own fate. We heard them doing it after we had gone — with shotguns![1]

Amid all the turmoil of that night and the day following, — for we took a long rest after daybreak and another at noon under the broiling sun and then pulled into Ragtown about 4 P.M., — some things are deathless memories. One is the stampedes caused by animals that heard or smelled water. In one case mules at the Desert Wells heard water being dipped up; they swung like wild horses, smashing a wagon-tongue and leaping straight over another team's tracings toward the sound. Again, near midnight, a team of mules passed us when one of our men was pouring water from a can. At the sound of the gurgling at the spout the wild beasts broke for our track and would have crushed our men had the latter not rolled headlong under a wagon. When, in the heat of the following afternoon, the scent of the Carson River was caught by animals of all descriptions, still floundering in that last ocean of soft sand, they portrayed such human symptoms of mingled terror and

[1] G. L. Cole, *In Early Days.*

delight that most women and many men saw their first glimpse of the line of green marking the Carson River's course through tears. Some drivers of mules with latent strength were too exhausted themselves to control their charges. Down the slope the teams tore at breakneck speed (for a desert road) and were never headed until they were belly deep in river water. One outfit had two insane men tied in a wagon. Such was the

at the river than did many of the so-called "sane." Reaching the cool sands at the water's edge, they threw themselves prostrate upon them, opened their clothing, and piled the cold sand on their stomachs.[1] Then, later, when safely cooled, they crawled to the water for their first drink. Many animals drank so much water that it was a long time before they could eat the lush green grass which the Carson waters also provided for them.

That wild desert run saw its many surprises and curious contradictions. Thissell, one of the Ohio boys I have mentioned (heroes of that long Humboldt swim!), saw imbedded in the sand beside that Humboldt-Carson track a wagon which he had helped to build at McConnelsville, Ohio,[2] on the Muskingum River, in the preceding March. A notch in the tailboard showed where a grave-marker had been sawed out to stand at the grave of "Hank" Seamon of McConnelsville, one of the original party. The names of the others, Jerry Sheppard and Ambrose and William Palmer, were inscribed with a red keel stone or red ochre on the side of the wagon-bed. I hope, Dad, if relatives of these men still live at McConnelsville, they

[1] W. Kelly, *An Excursion to California.*
[2] G. W. Thissell, *Crossing the Plains.*

will hear of this strange monument of Ohio carpentering and Muskingum River forests that stands now in "the Elephant's" lair on this bleakest of America's deserts.

Desert items, seen or reported : —

In fifteen miles someone counted 350 dead horses, 280 oxen, and 120 mules.

Someone stated that one thousand wagons have been abandoned in the forty-two miles between here and the Slough of the Humboldt.

Fifteen dollars was paid, by one report, for a glass of water from Cold Spring and one hundred dollars for a single pint.[1]

The suddenness with which cattle will succumb in the Desert is curious. They can appear to be going good and then fall as if shot and die instantly. Sand in dead animals' eyes gives them an unearthly glitter.

There are $43,000 worth of wagons to be had, free, within ten miles of Carson River.

Said one emigrant coming over, "Our cattle are getting so poor that it takes two of them to make a shadow." Another: "We were coming along and passed some men who said, 'For God's sake give us some water !' We told them that we had no water and it was water we were hurrying to get. Then they said, 'We will have to die.' We rode on, and presently looked back. Not a sign of them could you see. Probably they lay down to rest or die if they could." Sometimes you can't die, Dad. Think that over. Some said that they wished they were dead, while others would laugh in the face of calamity, which shows the difference in men.

The buried wagons we met first in the Desert after leaving the Slough are abandoned government wagons, George Smith says. They bogged down there, the story goes, and the drovers dug and got water for the animals, which killed them at once.

For all the noise and racket of night-marching, the Desert is very strangely quiet. The stillness is almost oppressive. It seems to come down, Boardy says, from the stars, quenching

[1] L. Sawyer, *Way Sketches*.

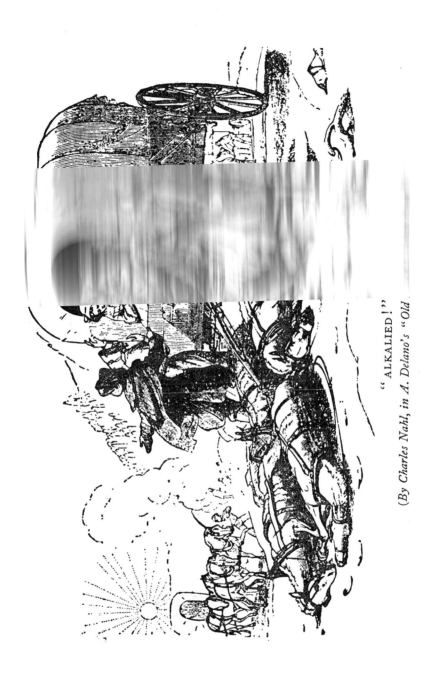

"ALKALIED!"

(By Charles Nahl, in A. Delano's "Old

all noises of its own force.   But not when wolves follow your train!

Except for what arrives in strong outfits like ours, the greater part of freight that comes over from the Humboldt is such as can be packed on animals' backs.   Someone made a list of things discarded along the road.   It is interesting because it shows *how very far* so many heavy things were carried : —

log chains	cross-cut saws
wagon-irons	iron-bound water casks
dishes	cooking implements
hollow ware	boots, shoes, clothing
life preservers	trunks
tin bakers	books, guns, pistols
gunlocks	gun barrels
planes	augers and chisels
mill saws	feather beds
tents and wagon-covers	

Ragtown here on the Carson River is named from the interminable piles of wind-strewn rags discarded by the emigration. And, despite all that has been left behind on the plains in the way of iron, it might just as well be called "Irontown." Hundreds get this far with wagons, but have broken their animals down in the process; the iron remains of burned wagons strew the plain and river shore.   And for that matter, Feathertown is a suburb of Ragtown — for, back up the trail a mile or two, someone ripped up a feather mattress to get the ticking, and an acre or two of goose feathers add their bit to the series of contradictions which meets the eye on arriving here.

I have just heard a story of singular bravery about a woman named Sarah Eleanor Royce, of Iowa City, Iowa.[1]

Mrs. Royce and her husband, with their little daughter Mary and a companion, driving as small an outfit probably as ever came unscathed down that Humboldt Valley, — consisting of four oxen, a wagon, and two cows, — traveling by night to escape the heat, missed the turnoff to the "Meadows" and actually entered upon the Desert beyond the Sink without

[1] Mother of Josiah Royce, the philosopher.

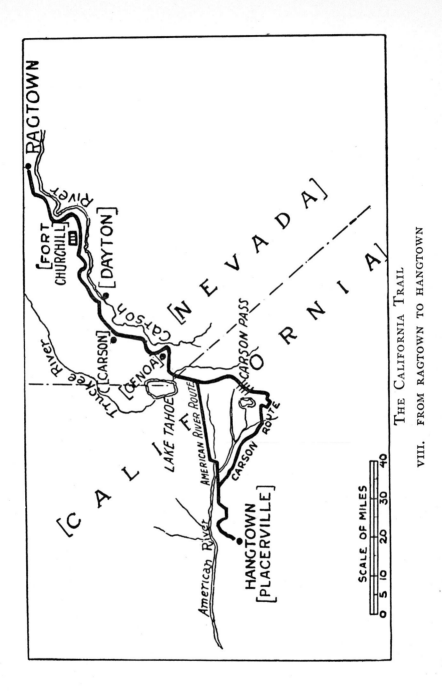

The California Trail

VIII. FROM RAGTOWN TO HANGTOWN

SECTION VIII

FROM RAGTOWN TO HANGTOWN

That evening of August 4, and the day succeeding, seem like a dream, punctuated with sun-baked lips that cracked open and eyes that burned in our sleep. We crawled off to one side and slept about thirty-five hours — except for some purposeful sleepwalking into that blessed cool Carson water and to the chuck wagon. Not until near evening of the fifth did either Boardy or I realize that, from our standpoint of analyzing the phenomena of which we were a part, this strange race-course from that rise of ground back there on the horizon to this river shore was the most exciting two miles in the whole 2200 to California. But even as we tried to watch its tragedies — we awoke to find we had slept again!

August 6. — If I have painted the Valley, Sink, and Desert of the Humboldt in their true colors, and clearly depicted their inevitable effect on our adventurers of '49, there is scarcely need to describe what this fine, cool Carson River and the shade of its giant cottonwoods and its alders mean to those of us who have gotten through. And, while I think of it, would you believe that it takes an hour or two for some of us who have just "come out of great tribulation" in the treeless desert to get used to the rustling of leaves overhead — and not, now and then, absent-mindedly duck our heads when a breeze sets them a-flutter?

Roughly, it is supposed that four fifths of each company of emigrants actually do arrive; and of the one fifth left upon the way, half would have succumbed to disease meanwhile even if they had stayed at home. Doubtless nearly half the wagons which start come through this far; but it is a question if more than a third of the total which start actually cross the Sierras. I should guess that one fourth are abandoned or destroyed east of Goose Mountains, one fourth between Goose Mountains and here; and that a goodly fraction more are lost on the mountains between here and the mines.

As to our reception in this ragged city, we get just what we want on arriving — gangway! I tell you no street corner in New York City is as dangerous as is the straightaway from the hilltop yonder to the margin of this Carson River! Not an hour out of the twenty-four but teams come tearing down it half-controlled. When rested and refreshed, outfits then move out of the way, upstream or down. But all day, and every day, some individuals wait there at the bottom of the slope to watch for lost relatives or friends!

Already gamblers from California have pitched their tents at Ragtown to welcome the unsuspecting; a Benevolent

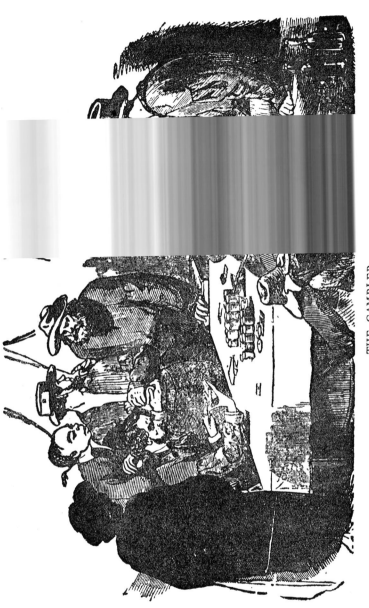

THE GAMBLER

(By Charles Nahl, in A. Delano's "Old Bl

Society [1] of the Coast is sending an agent here to extend charity to all in need. Forty-rod whiskey, at twenty-five cents a drink, was all that was for sale in Ragtown's trading post (a big tent) which did not cost a dollar a pound; but the most expensive thing here was experience in the thimble game operated by Lucky Bill, one of California's noted gamblers. Jerry Gullion staked his last ox and lost it; emboldened with whiskey, he lost his last dollar and five of G. W. Thissell's. But, to show how freakishly Fate can deal hands in this House of Cards that we call Life, Arthur Long, who was good and would not gamble, remained in camp and was stung by a scorpion and died in a few hours!

We move downstream five miles to-day to a cottonwood grove [2] and just lave in the water and shade while the mules do justice to the fine grass. By night, camp began to seem quite like those old jolly ones on the banks of the Little Blue and the Platte. There will evidently be more people and fewer teams from now on, since so many wagons have been discarded — and musical instruments went with them. It was fine to hear Carlo's voice again after nearly a month of silence — and that vitriolic obbligato of his complaining messmate whose nerves Carlo so enjoys rasping in song. To-night it was a fresh version of "Oh! Susanna" that came from a big cottonwood's shade. The new verses were: —

> "I had a dream the other night,
>   When everything was still,
> I dreamed I saw Susanna dear,
>   A-coming down the hill.
>
> *Chorus*
> "Oh, Susanna, oh, don't you cry for me,
>   I 'm going to California, some gold dust for to see.
>
> "The buckwheat cake was in my mouth,
>   The tear stood in her eye,
> And all that I could say to her
>   Was, Susanna, don't you cry."

[1] F. Langworthy, *Scenery of the Plains.*
[2] Later Cottonwood Station on the Pony Express and Overland Mail Line.

We are to take it very slowly now, for the task of getting wagon-loads as heavy as ours across the summit is no easy one. We watch for old friends along the trail — Pickpan, Brown, Jingo, Denny, and Jeremiah. We even get the old scrapbooks out and rehearse the incidents of our now-famous trek and listen again to the lore of the trail and the prairie. But the new incentive, the new lure is, beyond all description, domi-

that flow into it from the mountains is amazingly large. The wayfarers never seem to get tired of drinking from them; at each crossing-place you see eight, twelve, or twenty forms lying prostrate. They get up happy; eight, twelve, or twenty take their places.

Jerry Gullion, to prove he can gamble or leave gambling alone and still be happy, sang a Ragtown rigadoon along the trail to-day : —

> "I robbed a nigger of a dollar
>   And bought unguent to grease my collar;
>   I tried a pint, not one [1] had gone
>   Then it beat hell how I daubed it on.
>
> "The people threatened hard my life
>   Because I stole a miner's wife;
>   Went to the city, got a gambler's name,
>   And lost my pile at the thimble game."

August 7–9. — We made quite a march to-day of twenty miles. You can't imagine how like a storybook this traveling seems after what we have been through. So many are now on foot that it seems more like a pilgrimage than a migration of

[1] Meaning a louse.

many freighters, as heretofore. The recovery of health and courage fills these wandering crowds with levity. The commonest joke we hear, and it comes in various forms all day, is contained in such banter as: "Well, have you seen 'the Elephant' pass this way?" or "Have you eaten your 'Elephant's ears' to-day?"

We jog along from "point to point" again, meeting with the Carson River for our noonings and for a camp at night. The mules will be fully conditioned in another day, and Wagonhound, Meek, and Ox Bow are quite recovered from Uncle Bob's impromptu celebration over our safe passage of the Desert, duly held yesterday — for no one could have wanted a treat of that kind any sooner. After that dinner we chanced to see something of the other, and boyish, side of these serious, iron-jointed plainsmen of ours on whose shoulders so much responsibility has rested since South Pass was crossed. Such old-timers have a way of biding their time, and Wagonhound, with some four drinks of Uncle Bob's best whiskey in him, took this occasion to unload his mind of what had evidently been a long-festering determination to impugn Ox Bow's veracity. The talk had drifted around to old days and ways and from one topic or anecdote to the next when Wagonhound seemed to happen, rather by accident than otherwise, into a wandering résumé of some experiences that did n't have any head or tail or seem to get anywhere until he suddenly rounded up in the middle of a bear-hunt.

"Well, after a-lookin' all day fer bears in them rocks," he said, his eyes beginning to sparkle maliciously, "an' findin' none whatever, we turned down a draw toward a flat with a lot o' clover in it. The clover was in bloom and was full o' bees gettin' the honey. At the head o' the draw were all of the very bears we had a appointment with, holdin' a meetin'. By 'n' by it come to an end, and the bears lined out, single file, fur the bees an' their honey in that clover field. Now, no bear can ever catch a bee single-handed and get its honey; these bears knew that too well; so they posted themselves along down the draw and when all got set an' ready the nearest bear to the

clover took arter the first bee that left and chased it up the
draw; the next bear in turn took up the pursuit and they run
'em ragged that way, in relays, like Ox Bow's wolves done them
antelope over by Laramie's Peak — " Thump! The mortal
combat was on! What Ox Bow lacked in beard he offered in
the way of matted hair; and, as the two rolled in the grass like
boys again. Meek joined the jollification with a flat stave with

gear and *lares* and *penates* that (a moment ago, it seems) were
considered absolute necessities, the hundreds swarm through
these valleys, laughing, chortling, unconstrained and undismayed.

We saw an amusing illustration of this resignation to-day
as we lunched at noon above Clear Creek,[1] where you could see
our pathway ahead ascending a ridge. Up the road moved an
old scarecrow of a patriarch whose long struggle with "forty
years" in the wilderness and "forty-rod" whiskey had resulted
in a mighty beard and moustache with an ambition, at least,
to sweep the ground and which did successfully obscure from
sight almost every physiographic feature not hidden by a
fantastic apology for a hat. His mien indicated at once the
sense of his own importance and the subservient relation which
he thought the rest of the human race might well assume in his
presence.

"Well, strangers," he said, drawing himself up before us,
lounging at rest upon the grass, and pointing a long rifle at the
pathway high above, "I reckon we've got to climb that
mountain thar, hey?"

Boardy directed his attention to the thin line of a moving

[1] Near Carson City, Nev.

column, winding laboriously upward among the rocks and trees, and asked if he saw it.

"Ya-a-s," he replied, retrospectively.

"Well, sir, that is our road," said Boardy cheerfully.

The keen eyes surveyed the height, the road, the moving figures, and the forest, long and carefully. Then he turned, and dropped his chin upon the muzzle of his rifle in an attitude of profound submission.

"Gentlemen," he declared, "I am wholly resigned. I am prepared for anything that may come. I shall meet my fate with perfect composure."

No account of such an actual episode as this can bring to you a fraction of the humor and significance which — under those circumstances — it had for us.

Then occurred one of those impossible things that are scarcely believed afterwards even by the eyewitnesses themselves. A piece of paper came blowing along the ground from nowhere to Boardy's knee.[1]

"A message from the Army on the Heights," he said, whimsically, as he picked it up. He looked at it long and curiously until I demanded an explanation. He then handed it to me. The look in his eyes, how it spoke!

The paper bore these written lines : —

> Yes, my native land, I love thee,
>   All thy scenes, I love them well;
> Friends, connections, happy country,
>   Can I bid you all farewell?

"By Harriet Beecher?" he asked.

"No, by the Reverend S. F. Smith, who wrote 'My Country, 'T is of Thee,'" I answered.

We do several "Little Deserts," as they are called, these days, where old familiar Friend Dust greets us once more with millions of fingers which slink into every fibre of clothing and skin. But always back upon the river we find the glorious water and shade! At one place several trains, and more than a

---

[1] F. Langworthy, *Scenery of the Plains.*

hundred people, were resting under one giant cottonwood, the trunk of which measured ten feet in diameter; at twelve feet from the ground it divides into several branches which rise to a height of some fifty feet and have a spread of smaller branches of nearer sixty than fifty feet. Here we caught another view, across a chain of low hills, of the snowy peaks [1] of the Sierras.

ARRIVING IN SIGHT OF THE SIERRA NEVADAS, PAT MISTAKES
THE RAYS OF THE SETTING SUN FOR GOLD

(*In X. O. X.'s " The History of an Expedition to California "*)

Having been put on our guard against bands of hostile Indians, — two of which were killed by the William Kelly party hereabouts, — we were startled one day to see a cavalcade of Indians coming rapidly down our trail with an American flag fastened in an upright position to the saddle-horn of the

[1] Snow Valley, Genoa, Monument, Freel, and Job's peaks.

foremost mule; being thus assured of the friendly character of the caravan, we awaited the arrival of those behind. They proved to be Captain Sutter's Indians from Fort Sutter going with supplies to the head of the Humboldt to meet Mrs. Sutter, then on her way to join her quite-famous husband.

I doubt if any delegation could have brought us more certain and reliable news of just what we wanted to hear than did these men. The leader gave Meek and Wagonhound the last information about the road ahead and confirmed the reports of the successful finding of new "diggings"; but he warned us of "bad Indian, as he kill mule," against whom we should keep steadily on our guard.

August 10–12. — Boardy and I have endless hours these days to talk, sketch, and explore the country. We did another "Little Desert" on the tenth, but, arriving now at a great meadow-world,[1] our outfit spends two days gathering grass and merely shifting camp a few miles toward the mouth of the west cañon of the Carson. Day before yesterday, and again to-day, Boardy and I have visited some hot springs in this valley. The first was a fresh-water spring, the water a trifle warmer than blood heat. The basin is one hundred feet in length, sixteen in breadth, and the depth of water six feet. The water is very transparent. What a location for a bathing-house! Who knows but that such an establishment upon a grand scale may be erected here when "my" great Pacific Railway shall roll the tides of commerce and crowds of travel along this now lonely valley?[2]

Moving forward, we passed a remarkable hot spring. It gushes from the base of a mountain, between strata of horizontal rocks, in nearly a continuous thin sheet; the water being near the boiling point and the stream nearly a mile in breadth. This is by far the widest river of hot water that we have as yet seen. Indeed, we have not heard or read of anything like it. The quantity of water, however, is not so great as might be

[1] Carson Valley.
[2] Both the Southern and the Western Pacific pass north of Lake Tahoe.

inferred from its extraordinary width, the stream being very shallow, seldom more than an inch in depth; it flows down upon an extensive flat where it forms a large marsh, or pond, in which there is a dense growth of the most gigantic bulrushes. The road runs just above the line from where the water flows, the mountain above it being entirely destitute of trees and vegetation of every kind, though other mountains around are

Numerous fishbones, and other "signs," have made our "harsh masters" scold Boardy and me for roaming about, and led to another chapter of reminiscences by Ox Bow — who interestingly described the thing one hears so little about, Indian war psychology.   He was with Bill Williams and one Noble, among the Sioux, at a time when some Pawnees, in a foolhardy mood, ran off with a herd of one hundred Sioux ponies.   As soon as the news was received, fifty young warriors hastened to saddle their best ponies.   Williams signified his intention of going, but Ox Bow told him that he was too old and that Noble and he would go and bring back the stock.

"We started with the Injuns, under the leadership of Young Thunder," the narrator continued, "a bully specimen of a comin' chief.   I rode my pony 'Runner.'   We soon struck the trail of the 'Wolves' or 'Loups,' and followed it down the south side of the Platte about ten miles and then crossed to the north side.   We figgered by the appearance of the trail that they were only a lap 'r two ahead of us.   The Sioux now ripped off their clothing, 'cepting leggings and breechclouts, and mounted their

[1] Walley's Hot Springs section of Douglas Co., Nev.
[2] The upper or southern extremity of Carson Valley is known as Dutch Valley and Diamond Valley, Alpine Co., Calif.

war-horses, which they had been leading up to now. I put a pad on my 'Runner.' These pads are made by fillin' two sacks with antelope hair. The sacks are commonly made o' buckskin, seven or eight inches through, and rest on each side o' your critter's backbone, sewed together, like, on top with buckskin — with stuff rigged on to each side fer stirrups and cinch. These are a curiosity to Down-Easters, but are light and 'lastic, and a horse feels no heft from 'em and can travel twenty miles farther under 'em in a day than under a saddle.

"We now started at a canter, Young Thunder in the lead. After goin' about eight miles, we noticed that sand was still siftin' in the hoof-tracks ahead, proof that the Pawnees were n't fur in advance. We now slowed to about half-speed, the Injuns all eyes an' ears.

"Slidin' over a divide, we could plainly see a cloud o' dust about two miles off, an' in the same second the Pawnees must have seen us, for a big scatterin' follered as if stock was being

shoved ahead at more speed. We were soon close enough to see that there were twelve of 'em — humpin' their best to get the herd to a cottonwood grove at a bend o' the river. It was now I first saw the wonderful endurance of the Injun pony. Young Thunder gave a war-whoop, the signal for a charge, and their ponies slid for'ard like an engine when the

JEREMIAH AND THE CHIEF

throttle is thrown wide open. The Pawnees heard the yell and quit the herd of pilfered stock and dove for the grove, floggin' their ponies to top speed. Two of 'em went to sleep before they ever reached cover, ten getting safely to the grove, thankful of savin' their lives, knowin' that the Sioux would be satisfied with the two scalps and the recaptured herd.

"Several of the ponies were close to the grove, and Noble and I dashed in at full speed and turned them away. The Pawnees fired several shots at us, but the bullets

THE SURRENDER

if they did not intend to charge the Pawnees in the grove. Young Thunder, who had been a close observer of our actions in recovering the ponies, smiled, and shook us by the hand.

"I don't believe the Sioux would have recovered these ponies but for us. They will not monkey round a solid body o' timber with a heavy growth of underbrush. I thought then that

BOOT SOUP

Injuns were not such terrible fighters as some folks make 'em seem; and my first notion has never changed, though I 've

JERRY AND THE SERGEANT

met them as seemed to know no fear, but they are exceptions. When Bill Williams heard of my goin' close to the timber, he said: 'I shall have to keep you at home next time, if I expect to return you to your Dad. You are a young fool to go close to timber where hostile Injuns are hid.' I told Williams that three of our ponies was in the bunch and that I did n't want to quit without them. I thought the Sioux were cowards, but I have learned by experience, since, that a white man — on the plains, at least — will risk where an Injun dreads. Injuns are credited with being ter-

rible cunnin' in stealing horses, the Pawnees especially so, which is the reason other tribes call them 'Wolves.' We reached Black Moon's village on the Laramie River the next day, camping near the chief's lodge. The story of our recoverin' the stock and the takin' of two Pawnee scalps had got ahead o' us, and the young warriors wanted to see the young paleface who had

THE CAPTURE

ridden close to the grove. They looked upon that as a great feat, though older ones said that I was a young fool and would lose my scalp some day. I see now they were right — and you boys better learn afore you pay that price fer the same lesson."

The throngs pour by us as we loiter for our grazing and hay-making. By pure accident Boardy dis-

THE SQUAW

more substantial than footprints — *i.e.* a cut-off named for himself. But in the midst of the reconnaisance of this "Saddlebag Cut-off," he was most disagreeably confronted with an uncompromising Digger chieftain. An abject surrender was ordered and Jerry's life was saved by his adopting the native costume and handing over to the chief his bag of pilot bread, with all the rights, privileges, and prerogatives appertaining thereto.

Something, no doubt the meaty portion of his legs (in view of the approaching long, cold winter), influenced the

THE SERENADE

chief to send the prisoner back on the hills in charge of a sergeant, who promised faithfully to feed him regularly on boot-soup — the boots having recently been taken from Jerry's erstwhile companions. At every meal Jerry was reminded of the last time he dined upon the same with his friends!

The sergeant makes the mistake of farming out his job of looking after Jerry to his squaw — a lady long trained in making light of hard work.

Overcome in the presence of the fair sex, after so long a separation from their charms, Jerry pours forth his soul in a lament entitled, "We Miss Thee, Ladies."

"We miss thee at the washing-tub,
    When our sore and blistered digits
Have been compelled to weekly rub —
    Bringing blues, hysterics, fidgets.
'T is then we miss thy timely aids —
    Oh, do have pity, gentle maids!

"We miss thee when our Sunday shirts
    Are sadly rent and buttonless,
With not a thimble, button, thread,
    To help us in our dire distress.
'T is then we miss thy timely aids —
    Oh, do have pity, gentle maids!"

JERRY LEARNS TO DANCE

Man-like, he attributes his very evident conquest of the lady's interest to the exposition of his personality and his excellently modulated voice and intonation without half-recognizing the incidental factors which are strengthening his case, such as his success in drowning out the voice of Junior, and the long, appraising glances which the lady casts upon his four gold teeth.

JERRY TRIMS THE FORTY-NINER

Hero Jerry's life is spared on condition that he shall join the tribe and learn the tribal dance, which he does, as energetically as the nourishment provided by boot-soup permitted. The result, however, proves his salvation. For, accompanying Sarge on a raid on a returning gold-miner with sadly blistered feet, Sarge is killed, peace is made, and, wagering his boots against the miner's "pile," Jeremiah wins both and is certainly the only Forty-Niner who, with a bag of gold dust, is hurrying onward to California.

August 13. — In Boardy's sketchbook I found the following rhapsody to this lovely[1] valley, which I pilfer. He writes as

[1] Diamond Valley.

"BOARDY" AT SUPPER

(By Charles Nahl, in A. Delano's "Old Block's Sketch Book")

he talks, throwing in strange, irrelevant observations as he thinks of them, for what Boardy is saying requires no thought, once his massive brain has launched his tongue forth on any topic.

This Carson Valley just east of the Pass, for soil, situation, and natural charms, eclipsed the most highly favored localities in our

days.) It is some twenty miles long, of an oval shape, reclining in a sweet easy slope from the base of the Sierra to the river, intersected with numerous small streams, of the most crystal clearness, flowing down the mountain flank (Met a German who attended a meeting at Darmstadt last year to organize a "National Society for the Assistance of German Emigration" and has come with funds provided by that institution), the soil composed of a black unctuous loam, which throws up verdant fleeces of clover and rich indigenous grasses, enameled with beauteous flowers of the most delicate tints, like a lovely lawn, in contrast with the stupendous range of mountains that tower above it in the heavens, with a peculiarity entirely their own, rising immediately from a level surface, like a pyramid from the plain, their sides covered with gigantic pines that partake of their peaky character, standing so far apart that they feather out below to immense length, and tapering upwards with the most uniform graduation till they terminate in a point formed by a solitary leader.

(Beautiful illustration of mixed-drink metaphors, including clippers' tails, horns, and corns : —

> "The dark-eyed *señoritas*
> Are very fond of me :
> You ought to see us throw ourselves
> When we get on a spree ;

We are saucy as a clipper-ship
A-dashing round the Horn,
Head and tail up like a steer
A-rushing through the corn."

Alégrate! Amiguito!)

Our camp in the little Elysium was close under the mountains, at one of the several rivulets, the plain about us covered so profusely with clover blossoms that in fact the animals could lie down and fill themselves on the spot, it grew in such luxuriant abundance. We were busily engaged in supper preparations when two Indians came into camp, each carrying two glorious trout, weighing, I should say, five pounds, formed and speckled without any distinguishable difference from Irish salmon-trout; those we got for two tattered flannel shirts, and they furnished a supper that left nothing to be desired.

(For the family album: a picture of myself, showing what I might have had for supper but for the fish — trusting to my "trusty rifle.")

After supper some of the men took up the Indians' bows and commenced firing at a tree, without being able to hit it, whereupon they asked the Indians to shoot, which they appeared reluctant to do, but, on being pressed, consented, firing fully as wide of the mark as their white acquaintances. Suspecting, however, they were shamming, I took a bun that was left, and, sticking it in the bark of the tree, made signs that whoever hit it should have it to eat; on hearing which, one of them took up his bow and, without any studious aim, drove his arrow right into the dimple of the crust — showing, it was clear, they were disinclined to let us see their skill in the first instance, lest we should harbor bad impressions about them.

On leaving this resplendent valley, I looked back on it as a beautiful picture I was going to behold for the last time, and turned from it with a reluctant regret, my head and heart filled with all sorts of romantic and Petrarchal notions and ideas. (*Selah*, Boardy)

To-day's journey through the west cañon of the Carson[1] and on into the pretty valley[2] beyond fully justified all the loitering in the grassy meadows behind us which Guide Meek has been doing these last few days; our mules were fit for the fray, but you would not believe how rapidly this road could unfit them,

---

[1] West of Woodfords, Calif.   [2] Hope Valley.

THE GREEN DEVIL S

(*By Charles Nahl, in A. Delano's "Old*

nor how many it took to haul our wagons one by one up grades
that defied all of Newton's three laws.   Our cañon road wound
along in a chasm through which the river came in bawling cascades, the rocks on either hand standing so straight up (to
between three hundred and five hundred feet) that you feared
to watch an eagle alight on the pinnacle above you lest his
weight should destroy their equilibrium and grind you into

that the river here was already lined with the carcasses of
animals which, having conquered the Wakarusa, Ash Hollow,
the Three Crossings of the Sweetwater, Goose Mountains, and
the Sink and Desert of the Humboldt, broke their hearts on
this ledge in Carson Cañon almost within sight of El Dorado!

In fact, we are nearer our goal (if not our gold) than that,
for we are in Diggings, if not "the" Diggings, already.   While
toiling along up the west fork of the Carson, before the Elysium
Valley was reached,[2] we heard some men in an outfit ahead of
us yip out the same ironical "Quack, Quack!" that we had all
indulged in back on Goose Creek, to the discomfiture of those
who had there been fooled by Fool's Gold.   For here, too,
men from trains now delayed or in camp were panning gold.
"Quack ahead, you damned goose!" said one of these, swing-
ing down the road to his camp and holding out a hand that
trembled a little with excitement.   In the palm lay flakes of
real gold.   Their owner had already tested the metal in the
one superficial — but fairly correct — way possible on the
spot — namely, with his teeth.   The grains had adhered,
whereas "Fool's Gold" grains would have broken apart.

Gold!   We had seen some nuggets belonging to east-bound

[1] W. Kelly, *An Excursion to California.*   [2] Southeast of Sheridan, Nev.

Californians who had passed us on the road. But now, gold —
live gold — right out of the pan!

Fortunately there was but one fording of the Carson
necessary in this cañon. No one knows what the first-comers
with wagons by this route had suffered at this crossing place,
for the causeway of rocks in the stream's bed over which our
wagons rolled safely — fourteen miracles in succession! — must
have been laid no later than a month ago. By whom? And
at what cost? Little wonder there were graves hereabouts!

Two miles more brought us to a pretty glen where black-
tailed deer bounded gaily between our bullets along the shores
of Reed Lake. Here, within sight of our next impossibility,
Carson Pass, we spent the night.

The wind in these big trees! Since we first came into this
mighty tree-land how this army of Forty-Niners has appre-
ciated the whispering trees! It seemed as though they held a
cure for all our aching bones, creaking joints, blistered faces,
and reddened eyes. It is said that when one of these mighty
monarchs of the Sierras is burned the only thing left is what
it has taken in from the air through its leaves — carbon. It
almost seems that about all that is worth while in many of these
tired and broken bodies of men and women is some similar
elixir-of-life that is seeping in from the grass and trees of this
wonderful mountain kingdom at the edge of Goldland. Even
Carlo is singing again: —

"The Piutes stole what grub I had, they left me not a bite,
    And now the Devil was to pay, for the Desert was in sight;
  And as the people passed along they 'd say to me, 'You fool,
    You 'll never get through in the world unless you leave that
      mule.'

"But I pushed and pulled and coaxed, till I finally made a start,
    And his bones, they squeaked and rattled so I thought he 'd
      fall apart;
  We crossed the Truckee thirty times, but not a tear was shed;
    We crossed the Summit, took the trail that down to Hangtown
      led."

Out where you will read this, Dad, those words "not a tear was shed" will have little meaning, I suppose. But here, and to us on these mountains, there is a great cry of conquest and victory in that simple expression, "We crossed the Summit." A great many who started will never cross this Divide — their guideposts having directed them over another, where, let us hope, the very streets are paved with gold.

Reed Lake. This is narrow and about a mile and a half long; its western end is the key to our pathway over the first, and lesser in height, of our Sierra "summits," and the more difficult of the two on account of its steepness and the roughness of the road.

The first two miles of ascent are said by old-timers to be the most dreaded 10,560 feet out of the whole eleven and a half million feet between here and the Missouri River.[1]

The road is crooked, taking numerous turns around the roots of huge trees, and it is "paved" with huge, diabolically rounded rocks. Over these, cattle try to climb, but they generally compromise at last by creeping to the top on their knees.[2] Some outfits had thrown their wagons away here even after bringing them through the Humboldt Desert. A number of emigrants had no loads now left at all, but took their wagons along — three pairs of oxen were hauling up one empty wagon at a time as I came by. I saw horses being led to that steep ledge and looking at it with no more idea of what to do next than if it had been the side of a barn; while old "Sacramento," Meek's

[1] The height of Carson Pass is not given on the Markleville Sheet of the California-Nevada U. S. Geological Survey; adjacent Elephant's Back Peak is 9635 feet.
[2] W. Kelly, *An Excursion to California.*

mule, came to it, gave one look, and reared up for all the world like a hod-carrier at the foot of a ladder.　Several emigrants had dismounted their wagons and we found them putting the parts together on top after they had been hauled up piecemeal. A mule had been killed in the road the day before by a dislodged rock which rolled down and hit him in the head.　With all our mule-power and man-power it was only a question of time for us to get our wagons up; yet I really believe that there were moments when more mules were lying flat than were upright, and I am not sure but that, too, was a help, for they thus served as anchors to the upright animals, helping them to keep their feet and hold the wagon where it was until all could pull together in unison again.

Near the top a particularly ugly turn took the road around the base of a perpendicular rock near the edge of a singularly uninviting chasm far below, through which a mountain torrent roared its angry defiance.　But since there were, by actual measurement, at least eight inches to spare for the wagons, what did it matter if those of us not responsible were filled with qualms?

Enormous pine trees.　A gap.　Deep snow among the trees. A bubbling spring of water, so cold it made your teeth ache. Rough road downhill into a valley to an irregular lake [1] — and the first, and most dreaded, "Summit of the Sierras" had been conquered!　We pitch camp memorable for its giant camp-fire, arctic weather, and sixty almost wind-broken mules.

August 15. — Took an early breakfast and moved forward, leaving the lake at its southwestern extremity, and soon commenced the ascent of the western ridge, the loftiest chain in all these ranges of mountains.[2]　The last ascent is six miles, the first three through dense forests of ever-green timber; for the remaining three miles the mountain is mostly bare, except here and there a scattering tree.　The last two miles of the ascent

---

[1] Twin Lakes near Kirkwoods, Calif.

[2] Called "Carson Pass" on original township survey maps, near Thimble Peak (9870) on Pyramid Peak Sheet of the U. S. Geological Survey of California.

are terrific, being excessively steep, and a part of the way so
sideling that it was necessary for several men to brace themselves against each wagon to prevent its upsetting and rolling
down the side of the mountain. By doubling teams, and
assisting with manual strength, we succeeded in gaining the
top of this dreaded eminence by two o'clock in the afternoon.
Near the top of the ridge there is an immense embankment of

tnis we pass, and in an instant the New World of California
bursts at once upon our impatient sight. We are now 9300
feet above the level of the sea and nearly 2000 feet higher than
the South Pass of the Rocky Mountains.

Upon this stupendous observatory I halted a short time to
take a general view of the boundless panorama spread out
before me. At length, fixing my steady gaze towards the west,
the sight being assisted by a small telescope, I saw a waving
line of light blue at two hundred miles distance running along
the verge of the western horizon. This is the coast range of
mountains near the Pacific Ocean, and limits the view in that
direction. The intermediate space consists of the great valley
of the Sacramento and Joaquin rivers, embosoming the Bay of
San Francisco, which penetrates far into the plain, sending out
numerous arms in all directions. North and south, the view is
bounded only by the power of vision. I believe the extent of
country visible from this point to be at least two hundred miles
in breadth by five hundred in length. Immediately in front we
have a more distinct view of the great western slope of the
Sierra Nevadas. This slope consists of a great number of
ridges or chains of mountains, running a westerly course in
zigzag lines, starting from the main range on which we now

stand and gradually diminishing in height until they terminate at the eastern limit of the broad plain of the Sacramento. Between every two of these long ridges flows the American River or one of its branches, which, traversing the mountains and crossing the plain, falls at length into the Sacramento River.

Standing upon this towering eminence, the wayworn traveler experiences sensations similar to those felt by Moses of old when he climbed to the top of Mount Pisgah and for the first time caught a distant glimpse of the Promised Land.

I do not think it possible to drive teams over heights more difficult than those we have ascended, being twice the height of the Alleghenies and as high as the White and Green Mountains piled upon each other, and I think higher than any of the passes of the Alps into Italy. Hannibal and Napoleon gained deathless renown by crossing the Alps, which might not have been a more hazardous undertaking than crossing the Sierra Nevada, yet I am suspicious that thousands have crossed these tremendous heights the present year who will not acquire immortal honor by the exploit. One thing, however, is certain: that is, if the names of the California emigrants should not chance to be inscribed in the records of fame, you may yet see countless thousands of them very legibly written with chalk, wagon-grease, or paint upon the everlasting rocks that compose the towering ranges of these mountains. Volumes might be filled with these elevated names. Here are monuments that will stand until the "rocks fall to dust," though the inscriptions upon them will soon fade away, like those on Independence Rock and in the "City of Rocks."

At three o'clock in the afternoon we commenced the western descent, which we found to be less abrupt and not so rocky as the ascent on the eastern side.[1] We descended by a succession of sharp pitches, and in some places found deep, loose sand instead of naked rocks.

[1] By Tragedy Spring, Leek Spring, between the heads of Camp Creek and Plum Creek, and down the latter, which enters the South Fork of American River at Bullion Bend near Moore's, Calif.

BROWN AND JINGO IN SIGHT O

(By W. R. Ryan, in "Personal

Five miles of desert brought us down to a bench of the mountains, called Rock Valley, in which we encamped.

August 16–18. — The last three days of our journey before the memorable one on which we first saw the romantic, log-strewn flat of Hangtown, or Placerville, were days of rough traveling for the caravan, and Boardy and I outstepped its progress to visit halfway

tions of regret over parting from friends with whom you have shared hopes and fears, joys and sorrows, during never-to-be-forgotten days.

The rough road necessitated the slow progress of the train. Two wagons had been so shaken on the last summit that they had to be abandoned and their loads distributed among the other twelve. For the most part it was downhill work, but if that sounds easy to you it is because you cannot see the hills! On such roads almost any climb upward over sensible grades is safer to life and limb and cargo than even a gentle descent over a stony track.

The value and weight of our freight compelled our caravan to hold a steady equilibrium and to continue practising all the regular trail-routine which had been enforced from the beginning. Thus pursuing the calm tenor of our way, we presented a curious contrast to the excited mob about us — these hundreds who now "smelled" gold and rushed forward toward the Diggings with a precipitancy that left almost every encumbrance, and this now included even animals and cattle, in their wake.

You could not blame them; but from our brief jaunts to near-by diggings Boardy and I got some realization — and it came very quick — of what lay ahead of us all if gold was to be won.   The transcontinental trip had been hard, Heaven knows, but it had provided a continual variation; it was monotonous, but the monotony was lightened by change of scenery, by the various new conditions under which it was performed, and by all the give-and-take, ups and downs, of a life which brought sometimes as many laughs to lips as curses or groans.

Now, actually in the Diggings, what do we see — what is the impression? Whole mountains of dirt to be removed; hard labor of the stiffest kind known to man — shoveling. And for people in what condition, physically? The poorest imaginable. Even the healthy are unfitted for such back-breaking labor during the first few weeks after their arrival in this climate; for fever and ague are to be met and mastered. But no great percentage of us are at all well. Monotonous diet, poor water, and the strain and stress of desert travel have left its mark on most; scurvy and diarrhea have undermined 50 per cent of us or more.   For all these such work as shoveling dirt, sometimes waist deep in water, often knee deep, and seldom, if ever, with dry feet, is a hazard that only one man in fifty assumes without being made ill within four days. We have seen sad sights all along this California Trail; but just these momentary glimpses in these diggings have exhibited some just as sad — here, at the very goal! I refer to the sight of strong men compelled to sit around and become acclimated before going to work, and any number of sick men trying to recover from the result of refusing to do that before attempting hard work. And perhaps most regrettable of all is the sight of those who, either discouraged at feeling so miserable because of the enforced delay, or sick and needing to use great precaution, have taken the disastrous Gin or Rum Cut-off to "happiness" and thus postponed indefinitely the return of the health and strength necessary to tackle the work which they have come three thousand miles, maybe, to do.

Back in camp these nights, however, we banish our forebodings for humanity at large and enter into those eleventh-hour reminiscences and festivities common to travelers and friends who are about to separate forever. Within reason

Uncle Bob aids and abets this almost continual celebration of the successful prosecution of our eventful march from the supply of cheer in the noble Ark — though none of us can really believe that the thing has come through undamaged; the throngs which pass gape at it in a kind of holy awe, as though another Ark of the Covenant had crossed another Red Sea, not quite realizing that, though bulky, the weight is almost all in

nave forty young greasers to greet her,
  And fifty if put to the test.

"And fifty if put to the test,
  And fifty if put to the test;
Have forty young greasers to greet her,
  And fifty if put to the test."

"Ya-a-s," drawls Picayune, not far away, "you 're a little 'ero with the wimming with yer own lariat — but oh, let anybody else notice one, an' you around, an' a polecat has n't got you beat for wolfish nippin' in. 'Member the night I charaded fer you out on South Pass an' wanted me 'wife' to sit in me lap when I brung her the gold?"

"I 'll wear a right pert standin' collar,"

resumed Carlo, as though no one had spoken, —

"And smoke *cigarritos*, of course;
And when I run short on her dollars,
  I 'll try and obtain a divorce.

"I 'll try and obtain a divorce,
  I 'll try and obtain a divorce,
And when I run short on her dollars,
  I 'll try and obtain a divorce."

Around the fires we go back over that long trail behind us in retrospect and discuss at length its various aberrations, abnormalities, and absurdities — ask, "How can it be improved? — Will a railway ever follow it? In whole or in part?" Our old-timers talk about the spots along the way where grass was scant, even in this well-watered year of '49, and wonder how the later comers will fare. We wonder if the Black Pool of the Little Blue has dried up; if the islands on the "Coast of Nebraska" have been denuded of their green; if buffaloes block the road this side of O'Fallon's Bluffs; if the skunk that let his family float off in order to save his wagon-bed and team still goes unhung; if the magic-lantern man has arrived in this land wealthy; if the ice has all gone from Ice Slough.

We check the trail's course by its waterways and think of it as having these thirteen main divisions: Kaw, Little Blue, Platte, North Platte, Sweetwater, Green, Bear, Snake, Goose, Thousand Springs, Humboldt, Carson, and American. What will confuse people in after years, Meek thinks, will be the fact that the trail can never be in one year what it was in any other year. For instance now, in 1849, it is something wholly different from what it was in 1848. New military posts have been built; scores of trading-places have sprung up; a dozen or more ranches have been opened; a score of old crossing-places have been discarded because river banks at those points have grown into sloughs; old cut-offs have been abandoned because springs on them have been sucked dry; new cut-offs have been discovered by new Saddlebags; river camp-grounds, well-known until now, are deserted because the numbers of cattle dying at the water's edge have turned them into pest-places of putridity; the finding of new springs has swung the trail wide of the old track. The Golden Army of 1850 will find a new California Trail and mention points of which the Argonauts of 1849 never heard.

We ourselves, even, are confused by the multitude of memories and cannot agree as to where certain incidents occurred or when. As each one becomes more confirmed, through the years, of the correctness of his own view, who will ever reconcile the discrepancies? Where was the dragoon dandy dragged on his head across a parade-ground? Where did the "good boy" refuse to gamble and stay in his tent and get bitten by a scorpion? Where did the Indian medicine man try to revive the drunken Pawnee girl? Where did the naked boys bet on which could outlast the mosquitoes most courageously? Already few will agree on some of these incidents.

SADDLEBAGS INTRODUCING HIMSELF TO THE MINERS

Nebraska"; of O'Fallon's Bluffs; of Ash Hollow; the view from Scott's Bluffs; of Heart's Island as we left the Platte; of the strange "City of Rocks." Our nightmares — for how long? — will be Humboldt Desert nightmares.

The precipitancy of many who dropped everything in the Desert and joined the *sauve qui peut* race for the mountains, although at one time perhaps far behind us, has put them ahead of us in the days spent between Ragtown and here. Large numbers have arrived at Weaverville and Hangtown, I find, by way of the Truckee or Donner route to Yuba River, which branched from our Carson route near Humboldt Sink, where we heard those shotguns at work settling one unhappy company's debate as to which path to take. In our hasty round of the nearest diggings, however, we happened upon actual news of one of our friends; for the arrival of Jeremiah from out the burning Desert with a bag of gold had caused a sensation which nothing but his readiness to "treat" every-one as a friend could have allayed without an emergency jury's investigation. He certainly has a "head start" over the rest of us if he can wisely invest his capital.

SADDLEBAGS ENTERTAINING THE MINERS

We heard rumors that others resembling Brown, Jingo, and Pickpan had reached Hangtown and were already rich, hung, or both. Fancy, then, our joy at our noontime stop yesterday (August 18) to see Boardy rise up in his might at the appear-ance of approaching figures and yell with delight when a nearer view disclosed our friends. Uncle Bob had contracted a cold during the preceding snowy nights and was sipping a royal hot toddy at the moment; and, the essentials being at hand, the honors of the occasion were, shall we say, tossed off gallantly. The stately Brown announced, when asked how the firm had fared along the road, that it had had its ups and downs, but fewer *sideways*, since their horses (and Pickpan's also, by the way) had been gathered to their fathers along the Humboldt, and their decrepit wagons added to the roadside débris.

More than that, brother Pickpan had met a gentleman quite

as versed at cards as himself. The fortunes of war had swung first to one side and then the other, each contestant being in possession, at times, of practically all of their combined re-

sources. When morning broke, the larger fraction of the spoils lay with our friend — so far as bulk was concerned; but after his dejected comrade

A HOT TODDY ON THE SIERRAS

daylight, canceled customhouse receipts for the full amount of his winnings — *i.e.* $400. Pickpan was last seen in a characteristic attitude as he shouted good-bye on the run — hopeful of tracking that stallion to the mines. He

PICKPAN IN A CHARACTERIS-
TIC ATTITUDE

is doubtless ahead of us somewhere. We look for our other trail-companions, too — for "Boo" Johnson and her stalwart Iowans; for the Brotherhood, wondering if the salt of its stern convictions has survived the saleratus deserts to leaven these lumps of wickedness; for old "Indiana" — God bless him;

for the Ohio boys that swam the Humboldt; for Denny and his rare violinist, hoping that if we miss them a-trail we will find them (and the long expected "Elephant") in the sawdust arena.

We make our royal entry into Hangtown to-morrow!

"BRIGHT RED GOLD FOR DEARIE"

SECTION IX

All I can do, in conclusion, is to send the notes I have taken since we arrived and which, each day, I have expected to expand. But the days and nights have been too strenuous and I must send them as they stand; if you can make head or tail out of them you will perhaps do better than I could, anyway.

Down we rolled the morning of the nineteenth, excited as schoolboys, into Three Fingered John's or Jim's (whatever was the name of the first reprobate which that place honored itself by hanging) Hangtown — soon to be called Placerville if the genteel have their way — and found ourselves in a stumpy clearing filled with as weird a collection of shanties, tents, men, women, ardent hopes and spirits, and demoralized ambitions as could lie at the end of a trail 2266 miles from Independence, Missouri — figures not guaranteed. One thing regarding our journey as it comes to an end: Guide Meek was right when he said that the great task in making the California journey overland was to keep well enough and fit enough to do your fifteen or twenty miles a day — to grind on and not let the grinding tire or disgust you too much for health and happiness. "It is a test of character," says Boardy, who can settle any question with six words and a gesture, "more than of material resources. We have come through with an Army with Hearts of Gold."

There is little use of my telling the following incident. None but those who crossed the plains can have the slightest notion of its significance. We were coming down where "the road nears off tu Hangtown," as the fellow said who saw "the Elephant" sign pointing up. The jangle of the trace chains and wheels was just what it had been back on the Platte or Humboldt. The dust sifted up just as hateful as on Raft River. The mules grunted and cursed their luck as they always had, when what do you think burst out through the air? A rooster's crow. Oh, godlings! Chicken! Eggs! The train pulled up as if a warship had thrown a shell across our bows, and you should have heard the yelling from our maudlin mob![1] They had yet to learn that chickens were sixteen dollars each and eggs fifty cents apiece — but not one to his dying day will forget that welcoming salute of civilization by said chanticleer on the Hangtown Road that morning.

Powder is worth sixteen dollars a pound, the same as a quart of champagne and about what one gets for an ounce of gold dust, unless you know enough to stand out for eighteen dollars for gold. Uncle Bob, with his 11,000 pounds (more or less) will make a good haul (if the market holds up, of which there is doubt), even if what his shot and caps bring him amounts to the cost of living here awhile and going home in style. He is retailing his goods all the way from Hangtown to Sacramento, with side trips to numerous diggings with a single wagon, but finds that prices are dropping fast. Most of us are having a try at mining, but plan to meet at Sacramento September 15, if the rainy season does not set in before that.

At Fort Sutter we had the good fortune to meet the hero of the gold discovery of last year, James W. Marshall, and hear his story from his own lips. He first described building the mill at Coloma.

"While we were in the habit at night of turning the water

[1] F. Stimson, *Overland to California.*

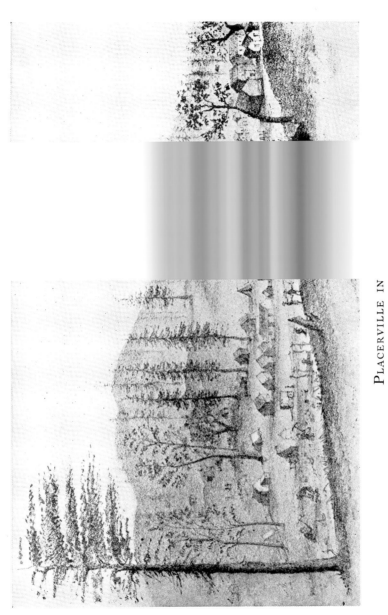

PLACERVILLE IN

(By F. M. Letts, in " A Pictorial

through the tail race," said Mr. Marshall, "I used to go down in the morning to see what had been done by the water through the night; and about half-past seven o'clock, on or about the nineteenth of January, — I am not quite certain to a day, but it was between the eighteenth and twentieth of that month, — 1848, I went down as usual, and after shutting off the water from the race I stepped into it, near the lower end, and there,

SUTTER'S MILL, IN 1848
(*In "The Miner's Own Book"*)

time. I picked up one or two pieces and examined them attentively; and having some general knowledge of minerals, I could not call to mind more than two which in any way resembled this — sulphuret of iron, very bright and brittle; and gold, bright, yet malleable; I then tried it between two rocks, and found that it could be beaten into a different shape, but not broken. Four days afterwards I went to the Fort for provisions, and carried with me about three ounces of the gold, which Captain Sutter and I tested with nitric acid. I then tried it in Sutter's presence by taking three silver dollars and balancing them by the dust in the air, then immersed both in water, and the superior weight of the gold satisfied us both of its nature and value."

The first piece of gold found by Mr. Marshall was worth about fifty cents. It was given, with other gold, to Mrs. Wimmer, the wife of one of Captain Sutter's workmen, and paid out for goods. So that the whereabouts of the first specimen is to-day unknown.

While stopping at Leidesdorff's rancho we had the gratification of seeing Captain Sutter and party ride up. He was accompanied by H. R. Schoolcraft, Esq., Chief Alcalde of Sacramento City, and Captain Smith, a Virginia gentleman for many years resident in Peru, who was at the head of a party engaged in extensive operations at the Mormon Islands of the American River. There were also with them several Indian attendants, all on horseback, the only genteel mode of traveling in California. One of our number was furnished with a letter of introduction to Captain Sutter, but we soon found such formality quite unnecessary with him, as he quickly manifested in himself the character of a perfect and most courteous gentleman of the old European military school; possessed of all its politeness, ease, and dignity, without its usual hauteur. He had just returned from a tour among the different *rancherias* of Indians in the mountains, and arranged for a talk with them, to be held in a few days, which he invited us to attend. He gave us much interesting information about the Indians in the valleys of the Sacramento and San Joaquin. When he first settled in California he had much trouble with them, but he adopted, and has pursued steadily from the first, a policy of peace, combined with the requisite firmness and occasional severity. Thus he had obtained all-powerful influence with them, and was enabled to avail himself of their labor for moderate remuneration. Now all was changed; the late emigrants across the mountains had commenced a war of extermination upon them, shooting them down like wolves, — men, women, and children, — wherever they could find them. Some of the Indians were undoubtedly bad and needed punishment, but

TRADING POST IN THE MINES

MINING IN THE STANISLAUS, 1849
(*By W. R. Ryan, in "Personal Adventures"*)

generally the whites were the aggressors. As a matter of course the Indians retaliated whenever opportunities occurred; and in this way several unarmed or careless emigrants had become, in turn, their victims.

Whatever curiosity most of us have about the art of digging in the ground for gold, it is not in the least shared by good friend Carlo. "I'm...

...picture of   Carlo the Mid-shipmite, Child of the Sea," which I append as a final salute to as good, honest, and hardworking a trail companion as ever crossed the plains. Uncle Bob sent him away happy on muleback — he might not have managed otherwise.

CARLO'S AMBITION

Captain Sutter's fort is an oblong pile, erected on a rising ground, with few of the characteristics of a fortress about it, built of adobes, the external wall being from eighteen to twenty feet in height and shedded down all round inside, with an adobe house two stories high in the centre. This was originally the Captain's residence, and all the sheds his stores, stables, etc. But now the house is an hotel and the sheds are fitted up into hospitals, billiard-rooms, and taps. There are two large gates, at each of which there were a pair of Indians on guard; but the whole is in a state of decline, fast crumbling into original dust in which it would not surprise me if there was a small percentage of the golden quality. I looked about the fort for Captain Sutter's immense fields of wheat and corn, which should be

ready for the sickle, but not a head of either was to be seen, the
Captain having declined agricultural pursuits about the time
they would have recompensed him best, if the pursuit was a
thriving one; but I suppose the Captain made the experiment,
and, finding the climate unsuitable for the maturation of grain,
discontinued it, for he is not the man to abandon a project if
he thinks it can be made to answer expectations by persever-
ance and industry. He no longer resides at the fort, his headquarters being at Suttersville, on the banks of the Sacramento,
about three miles below the city, where he is endeavoring to
found a new town, having sold his interest in the site of Sacramento before it grew into its present importance — a piece of
over-anxiety which threw a countless fortune into the hands of
the purchasers and which he will not be able to repair in his
new project, for it does not appear to prosper in the slightest.

Boardy is highly delighted with a new vital fact in the relation between Man and Nature. He heard to-day of a miner
who was considered the champion of profanity in the Diggings.
But while the valley reverberated with his elephantine trumpet-
roar of a voice (which usually awoke echoes at the slightest prov-
ocation), whenever he emitted the frightful curses which gave
him fame, — no matter in how loud a tone, — outraged Nature
revolted and no echo whatever came back from cliff, cove,
cavern, or cañon!

While part of us remained in charge of the trading, the rest
shouldered our shovels, buckets, and rocker, and proceeded to
the lower bar on the South Fork, to try our hands at digging and
washing out gold. The waters were so high that not many
miners were employed on the bars here, though there were
more on the Middle and North Forks. The great rush at that
time was to the diggings more recently discovered on the Stanislaus and other tributaries of the San Joaquin, where there were
about eight thousand miners, besides traders, etc. These
discoveries had excited much attention on account of the large
lumps of gold found there, but the most experienced miners
were already returning to the branches of the Sacramento.

DRIVING AWAY SQUATTERS FROM

(By Charles Nahl, in A. Delano's " Old

Arriving on the bar, the scene presented to us was new indeed and not more extraordinary than impressive. Some, with long-handled shovels, delved among clumps of bushes or by the side of large rocks, never raising their eyes for an instant; others, with pick and shovel, worked among stone and gravel, or with trowels searched under banks and roots of trees, where, if rewarded with small lumps of gold, the eye shone brighter for an instant, when the search was immediately and more ardently resumed. At the edge of the stream, or knee deep and waist deep in water, as cold as melted ice and snow could make it, some were washing gold with tin pans or the common cradle rocker, while the rays of the sun were pouring down on their heads with an intensity exceeding anything we ever experienced at home.

This "placer" or bar is simply the higher portion of the sandy and rocky bed of the stream, which during the seasons of high water is covered with the rushing torrent, but was now partially or entirely exposed. This is covered with large stones and rocks or, on the smooth sand, with clumps of stunted bushes of trees. Selecting a spot, we inquired of those nearest whether any other "diggers" claimed a prior possession, and, such not being the case, we went to work. First fixing our rocker firmly at the edge of the stream, we dug, and carried down, a pile of the earth to be washed; when sufficient was collected, one filled the machine with the earth and kept it in motion while the other supplied it with water. Getting but a small quantity of gold in that spot, we waded through a little inlet to another part of the bar nearer the stream, and, our labors not being well rewarded here, we again shifted our position nearer the other miners. There we fixed upon the edge of a bank where the ground had been broken by an old miner but soon deserted. Digging through about a foot of sand and stones which we rejected, we came to a clay deposit mixed with sand; with this we filled the buckets and carried it to the machine. The upper or sandy layer contains no gold, but the ore is caused by its specific gravity and the action of the water to sift through this into the clay, where it is found until the blue

MINERS DIVERTING THE WATE[R]

(In "The Miner's Own B[ook])

clay or granite formation is reached, which in these diggings is generally three to four feet; but in some of the others the miners dig ten to fifteen feet. This, we were told, was the fact in some parts of the Yuba diggings, and on the forks of the San Joaquin. It was now midday and the heat of the sun was quite

SOME OF THE CALIFORNIANS SPEND THEIR FORTUNES
IN DISSIPATION
(*In X. O. X.'s " The History of an Expedition to California "*)

intolerable to all but salamanders; finding in our machines about four dollars' value of gold to twenty buckets full of earth, we discontinued our labors for that day.

It is sad to see hard-working, eager men all but break their backs to fulfill the expectations of loved ones at home, and fail, while right at their sides are those who, having been successful, drink or gamble their fortunes away — the money going to those who have come only to prey on their fellow men.

With some of these latter men, who appeared good-natured in their excesses, we ventured to remonstrate. We said, "This digging gold is toilsome and hard labor. Why do you not try and keep some for a rainy day?' Their reply was, "Oh, we know where there's plenty more and when we want it we can dig it."

own hands and obtained of Indians some $23,000 in gold, we saw in this condition two or three days; he had now but about $7000 remaining. Some little boys came daily to our tent, sometimes twice or thrice, with gold dust tied up in the corners of their handkerchiefs, amounting each time to fractional parts of

HAVING LOST THEIR MONEY, SOME COMMIT SUICIDE

one, two, or three dollars, which they obtained by gathering and blowing or washing out the dust about the counters or doors of the stores and groggeries.

An Akron, Ohio, boy, George W. Smith, turned a trick in Sacramento in 1849 that showed ingenuity. Let him tell it in his own words, they are so lively: "My last ten dollars paid for an ice cream freezer I ordered and the material to make 2 gallons. I frose it in the Backyard of the Hotel where I boarded, near the horse market, where hundreds of people gather every day. I carried it over there and opened up business right next a saloon. It was a rush for ice cream by everybody. To my great amazement this 2 gals. of Ice cream netted me $32.00. Doubling my

capital three fold. I was congratulated by all who knew me. Next day I made and sold 4 gals. I then enlarged the capacity. It was a 4 gal freeser. To my astonishment my pockets were soon full of money. I followed this business till the ice famine struck Sacramento."

All hail to the rising fortunes of the memorable firm of "Brown and Jingo"! Those inimitable gentlemen have made a safe arrival at San Francisco (and more lately Sacramento), bringing with them supplies and an iron store building. The latter came knocked-down; but for some inexplicable reason

A "BURST" IN SAN FRANCISCO

all the pieces were found to have been shipped, and they actually went together. The grand "Opening" (it seemed to justify a "burst" in San Francisco) was somewhat delayed, but in the end it was all that the proprietors could have desired. The instant success (on paper) of the new concern seems to have resulted from some fast and excellent thinking on the part of the proprietors, who adopted a gala-day beflagged auction

BROWN AND JINGO AT WORK

system of salesmanship which permits any bid for goods to be accepted by the auctioneer whenever the usual market price of the article being sold has been exceeded. If "paper success" ever brought fame and fortune to any concern, the resplendent volume in which Brown and Jingo's debtors' names are enrolled bears testimony to their future opulence.

It appears that, while much gold has been panned, and vastly more will be panned, a regrettably small fraction will benefit the hands which actually lifted it from its resting place. We have fallen in with an estimable gentleman who was here when Marshall's discovery was made. He kept a diary through those bewildering days of 1848 and, upon sending it home, wrote a letter of which I acquired a copy. Nowhere have I read a briefer, franker statement of one person's ups and downs or so keen an analysis of exactly what is happening here : —

I assure you it is hardly possible for any accounts of the gold mines, and of what I may call gold gravel and sand [he wrote], to be exaggerated. The El Dorado of the early voyagers to America has really been discovered; and what its consequences may be, not only upon this continent, but upon the world, wiser heads — heads more versed than mine is in monetary science — must tell. There is much speculation here as to the effects which the late wonderful discovery will produce in the States and Europe. Of course we expect to be inundated with emigrants, coming, I suppose, from every part of the world, and truly, for all I can tell, there will be gold enough for all.

And now, the first question you will ask me is, whether I have made my fortune? I reply, my old bad luck has not forsaken me. I always seem to come in for monkey's allowance — more kicks than halfpence. Three months ago I thought my fortune was made, and that I might come home a South American nabob. Nothing of the kind. Here I was, almost on the spot, when the first news of the gold was received. I have worked hard, and undergone some hardships, and, thanks to the now almost lawless state of this country, I have been deprived of the great mass of my savings, and must, when the dry season comes round again, set to work almost anew. I have but fourteen hundred dollars' worth of the precious metal remaining, and, with the rate of prices which now universally prevails here, that will not keep me much over a couple of months. My own case, though, is that of many others. As the number of diggers and miners augmented, robberies and violence became frequent. At first, when we arrived at the Mormon diggings for example, everything was tranquil. Every man worked for himself, without disturbing his neighbor. Now the scene is widely changed indeed. When I was last there, as you will see by my diary, things were bad enough; but now, according to the reports we hear, no man known to be in possession of much gold dare say, as he lays down his head

at night, that he will ever rise from his pillow.[1] The fact is, that
there is no executive government of any strength here to put an
end to this state of things. The country is almost a wilderness,
whereof Indians are the principal inhabitants. The small government force here has been thinned very materially by desertions, and
the fidelity of those that remain is, according to the opinion of their
commanding officer, not to be over much depended on.

Of course, as you may expect, I am naturally much cast down at

that have happened, none could have had more interest for us
than the one which took place near Weaverville — could we
have witnessed it! For Pickpan surely met his man! All we
could get out of those who saw the combat was laughter and
more of it. But they did say that the surviving participant
was the poorest-dressed one at the beginning of the fray (as
there was no choice at the end), and that he was able to climb
on, and drive away, *a tolerably good-looking stallion!*

HANGTOWN GALS

(Air: "New York Gals")

They 're dreadful shy of '49ers
    Turn their noses up at the miners,
Shocked to hear them say "Gol darn it,"
    Try to blush but cannot come it!

    Chorus

Hangtown Gals are lovely creatures,
Think they 'll marry Mormon preachers,
Heads thrown back to show their features,
    Ha, Ha, Ha! Hangtown Gals!

[1] J. T. Brooks, *Four Months Among the Gold Finders.* This change from the halcyon
days of 1848 to the comparatively cruel days of 1849 has been mentioned by very few
annalists, because very few on the ground in both years left written records.

A FIGHT IN THE MINES

(By Charles Nahl, in A. Delano's "Old Block's Sketch Book")

To church they very seldom venture —
Hoops so large they cannot enter!
Go it, Gals! You 're young and tender,
Shun the pick and shovel gender!

For all the talk about the thousands of us that do come to California, you now and then hear folks express a curiosity as to why some famous plains-

HE MEETS A NATIVE   RENTS HIS CABIN

the keen-eyed Kit Carson. We hear that the latter is gathering six thousand sheep at Taos, New Mexico, to drive through to California by way of Raton Pass, Pikes Peak, Fort Laramie, and South Pass.[1] "How unromantic!" says Boardy, the philosopher, "for the dashing Kit!"

But speaking of dashing Bonneville and daring Kit Carson, how about our own intrepid Uncle Bob?

We have no proper record of the details of the adventure, but the main facts of his determination to locate a tentative

[1] Carson did not arrive in California with these sheep until 1853.

diggings of his own are agreed upon. Namely, that he left his own bed and board and went to a camp-site where he met a native who agreed at a price (looking at Uncle's purse, no doubt, carefully at the time) to rent him a miner's cabin.

In his home town the apartment would not have been considered adequate; but these are the California diggings.

RUDELY AWAKENED

Yet sweet sleep is the same in palace or hovel. Such Uncle was enjoying when rudely awakened in the middle of the night by an Indian attack. The Chieftain, who paid particular attention to Uncle, might have eaten the proprietor of the "hut" — so much did his voice resemble the latter's!

As a result of the raid Uncle was robbed of all his money and very many of his clothes. Making his way to us, and leaping unceremoniously into his chariot, he, for one, was cured of roaming the California wilds alone.

The "long tom" is becoming as famous in these diggings as

the cradle, but the stranger would not guess, offhand, that it is a sort of grown-up cradle. It was not long after the pan and cradle were in general use that it became apparent that some more expeditious mode was required for washing the gold from large quantities of earth. Men were not satisfied with the slow, one-man system, the use of pan or cradle; the situation demanded the invention of an implement by the use of which

"ROBBERS! HELP!"

the united efforts of individuals, as companies, could be made available and profitable.

The tom varies much in size, depending on the number of men intending to use it. It is an oblong box or trough about twelve feet in length, open at the top and usually at both ends; but always at the lower end. It is about eight inches in depth, and at the upper end from one foot to two feet in width, but increasing to nearly double that width at the middle; from thence its sides are parallel to the lower end. The bottom of this broad portion, for a distance of from three to six feet from the end, is made of strong, perforated sheet iron, in every respect similar to the sieve or hopper of the cradle, but of much heavier iron. The tom is not straight upon its bottom the whole length; but the sheet-iron portion is turned upward as it approaches the lower end, so that the depth of the tom is

HOME, SWEET HOME

diminished at that end to less than three inches. The object of this is that the water may all pass through the sieve or tomiron without running over the top.

Under this perforated iron portion is placed a rifle-box similar in principle to the bottom of a cradle; but larger and, alike with the tom, always to remain stationary or immovable while in use.

The tom is now placed in a proper position with reference to the dirt to be washed, generally as near the ground as possible, having to admit of the "tailings" passing off freely. The rifle-box is first fixed in proper position, then the iron-bottomed portion of the tom placed over it, with its open or narrow end several inches the highest. Water is now let in, either in open troughs of wood or through canvas hose, which, by its force, carries the dirt, when put in, down the tom; and while two or more men are employed shoveling the dirt into the tom at the upper end, one man at the side of the lower end, with hoe or shovel in hand, receives the dirt as brought down by the water; and after being violently stirred and moved about upon the perforated iron bottom until all has passed through it that will, the residue of stones and coarse gravel is thrown out by the shovel.

The manner of saving the gold by the rifle-box is precisely the same in principle as that of the cradle, with this advantage over it — that the falling of streams of water through the tom-iron serves to keep the sand upon the bottom of the rifle-box stirred up and loose, permitting the gold the more easily to reach the bottom, where it is retained by the rifle-bars; while the lighter matter, sand and pebbles, passes off with the water

The long tom has, of course, crept into local ballads, — along with everything else, — as witness this parody on Stephen Foster's "Oh! Susanna." It is called "Prospecting Dream" and introduces once more hero Joaquin : —

I dreamed a dream the other night
  When everything was still;
I dreamed I was a-carrying
  My long-tom down a hill.
My feet slipped out and I fell down;
  Oh, how it jarred my liver!
I watched my long-tom till I saw
  It fetched up in the river.

Chorus

Oh, what a miner,
  What a miner was I !
All swelled up with the scurvy,
  So I really thought I 'd die.

My matches, flour and chili beans,
  Lay scattered all around;
I felt so bad I wished to die,
  As I lay on the ground.

¹ *The Miner's Own Book.*

My coffee rolled down by a rock,
  My pepper I could not find;
'T was then I thought of Angeline,
  The girl I left behind.

I went to town and got drunk;
  In the morning to my surprise
I found that I had got a pair
  Of roaring big black eyes.
And I was strapped — had not a cent —
  Not even pick and shovel,
My hair snarl'd up, my breeches torn,
  Looked like the very Devil.

I then took up a little farm
  And got a señorita;
Gray-eyed, hump-backed, and black as tar,
  Her name was Marguerita.
My pigs all died, hens flew away,
  Joaquin he stole my mules;
My ranch burn "down," my blankets "up,"
  Likewise my farming tools.

I left my farm and hired out
  To be a hardware clerk;
I got kicked out "cos" I could n't write,
  So again I went to work.
But when they caught me stealing grub
  A few went in to boot him,
And others 'round were singing out:
  "Hang him, hang him, shoot him."

Last week we had rather poor success, having realized only nineteen ounces of gold — barely three to a man. Boardy has become interested in a Mexican boy named José who is with a party near us. José, like the rest, carries his gold on his person and, fearing it may be exhausted by perspiration or otherwise, is always weighing it and invokes every Saint in the calendar to keep his treasure safe. We feel sure he has found a method of recouping any such loss, whether fancied or real. He has been setting apart religiously one fourth of his winnings for the Big Woman, as he calls the Virgin Mary. We have reason to believe that he does n't play fair with her — *i.e.*, taking from her "pile" *both her share and his* of any and every supposed shrinkage or loss!

I have made a good friend, Henry Scamman, of the grand old State of Maine. He writes good letters to his folks and lets me read them and correct the spelling; he is such real Yankee
I think you will appreciate

themselves." . . . If I should come home without money all the old women in the place [1] would say that I was a good for nothing fellow and that they knew I would turn out so; but if I come home with plenty they will say: "I knew Henry was a smart lad, he showed it when he was a child." . . . I send . . . two ounces of gold dust which you can sell and out of the money I want all of you at home to have your daguerreotypes taken and sent to me. The balance of the money give to Mother. . . . I send in Package No. 4 the first gold I ever dug. I send it to you for safe keeping or, if you choose, you may have a ring made of it. Have all the gold there is made into it, in any device or shape you may choose, and wear it until I return. . . . If fate should so dictate that I should never return, keep it yourself as a memento. Do not have alloy put into it. . . . Say to Father that this is a great country for trout; there is a lake fifteen miles from Downieville where they catch them by the hundreds, but I had rather fish one day on Goose Fare and catch but one trout than to fish in the lake and catch an hundred. I am looking forward to the time when I can once more fish in Goose Fare and eat clam chowder on old orchard beach. Them was the times when I was happy. . . . I must go to bed for I have got a good deal of shovelling to do to-morrow in order to prospect a place I have in view. I think I have found something.

[1] Saco, Me.

We were prospecting on the north fork of Weber or Weaver Creek, twenty-five miles east of Hangtown. It was Saturday; the rain had been falling nearly all day, when Sam Hit came into camp with the joyful news that he had heard that a white woman had come to Snow's camp, sixteen miles away. Next morning he put on his best jeans pants his mother had made, a pair of alligator boots that he gave an ounce of gold dust for ($18), a red flannel shirt that cost him four dollars, and his old wool hat, lopped down over his ears, and struck out on foot to

see such a wonderful thing as a white woman. When he arrived at Snow's camp it was late in the day, and, as Mrs. Snow kept a restaurant, he ordered dinner at $1.50. While eating he saw some eggs in a pan. On inquiry he learned they were worth one dollar each, so he ordered one cooked. This brought his dinner up to $2.50. It was dark long before he reached camp. He had had a long, weary walk over a steep mountain trail, and, should he live to be a hundred years old, he says he will never forget the day he walked thirty-two miles to see a white woman in California.

PICKPAN TRYING TO RE-MEMBER THE LOCATION

The last meeting of our overland campaigners, minus chortling Carlo but happily including the unexpected Pickpan, — who believes he discovered a mine of solid gold just before he found and fought his gambler-friend, but cannot yet remember its location, — was duly held September 15 at Sacramento. The resourceful Boardy from his cartoon books illustrates what happened — as you will see. Here Brown and Jingo awaited the rest of us in a characteristic pose; and, tête-à-tête at a table, Jingo figured up the

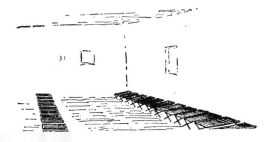

 washing materials, the rooms unfortunately had occupants who were not registered.

The tavern was, also, serenaded o' nights. The three had taken Picayune into custody because the slight training in

theatricals given him on the trail by Carlo, combined with the beverages afforded by Sacramento, had given him the unholy ambition to become a theatre-hall star. As Uncle Bob could play the piano, the three brought about Picayune's sobering-up by renting a "place of entertainment" during its unoccupied

"THE TAVERN WAS SERE-NADED O' NIGHTS"

hours, namely, from seven to nine A.M., and letting the poor
galoot sing "Seeing the Elephant," with the result, as Uncle
Bob curtly remarked, by way of dismissing a regrettable topic,
"that if Picayune did n't see 'the Elephant' it was the only
animal he missed."

Wagonhound and Ox Bow spied Boardy and me and directed
us to headquarters, where we in turn awaited the arrival of

PICAYUNE'S PERFORMANCE

Jeremiah, who was delayed by a business deal concerning a wig.
He had also purchased (from what looked to Uncle like the most
fascinating crook in California) a claim to a gold-and-silver
mine, but was having difficulty in getting a clear idea of the
road to it.   The salesman's map showed the road plainly to its
final destination; but it did not show the mountainous peaks
which necessitated the many curves in the route and prevented
a cut-off which Jeremiah thought would shorten the distance
materially.   The bill of sale, however, gave him full rights to

any cut-off which he might discover in or on or across the premises.

We had a grand night of it — milling with the crowd, visiting the saloons, keeping Picayune from singing "Seeing the Elephant," trying to remember where Pickpan had located his mine, and arguing away a good half of the Sierras

Creek, Horse Creek, and the Sweetwater; or compared ferrying over the South Platte at "Lower Crossings" with the North Platte below Red Buttes and the Green. Together again we saw the squaws at play in the waters of the Little Blue; Carlo singing "Pancakes" amid the dust of O'Fallon's Bluffs; the wagon crash

JEREMIAH'S MINE

the mule to nothingness in Ash Hollow; the woman laughing insanely in the heat of the Humboldt Valley because her man had suddenly gone cross-eyed and "could n't come back"; the Ark a-tilt on one wheel in the midst of the Platte River; the Goosie Goosie Ganders panning Fool's Gold in Goose Creek. In one "palace of refreshment" a "Sacramento Gal" waved a scarf in Ox Bow's face as she passed, to the mild amusement of Wagonhound; suddenly the latter, just mellow with beer, leaned over to his old pal and said : —

"Now, old Ox, if you really want one o' them there gals what yer can't git on yer merits, less adopt a strategy. Less half on

DOWN THE SACRAMENTO

us go daown one sider the room, an' t'other half t'other side, and run 'em up the room in relays like them wolves. . . ." Ox Bow's uncertain lunge at Wagonhound was smothered as the latter gripped his old chum in an iron bear hug.

The laughter was lost in a sudden silence that filled the room. The rattle of dice, click-clock of little heels, the tinkle of glasses, and all voices stopped.

"Forty-Niners," rang out a voice at the door, "there ain't no

JEREMIAH'S CUT-OFF ACROSS THE PEAKS

more grass on the Humboldt! The last o' the migration is pilin' up at Ragtown in heaps o' starvin' folks! We gotta send food to 'em. Who 'll go?"

Do you know, Dad, the roar that greeted that man's words could only be described by a man with Boardy's flow of language. "Did you hear that?" he shouted. "Did you hear them yell 'yes'? Did you see them drop their glasses and harlots and cards and pictures of sweethearts and love-letters from home? That's something to hear!"

P. S. A last word, Dad. We're separating like an explosion. Brown and Jingo are setting sail down the Sacramento, and Jeremiah is on his way to explore his cut-off across the peaks to his "gold mine"; but Boardy and I, with Wagonhound and Ox Bow and two thousand dollars of Uncle Bob's

BIBLIOGRAPHY

Writings of the California Argonauts, 1848–18͡5͡2   ̵   ̵ ̵

                                        ̵ ̵ ̵.ıuıicɛɪ Association *Transactions*
 ̵ ̵ ̵, ̵. ̵., ʊold Seeker's Manual (New York, 1849)
AUGER, ÉDOUARD, *Voyage en Californie* (Paris, 1854)
AUTENRIETH, E. L., *A Topographical Map* (pub. by J. H. Colton, New York, 1851)
Avis pour guider les émigrants (Paris, 1849)

BAILEY, WASHINGTON, *A Trip to California* (Le Roy, Ill., 1915)
BALL, NICHOLAS, "Pioneers of '49," Society California Pioneers of New England *Publications*
BALLARD, A. A., *A Forty-Niner's Scrapbook*, MS. Chicago Historical Society
BALLENSTEDT, C. W. T., *Beschreibung . . .* (Schöningen, 1851)
BARTLETT, J. R., *Personal Narrative* (New York, 1854)
BEACHER, REV. DR. E., "Address to Members of the New England and California Trade Manufacturers Association," *Boston Daily Times*, Jan. 29, 1849
BELISLE, D. W., *American Family Robinson* (Philadelphia, 1854)
BENNETT, W. P., *The First Baby in Camp* (Salt Lake City, 1893)
BENTON, J. A., *California Pilgrim* (Sacramento, 1853)
BERRY, G., *The Gold of California: Its Probable Effect*
BESCHKE, W., *The Dreadful Sufferings* (St. Louis, 1850)
BIDWELL, J., *John Bidwell's Trip to California* (St. Louis, 1842)
BIGLEY, C. A., *Aurifordina, or Adventures in the Gold Region* (New York, 1849)
BLOK, G., *A Short Geographic and Statistic Description of California* (St. Petersburg and Moscow, 1850)

BLOOD, JAMES A., *Diary*, MS. Newberry Library

BOEHMER, FRITZ, "Experiences," Society of California Pioneers *Quarterly*, IV, 87

BORTHWICK, J. O., *Three Years in California* (London, 1851)

BOUCHACOURT, M. CHARLES, *Notice industrielle sur la Californie* (Lyons, 1849)

Bound Home, Diary on SS. *Northerner*, MS. Bancroft Library

BREEN, P., "Diary" (of Donner party), Academy Pacific Coast Historical Society *Publications*, I, 6

BREWERTON, G. D., "A Ride with Kit Carson," *Harper's Magazine* (1853–4)

BRIER, J. W., "The Argonauts of Death Valley," *Grizzly Bear*, IX

BRODIE, WALTER, *Pitcairn Island in 1850 & a Few Hints on California* (London, 1851)

BROOKS, J. T., *Four Months among the Gold Finders* (London, 1849)

BROWN, H. S., *Statement*, MS. Bancroft Library

BROWN, J. S., *California Gold* (Salt Lake City, 1900)

BRUFF, J. G., *Journals*, MS. Huntington Library

BRYANT, E., *What I Saw in California* (New York, 1848)

BUFFUM, E. G., *Six Months in the Gold Mines* (Philadelphia, 1850)

BURCH, J. C., *Missouri to California*, MS. Huntington Library

BURNETT, P. H., *Recollections* (New York, 1880)

Burns Ranche Gold Mining Co., MS. Bancroft Library

BUTLER, B. F., *Map of the State of California and the Gold Regions* (San Francisco, 1851)

California Broadsides (1850)

California Characters and Mining Scenes

California: Gold Discoveries, *Hunt's Merchants' Magazine*, XXI–XXXIII (For newspaper bibliography see R. P. Bieber, "The Southwestern Trails to California in 1849," *Mississippi Valley Historical Review*, XII, 3)

California Gold Regions (New York, 1849)

California Guide Book (New York, 1849)

California: Its Past History . . . Present Condition of Mormon Settlements (1850)

California Pilgrims

California, Sein Minen-Bergbau (Cassel, 1867)

California Songster (1855)

California und Seine Goldminen (Kreuznach, 1849)

CANFIELD, C. DE L., *The Diary of a '49er*

CARDINELL, CHARLES, "Adventures on the Plains," *California Historical Society Quarterly*, I, 57

CARICOF, M., MS. Bancroft Library

CARLETON, J. H., "The Overland Route," *Stryker's Magazine* (1850)

CARSON, J. H., *Early Recollections* (1852)

CARVALHO, S. N., *Incidents of Travel* (New York and London, 1856)
CARY, T. G., "Gold," *Hunt's Merchants' Magazine* (1858); *Alta California during the Mexican War and the Discovery of Gold*, MS. Library of Congress
CHAMPAGNAC, J. B., *Le jeune voyageur* (Paris, 1857)
CHAVANNES DE LA GIRADIÈRE, H. DE, *Les petits voyageurs en Californie* (Tours, 1853)
CHILD, A., *Overland Route* (Milwaukee, 1852)
CHOUINARD, E., *Sur mer et sur terre* (Quebec, 1919)
CLARK, B. C., "Diary of a Journey from Missouri to California in 1849,"

CODMAN, JOHN, *California and Mining Scenery* (New York, 1879)
COKE, HENRY J., *A Ride over the Rocky Mountains* (London, 1852)
COLE, G. L., *In Early Days along the Overland Trail* (Kansas City, 1905)
COMSTOCK, J. L., *History of Precious Metals* (Hartford, 1849)
COUTTS, C. J., *Diary*, MS. Bancroft Library
COX, C. C., "Diary," *Southwestern Historical Quarterly*, XXIX, 36
COX, P., *Poems and Illustrations* (1874)
COYNE, J. S., *Cockneys in California* (New York, 1850)
COYNER, DAVID H., *The Lost Trappers* (Cincinnati, 1847)
CRAWFORD, P. V., "Journal," *Oregon Historical Society Quarterly*, XXV
CREUZBAUR, R., *Route from the Gulf of Mexico* (New York, 1849)
CROSS, O., "Report to U. S. Quartermaster General," *31 Cong., 2d Sess.*, I
"CROWQUILL, ALFRED" (*See* A. H. Forrester)

DE COSTA, W. H., *Journal*, MS. Huntington Library
DE GROOT, H., *Recollections of California Mining Life*
DELANO, A., *Life on the Plains* (Auburn, N. Y., 1854); *Old Block's Sketch Book* (1856); *Pen Knife Sketches*
DELEVAN, J., *Notes on California*
DENISON, BILL, *The Letter of a '49er*, MS. Library of Congress
DE QUINCEY, THOMAS, "Letters of a Young Man," *Works*, IX, 199–246
DERBY, E. H., *The Overland Route* (Boston, 1869)
DERR, P., *Account of Experiences*, MS. Bancroft Library
DEWOLF, DAVID, "Diary," Illinois State Historical Society *Transactions* (1925)
Diary of a Young Girl, MS. Huntington Library

DICKINSON, MRS. L., *Trip across the Plains in 1846* (San Francisco, 1904)
Diggers' Hand-Book (Sydney, N. S. W., 1849)
DILLON, PATRICE, "La Californie dans les derniers mois de 1849," *Revue des Deux Mondes*, V, Jan. 15, 1850
"Discovery of California Gold," *Stryker's American Register*, II, 17
DISTURNELL, JOHN, *Emigrant Guide* (New York, 1849)
DORÉ, BENJ., "Journal," *California Historical Society Quarterly*, II
DORNIN, G. D., *Thirty Years Ago*
DOWELL, B. F., *Letters*, MS. Bancroft Library
DRAPER, S., *Voyage of Bark Orion*, MS. Huntington Library
DRESSLER, A. (ed.), *California Pioneer Circus* (San Francisco, 1926)
DUNBAR, E. E., *The Romance of the Age*
DUNIWAY, MRS. A. J., *Captain Gray's Company* (Portland, 1859)

EARNSHAW, WILLIAM, *Across the Plains*, Waterford, Wis., *Post*, June 5– Sept. 4, 1897
"Emigrants and Routes to California," *Little Rock Gazette*, July 26, 1848

FABENS, J. W., *A Story of Life on the Isthmus* (New York, 1853)
FARNAHAN, E. W., *California Indoors and Out* (1856)
FERRY, H., *Description de la Nouvelle Californie* (Paris, 1850)
FLEISCHMANN, J. C. L., *Neueste Officielle Berichte* (Stuttgart, 1850)
FLINT, DR. THOMAS, *Diary* (Los Angeles, 1923)
FORRESTER, A. H. ("Alfred Crowquill"), *A Good-Natured Hint about California* (London, 1849)
FOSTER, G. G. (ed.), *The Gold Mines of California* (New York, 1848)
FRANZ, T. M. F., *From E. Prussia to the Golden Gate*
FRÉMONT, J. C., *A Report on an Exploration* (Washington, 1843)
FRENCH, S. G., "Report of Southern Route," *Sen. Ex. Docs., 31 Cong., 1st Sess.*, No. 64
FRINK, MRS. MARGARET, *Journal of a Party of California Gold Seekers* (Oakland, Cal., 1897)
FRIZZELL, L., *Across the Plains* (New York, 1915)
FROTHINGHAM, N. L., *Sermon*, Huntington Library

GARNER, WM. ROBERT, "Letters from California," *Supplement, Philadelphia North American*, April 26, 1847
GARRARD, L. H., *Wah-To-Yah* (New York, 1850)
GAY, F. A., *Sketches of California*
GENTRY, M. A., "A Child's Experience in '49," *Overland*, LXIII
GERARD, ULRICH, *Kalifornia* (Amsterdam, 1849)
"German Emigration," the *Californian*, May 24, 1848
GERSTACKER, F., *Kaliforniens Gold* (Leipsic, 1849); *Aventures d'une colonie d'émigrants* (Paris, 1855)

Gids naar California (Amsterdam, 1849)

GILL, WILLIAM, *California Letters*

GOBSON, J. W., *Recollections* (St. Joseph, Mo., 1912)

Gold Digger's Song Book, The

"Gold Mines of Sacramento," the *Californian*, May 3, 1848

GOLDSMITH, O., *Overland in '49*

GOODWIN, G. K., *Reminiscences* (Philadelphia, 1881)

GOODYEAR, A., *Memo.*, MS. Bancroft Library

GOULD, CHARLES, *Diary*, MS. Newberry Library

HALE, R. L., *Log of a 49er*

HALL, J. J., *Around the Horn*, MS. Huntington Library

HAMILTON, W. T., *My Sixty Years on the Plains* (New York, 1905)

HAMMON, C. J., *Diary*, MS. Huntington Library

HANCOCK, S., *Narrative* (New York, 1927)

HARLAN, A. W., "Journal," *Annals of Iowa*, XI, 3rd Ser.

HARRIS, J. M., "A Paper on California," Maryland Historical Society *Publications*, II, No. 6.

Hartford Union Mining Journal, MS. Bancroft Library

HASKINS, C. W., *Argonauts of California* (New York, 1890)

HASTINGS, L. W., *Emigrant's Guide* (Cincinnati, 1845)

HATHEWAY, E. P., *Letters*, MS.

HAUN, C. M., *A Woman's Trip*, MS. Huntington Library

HAYES, B. I., *Diary of a Journey*, MS. Bancroft Library

HAYNIE, S. G., "Circular regarding Emigration to California, Austin, Texas, Mar. 1, 1849," MS. Library of Congress

HELMS, L. V., *Pioneering in the Far East* (California, 1849)

HELPER, H. R., *The Land of Gold*

HERBERT, W. A., *Journal*, MS. Huntington Library

HICKMAN, R. O., "An Overland Journey," the *Frontier*, Mar. 1829

HICKSON, J. M., *A Gold Hunter*, quoted in O. C. Coy, *The Great Trek*

HOLYNSKI, A. J. J., *La Californie* (Bruxelles, 1853)

HOPPE, J., *Californiens Gegenwart und Zukunft* (Berlin, 1849)

HORN, H. B., *Overland Guide* (New York, 1852)

HOVEY, J., *Journal of a Voyage*, MS. Huntington Library

HOWE, O. T., *Argonauts of '49* (Cambridge, Mass., 1923)

HUNT, NANCY A., "By Ox-Team to California," *Overland*, LXVII, 317
HUNTLEY, SIR H. V., *California and Its Gold* (London, 1856)
HUTCHINSON, R., *Journal*, MS. Huntington Library

Idle and Industrious Miner, The
INGALLS, E., *Journal* (Waukegan, Ill., 1852)
IRBY, MRS. ALFRED, "Pathfinders of '49," *Overland*, LXIX

JACKSON, A. T., *Diary of a '49er*
JACOBS, E., *Journal of a Voyage*, MS. Huntington Library
JOHNSON, S. R., *Sermon to Departing '49ers*, February 11, 1849, at St. John's Church (Brooklyn, 1849)
JOHNSON, T. T., *Sights in the Gold Region* (New York, 1849)
JOHNSON, W. G., *Experiences with First Wagon*
JOSSELYN, A. P., *Journal*, MS. Newberry Library

KANE, T., *The Mormons* (Philadelphia, 1850)
KELLER, G., *A Trip across the Plains* (Massillon, Ohio, 1851)
KELLS, C. E., *California* (New York, 1848)
KELLY, W., *An Excursion to California* (London, 1851)
KENT, C. F., *Journal of a Voyage*, MS. Huntington Library
KERN, E. M., *Journals*, MS. Huntington Library
KERNS, J. T., "Journal," 42 Annual Report Oregon Pioneer Association *Transactions*
KINDGREN, CARL REINHOLD, *Californien en Skildring* (Stockholm, 1850)
KING, T. B., "California the Wonder of the Age," *H. Doc. 59, 31 Cong. Sess.*
KINGSLEY, N., "Diary," Academy Pacific Coast History *Publications*, III, 3
KINWORTHY, C. W., *Amelia Sherwood*
KIP, L., *California Sketches* (Albany, 1850)
KIRKPATRICK, C. A., *Journal*, MS. Bancroft Library
KNOWER, D., *The Adventures of a '49er*
KRAKENFUSS, A., *Munchausen in Californien* (Bremen, 1849)

La Californie: Recit d'un chercheur d'or (Cambria, 1851)
LACOSTE, A., *Fragments inédits* (Paris, 1849)
LAKE, D., *Letters from a Gold Hunter*, MS. Bancroft Library
LAMBERTIE, CHARLES DE, *Voyage pittoresque* (Paris, 1853)
LAMBOURNE, A., *The Pioneer Trail* (Salt Lake City, 1913)
LANGWORTHY, F., *Scenery of the Plains* (Ogdensburg, N. Y., 1855)
LARIMER, A., *Journal*, MS. University of Southern California Library
LAUTS, G. (*See* Ulrich Gerard)
La vérité sur la Californie, par K. E. (Paris, 1849)
LEEPER, D. R., *The Argonauts of Forty-Nine* (South Bend, Ind., 1894)

Le magasin pittoresque (Paris, 1849)

LETTS, J. M., *California Illustrated* (1852)

Le voyage en Californie, présenté pour la première fois au public sur le théâtre des Variétés le 8 août (Paris, 1850)

LIENHARD, HEINRICH, *California unmittelbar* (Zurich, 1900)

LINFORTH, J. (ed.), *Route from Liverpool to Great Salt Lake* (Liverpool, 1855)

LOBENSTINE, WILLIAM C., *Diary* (New York, 1920)

LONGSWORTH, B. N., *Diary* (Denver, 1927)

LOOMIS, J. V., *Journal of the Birmingham Emigration Co.* (Salt Lake

MASON, COL. R. B., *Official Report, H. Ex. Docs., 30 Cong., 2d Sess.*, No. 1

MASSEY, "Frenchmen in the Gold Rush," *California Historical Society Quarterly*, 1926, III

MAURY, P., *La Californie en février 1852* (Paris, 1852)

MAXWELL, WILLIAM A., *Crossing the Plains* (San Francisco, 1915)

MAYRE, G. T., "The Journey to California in '49," *Overland*, LXIII, 139

M'COLLUM, W. S., *California As I Saw It*

MCGAFFEY, JOSEPH, *Journal of a Voyage, 1849*, Photostat Newberry Library

MCGAFFEY, J. W., "Across Mexico in the Days of '49," *Touring Topics*, May 1929

MCGLASHAN, C. F., *History of the Donner Party* (Sacramento, 1890)

MCILHANEY, E. W., *Recollections of a '49er* (Kansas City, 1908)

MCILVAINE, W., JR., *Sketches of Scenery* (1850)

MCKEEBY, L. C., "Memoirs," *California Historical Society Quarterly*, III

MCNEIL, S., *Travels in 1849* (Columbus, 1850)

MCPHERSON, JOHN C., "Diary," the *Californian*, Oct. 1848

MEYER, C., *Nach dem Sacramento* (Aarau, 1855)

MILES, WILLIAM, *Journal* (Chambersburg, Pa., 1851)

MILLER, S. V., "Letter," Wyoming Historical Society *Publications*, Misc. 31

Miner's Lamentations, A

Miner's Own Book, The

Miner's Progress, The

MITCHELL, S. A., *Description of Oregon and California* (Philadelphia, 1849)

MONTAGU, Montagu, *California Broadsides* (1850)

MORGAN, M. M., *A Trip across the Plains* (San Francisco, 1864)

MULLER, J., *Das Goldland Californien* (Leitmeritz, 1850)

Nécessité d'une intervention armée en Californie (Paris, 1849)
NEWCOMB, S., *Journal*, MS. Coe Collection
NEWMARCH, W., *The Supplies of Gold* (London, 1853)

Opis Kalifornii, pod zgledem (Krakow, 1850)
OSWALD, H., *Californien und Seine Verhältnisse* (Leipsic, 1849)
Overland Diary, MS. Chicago Historical Society

Pacific Song Book, The (1861)
"Pacific Wagon Roads, Reports upon," *H. Ex. Docs., 35 Cong., 2d Sess.*, No. 36
PALMER, J., *Journals*, Cincinnati, 1852; *Wagon Trains*, MS. Bancroft Library
PANCOAST, C. E., *A Quaker Forty-Niner* (Philadelphia, 1930)
PARBURT, G. R., *Oration on the Sylph*, MS. Huntington Library
PARKMAN, F., *The California and Oregon Trail* (New York, 1849)
PATTERSON, E. H. N., "From the Plains," *Deseret News*, I, No. 19
PATTERSON, L. A., *12 Years in the Mines* (Cambridge, Mass., 1862)
PAULSON, *Across the Plains* (New York, 1867)
PAYSON, GEORGE, *Golden Dreams* (New York, 1853)
PEARSON, G. C., *Recollections*, MS. Bancroft Library
PECK, S. W., *Aurifodina* (New York, 1849); *Sermon to Pacific Pioneers*, Huntington Library
Pencillings by the Way (Buffalo, 1850)
PIERCY, F., *Route from Liverpool.* (*See* Linforth)
POLK, J. K., "Presidential Message," *H. Ex. Docs., 30 Cong., 2d Sess.*, No. 1
POTTER, T. E., *Autobiography* (Concord, N. H., 1913)
PRATELLES, V. M., "Sufferings of the Overland Emigrants in 1849," *Overland*, LXII, 342
PRATT, J. W., *Reminiscences* (New York, 1910)
PRATT, ORSON, "Interesting Items," Liverpool, *Millennial Star*, XI, XII, 1849–1850
PRAY, W. H., "Diary," West Killingly, Conn., *Arena*, 1849
PRICE, J., "Diary," *Mississippi Valley Historical Review*, XI, 2
PRINGLE, J., "Diary," 48th Annual Report, Oregon Pioneer Association *Transactions*
PUTNAM, C. AND N., "Journal," the *Frontier*, IX, 1

Rathgeber für Auswanderer (Bremen, 1849)
READ, G. W., *A Pioneer of 1850* (Boston, 1927)
READ, J. A. AND D. F. ("Jeremiah Saddlebags"), *The Journey to the Gold Digging Regions* (Cincinnati, 1849)
REDMITZ, L., *Getreuester und Zuverlässigster* (Berlin, 1852)
REED, J. F., "The Donner Tragedy," *San José Pioneer* (1877)

REID, J. C., *Tramp or a Journal*
REVERE, J. W., *A Tour of Duty* (Boston, 1849)
RICHARDS, R., *The California Crusoe* (New York, 1854)
RILEY, B., "Official Report," *H. Ex. Docs., 31 Cong.*, No. 17
ROBERTS, S., *To Emigrants to the Gold Region* (New Haven, 1849)
ROBINSON, F., *California and Its Gold Regions* (New York, 1849)
ROSSIGNON, J., *Guide Pratique* (Paris, 1849)
ROYCE, S. E., "From Salt Lake to the Sierras in '49," *Yale Review*, XX
    (June 1931)

SAXON, *Five Years within the Golden Gate* (1851)
SAYD, ERNEST, *California and Its Resources* (New York, 1849)
SCHARMANN, HERMANN B., "Overland Journey," New York *Staats-Zeitung*
    (1852)
SCHERER, J. A. B., *The First '49er*
SCHMÖDLER, C. B., *Neuer praktischer Wegweiser* (Mainz, 1848)
SCHWARZ, J. L., *Briefe* (Berlin, 1849)
SEDGLEY, J., *Overland in '49*, MS. Huntington Library
SEYMOUR, E. S., *Emigrant's Guide* (Chicago, 1849)
SHALLENBERGER, MOSES, *Overland in 1844*, MS. Bancroft Library
SHAW, D. W., *Eldorado* (Los Angeles, 1900)
SHAW, PRINGLE, *Rambling in California* (Toronto, 1856)
SHAW, R. C., *Across the Plains in Forty-Nine* (Farmland, Ind., 1896)
SHAW, W., *Golden Dreams* (London)
SHERWOOD, J. E., *Pocket Guide* (New York, 1849)
SHIVELY, J. M., *Route and Distances*
SIMPSON, H. I., *The Emigrant's Guide* (New York, 1848)
SLATER, N., *Fruits of Mormonism* (Coloma, Cal., 1851)
SMITH, C. W., *Journal of a Trip* (New York, 1920)
SMITH, GEORGE W., *Account of a Journey from Bowling Green, Ohio, to
    California*, MS. Harvard Library
STANSBURY, H., *An Expedition to the Valley of the Great Salt Lake* (Phila-
    delphia, 1852)
STEEL, J., *The Traveller's Companion* (Galena, 1854); *Across the Plains*
    (Lodi, Wis., 1901)
STEPHENS, L. D., *Life Sketches of a Jayhawker of 1849* (San José, 1916)

STIMSON, FANCHER, "Overland to California," *Annals of Iowa*, 3d ser., XIII, 403

STREET, F., *California in 1850* (Cincinnati, 1851)

STUART, GRANVILLE, *Forty Years on the Frontier* (Cleveland, 1925)

STURDIVANT, H., *Journal*, MS. Huntington Library

SUBLETTE, S., *To F. Sublette* (1849), MS. Missouri Historical Society Library

SWAN, JOHN A., *Trip to Gold Mines in 1848*, MS. Bancroft Library

SWASEY, W. F., *Early Days in California* (Oakland, 1891)

TAYLOR, B., *Eldorado*

TAYLOR, S. H., "Letters," Oregon Historical *Quarterly*, 117

THISSELL, G. W., *Crossing the Plains in '49* (Oakland, Cal., 1905)

THOMPSON, G. A., *Handbook* (London, 1849)

THORNTON, J. Q., *Oregon and California* (New York, 1849)

THURSTON, S. R., "Geographical Statistics," *Stryker's Magazine* (1850)

TOMPKINS, E. A., *Diary*, MS.

TUCKER, J. C., *To the Golden Goal*

TURNBULL, T., *Travels across the Plains* (Madison, Wis., 1914)

TYSON, J. L., *Diary of a Physician* (New York, 1850)

UDELL, J., *Incidents of Travel to California* (Jefferson, Ohio, 1856)

VANDYKE, W., "Overland to Los Angeles," *Annual Publications Historical Society of Southern California*, III

VAN SCHAICK, H. D., *Journal*, M.S. Newberry Library

VILLARS, MIETTE DE, *Manuel des émigrants* (Paris, 1849)

Voyage en Californie (Paris, 1851)

Vue de San Francisco (Paris, 1850)

WADSWORTH, W., *National Wagon Road Guide* (San Francisco, 1858)

WALTON, D., *The Book Needed for the Times* (Boston, 1849)

WARD, D. B., *Across the Plains* (Seattle, 1912)

WARE, J. E., *The Emigrant's Guide* (St. Louis, 1849)

WARNER, WILLIAM, "Overland in 1853," *California Historical Society Quarterly*, V, 289

WEBB, J. J., "Papers" (R. P. Bieber, ed.), Washington University *Studies*, XI (*Humanistic Series*, No. 2)

WEBSTER, JOHANN, *Californien wie es ist* (Philadelphia and Leipsic, 1849)

WESTON, SILAS, *Four Months in the Mines* (Providence, 1854)

WHITE, W. F., *A Picture of Pioneer Times*

WIDBER, J. H., *Statement of a Pioneer of 1849*, MS. Bancroft Library

WIERZBICKI, F. P., *California As It Is* (San Francisco, 1849)

WILKES, CHARLES, *Western America* (Philadelphia, 1849)

WILLIAMS, J. W., *Journal of a Voyage*, MS. Huntington Library

WILLIAMS, V. A., "Diary," 47 Annual Report Oregon Pioneer Association *Transactions*

WISTAR, V. A., *Autobiography* (Philadelphia, 1914)

WITHER, G. W., *Letter to R. H. Miller*, Miller Papers *Sen. Ex. Docs., 28 Cong., 2d Sess.*, No. 174

WOOD, ELIZABETH, "Journal of a Trip to Oregon in 1851," Peoria *Republican*, Jan. 30 and Feb. 13, 1852

WOOD, JOHN, *Journal* (Columbus, Ohio, 1871). *Cf. Motor Land*, December 1928–April 1929

X. O. X., *Outline to a History of an Expedition to California* (New York, 1849)

ZEIBER, J. S., "Diary," 48 Annual Report Oregon Pioneer Association *Transactions*

INDEX

DATE DUE

DEC 7 '65			
NOV 30 '66			
NOV 26 '68			
DEC 8 '70			
OCT 18 '7			
GAYLORD			PRINTED IN U.S.A